A Brilliant Red Thread

Revolutionary Writings from Don Hamerquist

A Brilliant Red Thread

Revolutionary Writings from Don Hamerquist

Edited by Luis Brennan

KER
SPL
EBE
DEB

2023

A Brilliant Red Thread:
Revolutionary Writings from Don Hamerquist
Edited by Luis Brennan

ISBN 978-1-989701-22-5

Published in 2023 by Kersplebedeb

To order copies of the book:

Kersplebedeb
CP 63560, CCCP Van Horne
Montreal, Quebec
Canada
H3W 3H8

info@kersplebedeb.com
www.kersplebedeb.com
www.leftwingbooks.net

Printed in Canada

# Contents

## VI. Analysis

## ACRONYM KEY

| | |
|---|---|
| ARA | Anti-Racist Action |
| CWP | Communist Workers Party |
| BRIC | Brazil, Russia, India, China |
| BTR | Bring the Ruckus |
| CIO | Congress of Industrial Organizations |
| COINTELPRO | Counter Intelligence Program |
| CP | Communist Party |
| CPSU | Communist Party of the Soviet Union |
| CPUSA | Communist Party USA |
| DAN | Direct Action Network |
| ILWU | International Longshore and Warehouse Union |
| IMF | International Monetary Fund |
| IWA | International Woodworkers of America |
| IWA | International Workingmen's Association |
| IWW | Industrial Workers of the World |
| LSW | Lumber and Sawmill Workers |
| M-L | Marxist-Leninist |
| NEP | New Economic Policy |
| NGO | Non-Government Organization |
| NLRB | National Labor Relations Board |
| OWS | Occupy Wall Street |
| POC | People of Color |
| SDS | Students for a Democratic Society |
| STO | Sojourner Truth Organization |
| WTO | World Trade Organization |
| WUO | Weather Underground Organization |
| WVO | Workers Viewpoint Organization |
| ZANU | Zimbabwe African National Union |

## Acknowledgments

I want to thank some people who have contributed to this collection and been important parts of the political experiences on which they are based.

First is Janeen, my comrade of more than forty years, who prodded me to agree to the project and helped gather a core of people to do the work. I am regularly amazed by her judgment and political courage that far outweigh my own and that of the hundreds of radicals that we have worked with over the decades. This is a reality I often recognize partially and belatedly, so I'm determined to make it absolutely clear here. I won't dwell on her ability to deal with daily life with me.

I'm grateful to Luis Brennan who has done yeoman work sifting through a very large disorganized and fragmentary inventory of writings and recruiting a few others to help. Also, thanks to Karl and Casey at Kersplebedeb for pulling things together in an essential late intervention, and to Ian Wallace for his help with the cover art.

Our relationship with a core group of Chicago comrades—Kieran Knutson, Christian Ogilvy, Trisha Rushkys, and Sprite—kept Janeen and myself politically functional and somewhat relevant from the mid-nineties. Kingsley Clark and Mike Morgan have been valued and trusted comrades even longer—from the seventies. Also, from the seventies in STO till now, I have been able to depend on Nick Paretsky to read what I write and find whatever meaning might be there.

I owe a great deal to the political activity and discussions with many comrades in STO from 1969-84. Some of this I remember favorably, some not so much. Ira Churgin in particular was always a source of reasoned and clear argument. We went different ways at the end of the sixties, but I benefited substantially from a close relationship to Gill Green during my long decade in the Communist Party.

Very little of what I have written was intended for public circulation or general interventions in broader academic or political frameworks. The political questions raised were normally intended to facilitate cooperative, collective political activity and organization on specific projects in organized collectives, and some may be difficult to understand and evaluate outside of this context. At times the attitude towards discussion was more significant than the specific positions I advanced and defended. Unfortunately, this frequently meant that as new issues emerged, other questions were left behind in an unfinished state. And since many of them were shaped by oppositions and alternatives that may have disappeared into the historical dustbin, it's certainly possible that various broader motivations and intentions may not always be clear.

Don Hamerquist
September 2022

Janeen and Don, decades ago in Austin, Texas

## Editor's Preface

The foundations of our society are crumbling. In such times of great instability our actions may fundamentally affect history's trajectory—toward the more beautiful or the more brutal. For those committed to the former, this book's arrival should be recognized as a significant event. This is not an academic, scholarly, or historical collection. This book is a weapon to be turned on the powerful for maximum impact.

It is also the first widely available collection of Don Hamerquist's writing. Over six decades of active political engagement and intellectual work Hamerquist has remained mostly unknown outside of those "in the know." This has not been out of vanity or elitism; instead it has been due to Hamerquist's humility and the primacy of his commitment to the work of politics rather than money or notoriety. As his longtime political sparring partner Noel Ignatiev once remarked, "The thing with Don is that his ego just isn't involved."

Instead, Hamerquist always preferred to be in close discussion with active militants. Most of the works collected in this book began as emails with comrades, either in personal correspondence or over various discussion lists that included movement veterans and fresh radicals. They are, as Hamerquist has said, "political discussion among political people." As such, they are not authoritative proclamations. They are argumentative positions aimed to spur others to think harder and more critically about how to act in the world. A serious engagement with their methods and goals will not necessarily result in agreement, but rather in a sharpening of your own positions.

Beyond being object lessons, these essays grapple with some of the most important questions concerning the movement today.

In fact, despite Hamerquist's long career, all the essays here were written since 2000, as it was decided to include only more recent pieces that speak to the current situation. Today we face a bewildering conundrum: millions of people are ready to engage in active combat with the ruling capitalist order, but we have not seen the emergence of a viable social force that articulates a promising alternative to that order. Hamerquist's great strength is to envision a political trajectory that does: one that aims directly at revolutionary social transformation without detours into reformist blind alleys or corrupting engagement with the state. He does this while still remaining concerned with building a mass participatory movement that matters to regular people, and remaining realistic about the challenges facing such a project. He recognizes that we are not alone on the playing field and that it is our duty to deeply understand our enemies, both the insurgent right and the bearers of capital. Moreover, he rejects a politics that leaves history to some spontaneous fate. In his view it is not incompatible to embrace our role as agents and even leaders in struggle as well as remaining committed to the "self-emancipation" of the working class.

The book is designed to support your deep engagement. It has a roughly thematic structure: essays are divided between sections on "Organization" and specific "Events," as well as "Anti-Fascism" and "Anti-Repression," with a more in-depth and theoretical essay on revolutionary organization and history ("Lenin, Leninism, and Some Leftovers") and ending with and set of longer essays contemplating questions pertaining to capitalism's global and historical trajectory ("Analysis"). You are encouraged to read out of order and to seek out pieces that speak to practical problems you are currently facing. At the same time, the essays are ordered chronologically so that you can trace the development of the ideas, and a thorough bibliography includes, wherever practical, references to free online resources. We have also attempted to provide helpful editorial material, including endnotes and brief introductions to certain pieces. Because most pieces are embedded in an active conversation, they are full of references and acronyms. To assist the curious reader, we have provided a Glossary with entries on terms and concepts that recur in various texts; these are usually indicated in the text itself by an asterisk (*). We have also provided a short acronym key. However, the core issues addressed are more general, and grasping the full effect does not require carefully tracing each off-hand comment. You're encouraged to delve into this complementary material, but there is no need to get too hung up on it.

Hopefully with these efforts and the energy of you the reader, the essays included here can advance our collective project for the abolition of all forms of oppression and for the creation of a future worth struggling for.

In that collective spirit, this book would not be possible without the generous support of many people. Notably those who helped with sifting through and editing the massive quantity of raw material: Dave Ranney, Kingsley Clarke, Hugh Farr, Cole Nelson, and Fiona Marten. Also, those who helped in a myriad of small and big ways to get this project completed: Amelia Cates, Kristian Williams, Peter Little, Nick Paretsky, John Steele, Scott Nappalos, Tamara Smith, Cloee Cooper, Karolyn Burdick, Xtn, Matthew Lyons, Kieran Knutson, Sinead Steiner, Kevin Van Meter, Craig Johnson, Ian Wallace, Dustin Hawks, and Michael Staudenmaier. And finally, the biggest thank you to Don and Janeen for filling a flash drive with hundreds of documents and wishing me luck (and of course, for all their support along the way).

Luis Brennan
Portland OR, September 2022

## An Introduction to Hamerquist's *A Brilliant Red Thread*

In the early 1970s I was tasked with moving the national office of the New American Movement (NAM) from Minneapolis to Chicago. NAM considered itself a "multi-tendency socialist organization" and had chapters across the US. At that time, I was clear that I was anti-capitalist and quite optimistic about the prospects for some sort of socialist revolution. But I was not at all clear on what a new socialist society might look like, nor did I have much of a sense of how to get from "here to there."

While unpacking pamphlets representing a range of politics on these topics in our new Chicago office, a man stuck his head in the door and introduced himself as Don Hamerquist. He told me he had a print shop down the hall and wondered if we might be interested in having "C and D Printing" print our future pamphlets. While touring the print shop, I was intrigued to discover that Don was one of the founders of Sojourner Truth Organization (STO), a New Left revolutionary organization. I had been exposed to some of STO's pamphlets through a workshop I attended while living in Iowa City. Don characterized these works as discussion documents. They included STO's views on revolutionary organization ("Toward a Revolutionary Party"), an explanation of STO's emphasis on industrial organization ("Mass Organizations at the Workplace" and "Reflections on Organizing"), and their well-known stance on the role of white supremacy in maintaining capitalism in the US ("White Blindspot" and "Black Worker, White Worker").[1] During the next year I left NAM and joined STO. NAM merged with Michael Harrington's Democratic Socialist Organizing Committee (DSOC) and became the Democratic Socialists of America (DSA). I took a different path. And it was greatly influenced by Don Hamerquist.

Don grew up in a logging family on a farm near the small town of Clallam Bay on Washington's Olympic Peninsula. Both his parents were active union militants and known communists. His father had been an activist in the IWW's logging and maritime sections until the 1930s, when he became a major organizer of the Congress of Industrial Organizations (CIO) logger's union, the International Woodworkers of America. Differences over policy and stance with the union and its Communist Party (CP) leadership led him to quit his union position and return to work in the woods. Except for a period in the Merchant Marine during WWII, he worked as a logger for the rest of his life, widely blacklisted, with great difficulty finding and holding jobs.

Differences with CP leadership and policy in the Browder period led to Don's parents' expulsion and official "shunning" by the Washington CP. In the 1950s they both were re-recruited, however they always retained substantial skepticism about the CP's politics and personnel.

Don joined the Communist Party at age twenty and became the District Organizer in Oregon in 1962, one of the few open members of the CPUSA in the country. After dropping out of college he worked as a truck driver for a number of years before becoming a paid CP organizer in 1966. Don's break with the CPUSA, politically and organizationally, is described in the essay, "More on the CP and Me."

Documents from the FBI's COINTELPRO* operation against Don trace his political trajectory in the CP. Early entries focused on attempts to discredit him—including "an anonymous 'tip' to the appropriate Oregon Department of Health official that subject is a possible vencreal disease carrier." However, their approach was quickly modified to "building up ... [his] stature as a future leader ... in the hopes he will continue to be a disruptive influence" on the party.

Shortly after breaking with the CP, Don joined a few dozen other activists in forming STO in Chicago. This led to three decades of radical activism that provide the context for many of the writings in this collection. The activism was never separated from an analysis of capitalism's practice and the responses of the masses and the left. His work offers a rich meeting of theory and practice at various historical junctures.

After joining STO, I participated in the STO concentration in industrial organization by working in a series of factories over the next seven years. I left STO after five years when the group decided that industrial insurgency was in a "state of lull" and that we should therefore de-emphasize such organizing. But those five years were years of tremendous learning and political development for me, and my thinking continues to be shaped by them; I have retained much of what I learned in STO to this day.

STO was founded in 1969 and was dissolved in the mid-1980s. Subsequently, Don remained an active participant in revolutionary struggles and is active to this day in developing the ideas that began with STO. The essays in this book were all written after 2000; they show how Don's thinking continues to develop more than three decades after he broke with the CPUSA.

This book will be valuable for today's radical activists as well as for historians. The essays contained within demonstrate how the author has translated the current trajectory of capitalism and responses to it into timely adaptations and sometimes changes to his ideas on a whole range of topics, including: revolutionary organization, the nature of the capitalist state, capitalist institutions including government and trade unions, state repression and how to combat it, and the nature of fascism and prospects for organizing against it.

A key to understanding Don's method can be found in an email to a young activist involved in the Occupy Wall Street* movement in 2011: "it is important to always look at what is new," he wrote, before going on to discuss the possibility of "a new capitalist equilibrium." (See "Email on the Historical Situation" on page 104.)

When he led STO to question our focus on the industrial workplace, the discussion concluded that we were in a period of "lull." As he puts it in his recent essay that is part of the introduction to this book:

> Decreasingly frequent examples of class militancy and self-organization were increasingly associated with tactical and strategic defeats that didn't provide a promising terrain for the future growth of a culture and community of class struggle. … It was increasingly evident that we were dealing with processes that raised questions about some basic assumptions about the trajectory of capitalism. (17)

These were his thoughts about what was new as he presided over his punch press at an electronics firm in Chicago. I, on the other hand, while working at a factory on Chicago's Southside that mixed lard and tallow to make a disgusting mess called "shortening," was not ready to let go of STO's industrial organizing emphasis, so I left the organization. It turned out that we were both right, but for the wrong reasons! Don was right about the fact that militant struggles on the factory floor were on the decline. He saw this as a "lull" that justified a shift in emphasis for STO. At Chicago Shortening, we were on the cusp of what turned out to be a very militant wildcat strike, and there were other shop-floor struggles still going on in Southeast Chicago, so I was right not to let go of the militancy of the workers I was associated with.[2] But what neither of us understood at that time (late 1970s) was that global capitalism was launching a major reorganization that would result in the closing of factories across the US and Europe. Between 1980 and 1990 in the Chicago Metropolitan Area alone there was a net loss of nearly 152,000 manufacturing jobs. The strategic shift that led to such losses was what today we call "neo-liberalism" or what President George H.W. Bush called a "new world order." Many of the essays in this book show the development of Don's thinking about this strategic shift.

Most readers know that the 1960s and 1970s were a time of great possibility. Insurgencies took place throughout Europe and the US, at the workplace and in communities. And black and brown people were leading the way. Massive civil rights movements that included both communities and workplaces challenged the assumption of white supremacy. A women's movement targeted not only "women's issues" like abortion rights but also challenged all appearances of male supremacy, including those within the left. A strong anti-war movement developed in response to the war in Vietnam. A massive demonstration at the 1968 Democratic National Convention denounced the party's liberals and called into question the two-party system, and in some cases even the value of electoral politics. And a vibrant counterculture challenged the dominant mores of society. Meanwhile, the Vietnam War was part of a much broader armed struggle against colonialism throughout the "Third World." Anti-colonial wars arose all over the globe. The ability of the major capitalist nations to dominate the other countries of the world was being challenged as one nation after another fought both colonialism and imperialism. For those of us on the left it was a very hopeful time. We believed we would experience a new society in our lifetime.

The left, however, was very divided on the issue of how to get there—what revolution means. And we were divided on exactly what "there" entailed—what we were for. STO weighed in, challenging the theory and practice of much of the rest of the left. But most importantly, none of us recognized that global capitalism was facing what Don calls a "secular crisis." Put simply, a secular crisis indicates that the crisis is the result of the long-term tendency (the "secular" trend) within capitalism. Crises have occurred throughout the history of capitalism itself, and Marx explained why that is so in his writings. Cyclical crises, recessions and inflation, can be manifestations of the longer term, secular crisis. Don, in the essays in this book, grapples with the implications of the secular crisis, challenging the traditional left notion that capitalism will simply self-destruct as a result, and at the same time has delineated the difference between the secular crisis and the episodic cyclical crises. He explains how, in response to the latter, capital has historically created "new equilibriums" to enable it to pick itself up and start over. In a 2011 essay called "Financialization and Hegemony," Don says:

> Without a functioning revolutionary subject, any new equilibrium will be essentially capitalist. ... [c]apitalism will not topple "through ... exhaustion." It will not stop running "on its own." It must be overthrown by a politically conscious, mass counter-force, and the primary issue for us concerns how such a force might develop. (268–69)

As we tended our punch presses and wallowed in shortening, there were forces in play that would change, as Don puts it, "the basic trajectory of capitalism" in response to the crisis. The activities of the capitalist class turned out to be far more effective than the efforts of the left and working-class struggle. Without a significant mass and left response, the result was indeed a "new equilibrium."

### Transnational Capitalism and Financialization

In a note on his recent thinking about global capitalism titled "On Transnational Capitalism," Don points out that his position evolved piecemeal over a period of fifty years. It truly wasn't obvious what was happening as it was happening. But his understanding of the "new equilibrium" is important for us all to understand today, because it has profound implications for our understanding of the role of a weakened and "hollowing" capitalist state in meeting an ongoing secular crisis. Don states:

> The basic economic premise of this transnational capitalist system—the unfettered flow of capital to areas of maximum returns—constantly undermines and hollows the brittle and corrupt state and regulatory institutions that are its major hopes for maintaining and renewing a stable legitimacy. Though this social formation is extremely unstable, there is no real possibility that its basic financial

architecture will collapse back into a nation-state-based imperial structure. (237)

The "transnational capitalist system" constitutes a "new equilibrium" that we couldn't see coming in the late 1970s. While it was first rolled out with a CIA-backed coup in Chile in 1973, many other ruling-class ventures were in play around the world that would make the Chile model into today's "transnational capitalism." An international agreement known as Bretton Woods, officially put in place in 1944, specified that the US dollar—with a value fixed in gold—would be the international medium of exchange. That agreement reflected the fact that the US nation-state emerged from World War II as a global superpower. But as the secular crisis deepened in the 1960s, the dollar's role in capitalist development was being challenged, and in 1971 and 1973, President Nixon essentially canceled the 1944 agreement by taking the dollar off the gold standard and creating a global "money market" that would determine the value of the dollar against all other currencies.

Other initiatives by the governments of the global capitalist state changed the functioning of the institutions established by the Bretton Woods Agreement to achieve a goal of maximum mobility of capital. IMF and World Bank mandates pushed developing nations—many of them former colonies—to accept loans with strings attached that would alter the structure and functioning of their economies and make their nations open to penetration, termed "foreign investment." Floating currency exchange mechanisms began to be developed in the 1980s and 1990s. The GATT that had governed trade since 1948 was replaced by the World Trade Organization (WTO) in 1995. International commerce was increasingly structured by multilateral and bilateral "free trade agreements" like the North American Free Trade Agreement.

Meanwhile, important technological developments occurred that were not tied to any particular nation-state but allowed production to flow to parts of the world with the fewest governmental regulations and the lowest wages. These changes included the development of technologies that made long, Fordist assembly lines outmoded. The manufacturing of nearly all consumer or producer goods could be broken up into pieces, with different parts produced in different locations and assembled somewhere else. Transportation innovations, including standardized big box containers, massive container ships, and computer-based inventory controls, facilitated the movement of goods, creating giant, global supply chains. This development made scattered-site production feasible.

All of these mechanisms built the global supply chains that have become a key feature of today's "transnational capitalist" economy. But none of this would have been possible without a greatly expanded role for finance. Government debt generated by private banks, national governments, and the IMF and World Bank placed less developed nations in thrall to the finance industry, which forced them to welcome foreign investment, moving not only manufacturing but financial services themselves around the world, accelerating the hypermobility of capital. Much of this activity happens out of the reach of government regulators. IMF, World Bank, and WTO rules have opened the world to global finance networks. The global flow of finance capital has been enhanced and taken further outside of the realm of state-based regulators and central banks by the expansion of "shadow banks." These institutions include many different creditors, including pension funds, private equity firms, and a variety of asset managers. Their assets have been estimated to be in the trillions of dollars.

But the rise of this "financialization" brought with it its own set of contradictions. All sorts of exotic financial "products" became commodities in their own right. Bundles of debt called "collateralized debt obligations"—including mortgages, corporate debt, student loans, and car loans—were bought and sold as if they were automobiles, apples, oranges, and computer chips. And traders began to speculate on their "value." But in reality these financial products were simply claims on the value of real products yet to be produced. The tail began wagging the dog, so to speak. And this led to a new crisis that manifested itself in the financial meltdown of 2008–9, which has been mislabeled the "greatest recession since the great depression." In "Financialization and Hegemony," Don says, "I see the development of financialization as a significant disturbance to the capitalist equilibrium of our recent past that is central to this current crisis." (269)

The appearances of the current crisis are many and began with the 2008 financial meltdown. But even more recently a mishap in the Suez Canal,[3] the COVID-19 pandemic, and the war in the Ukraine have made "supply chain" a household phrase, and not in a good way. The huge container ships are piling up at ports in the US and in Europe, prices are skyrocketing, and the shelves of US supermarkets are periodically empty of goods like toilet paper and vital baby formula. There is indeed a significant disturbance to the capitalist equilibrium that had evolved from the 1960s crisis. The hollowing of the capitalist nation-state is being exposed as governments struggle to contain inflation with outmoded fiscal and monetary policies, just as they are unable to stop the pandemic with their weakened public health systems.

In the US, the collapse of living-wage manufacturing jobs has left major parts of the working class superfluous to the economy. In large cities many black and brown youth, whose fathers and grandfathers once worked in the manufacturing sector, are without prospects. They are being contained in US prisons and by violent police actions. Shootings and police killings of black youth have set off spontaneous insurgencies. But global conditions have also eaten away at the prospects of many in the white working class as well, giving rise to a populist movement driven by the fear of being replaced by a growing black and brown population.

Don argues today, as he has his entire revolutionary life, that capitalism and the nation-states that support it will not simply "wither away." This is a time of opportunity for the left but also one of great peril. The essays in the final section of this book, "Analysis," spell much of this out. We need revolutionary organization, theory, and practice to combat today's perils and to offer an alternative to the barbarism of fascism that is knocking on our door.

As Don has continued to look at "what is new" over the past fifty years, he has attempted to address this need. The essays in this book reflect that, and by considering his method and analysis, today's young revolutionaries can find a path to combatting today's perils, offering a positive outcome to the old admonition of "socialism or barbarism."

In the present era of "transnational capitalism" and the secular crisis discussed in this book, a number of issues present themselves where the development of Don's revolutionary politics seem particularly important to me: Fascism, Contract Unionism, and Social Democracy.

### *Fascism, Anti-Fascism*

One of these issues is the rise of far-right political movements. The crisis-ridden system, which is unable to feed, clothe, house, educate, and care for the people that capitalism presently rules over, produces a reaction from what we may broadly call the right wing. In the US, the Trump phenomenon and the appeal of fantastic conspiracy theories raise the possibility of various forms of barbarism, including fascism. Don has written a great deal about fascism and has worked with anti-fascist groups, including engaging in street battles, over the last thirty years. A section in this book contains four essays on fascism written between 2001 and 2015. His approach to what fascism is and what to do about it is quite well developed and distinct from those of many other leftists.

In an essay written in 2015, "Mistakes in our Previous Approaches to Fascism," he has this to say:

> Virtually all leftists (including anarchists) see fascism as a tactical form of capitalist rule; a more consistently reactionary and authoritarian capitalist policy option particu-

> larly appropriate to moments when the power of capital is under greater-than-usual stress. (162)

> For some time, I've argued for a different approach to the analysis of fascism, one that doesn't see it as a potential form of capitalist rule but as a reactionary response (potentially a mass one with radical or even revolutionary characteristics) to an increasingly crisis-ridden late capitalism. In this perspective, neo-fascism and various forms of warlordism are understood, not as a "worse" form of capitalism, but as the barbarism side of the "socialism or barbarism" options to it. (164)

As Don's analysis of "late capitalism" began to develop, he made an important contribution to a growing anti-fascist movement. In an essay written in 2001 called "Third Position Fascism," he examined a tendency within the German Nazi movement led by rivals of Hitler's, the brothers Gregor and Otto Strasser. The Strassers, unlike Hitler, Mussolini, and Franco, were anticapitalist revolutionaries. Applying this to conditions in 2001, Don argued that "Third Position Fascism" needed to be studied and combatted. This analysis led Don and young anti-fascists at that time to articulate the notion of a "three-way fight" and to create a blog by that name (threewayfight.blogspot.com). Here is an explanation from the blog:

> Leftists need to confront both the established capitalist order and an insurgent or even revolutionary right, while recognizing that these opponents are also in conflict with each other. The phrase "three-way fight" is short hand for this idea (although in concrete terms there are more than three contending forces).[4]

## *Contract Unionism*

The right-wing response to the secular crisis of transnational capitalism is far stronger than anything coming from the liberal left, never mind the revolutionary left. One initiative coming from the liberal left is the rise in union organizing and unionization. In the 1960s and 70s, a great deal of leftist activity happened within the trade union movement. In the 1950s, individuals known to be "reds" were purged from unions. Labor law was also passed that greatly weakened unions. Still, many left organizations had a perspective of getting their members into trade unions that they believed they could eventually take over and turn into progressive, working-class organizations. STO took a different path, and as a result we were often accused of being "anti-union" or promoters of "dual unionism."

Much of the left-wing union organizing ceased when factories shut down across the US and Europe. In the US, union membership plummeted. But in the last few years we have seen a rise in union organizing, especially in workplaces that are part of the logistics industry (like Amazon warehouses), fast food companies like Starbucks, hospitals, schools, government agencies, and a variety of service sector corporations. And the left, once again, seems to be back to trying to organize such workplaces and playing a role in the unions there.

The idea that STO was "anti-union" in the 1970s was a misrepresentation of our position. We did oppose certain union activities when unions attempted to discipline their members on behalf of companies or when there were obviously corrupt practices. We also believed that labor legislation, especially that enacted in the 1950s, put unions in a position of being enforcers of rules dictated by contracts, especially the prohibition of "secondary boycotts" (strikes supporting striking workers at other workplaces). Unions also enforced no-strike clauses between contracts by joining companies in trying to crush "wildcat" strikes. We supported the wildcats and hence opposed the unions trying to stop them. The

1960s and 70s was a time of a great deal of extra-union insurgency in industrial workplaces, and Don and STO as a group took the position that the revolutionary left ought to be supporting those insurgencies rather than confining themselves to the government-enforced strictures of labor law.

These ideas are articulated in a number of essays in this book. The old STO position is brought into the context of twenty-first-century union organizing. In a 2009 essay regarding revolutionary organization, "Lenin, Leninism, and some Leftovers," Don addresses, among other things, issues in workplace organizing:

> I ... have always favored organizing direct-action, mass groupings of workers at the point of production that can begin to understand the relevance of class issues beyond their particular shop floor—whatever the nature of the union or whether there is one or not. ... The focus on contract unionism is usually a diversion from the issues of power in the workplace. ... [The] quasi-parliamentary struggle for influence within the union [is] a form of struggle that the overwhelming majority of workers avoid like the plague. (213–14)

### Social Democracy

The idea of leftists "taking over government through elections" and bringing about a fair and democratic society is similar to the idea of leftists taking over unions and turning them into working-class institutions. While "social democracy" is an old idea, the enthusiasm of so many old and new leftists for the Bernie Sanders campaign and the rapid rise of Democratic Socialists of America show that it is also a very persistent one.

Throughout this book, Don discusses the limitations of this approach in different contexts. In general, the critique of social democracy rests on the view that the function of the state is to preserve capitalist rule. In response to a charge that "Hamerquist is still for the seizure of state power," he says quite clearly, "I am for smashing, not for seizing, the capitalist state." In addition, he argues that too many leftists hold onto the idea that there is such a thing as "good capitalism" and "bad capitalism," which can justify running an institution designed to secure the capitalist system. In a 2010 essay critiquing Naomi Klein's work, he says:

> The issue is capitalism, not "shock capitalism" or "disaster capitalism"; the issue is capitalist ideology, not a bad "Chicago School" neoliberal trend versus a good "Cambridge School" neo-Keynesianism. …
>
> It has always been difficult for the left to understand that capital rules through force *and* through hegemony—through repression *and* through concession, through incarceration *and* incorporation—and that it uses both tactics simultaneously. (44–45)

The idea that you can't seize institutions designed to preserve capitalist rule and expect to gain anything but more capitalism becomes even more urgent as the nature of the capitalist state goes through the sorts of transformations that are discussed throughout this book. The secular crisis is proceeding in the context of "transnational and financialized capitalism" with an ongoing "hollowing" of the capitalist nation-state. So new forms of state power are likely in the making. Don's writing about the "hollow state" becomes an important part of the critique of social democracy (which at its best aims to seize nation-states that are themselves increasingly unable to control global capital).

> [We are witnessing] the increasing influence of the suprastate elements of capital accumulation: transnational corporations; global productive processes and labor flows; and, above all, global financial markets dealing with magnitudes far in excess of any measure of the values of actual production—and more and more commonly far in excess

of the economic resources commanded by and encompassed within any state formation. All of this becomes less and less compatible with the viability and the success of any of these, "competing political jurisdictions." (273)

Thus, the capitalist crisis and new state forms point to the futility of "seizing the state," whether by parliamentary or other means.

As capitalists, the nation-states that support them, revolutionaries, and other activists left and right churn and flail away, trying to figure a way out of the mess of yet another crisis, the historical choice of socialism or barbarism once again presents itself. As one reads these essays, an unfettered brilliant red thread emerges that offers a much-needed revolutionary vision.

Dave Ranney
Chicago, August 2022

# BACKGROUND

## Family History

I grew up as a "red diaper" kid, but in an atypical "red diaper" situation. My father worked in the woods as a high climber and a rigger and later a busheler. During most of my childhood he was blacklisted for communist politics and past union organizing, so he worked sporadically and often at a substantial distance from home. We lived close to the bone on a subsistence farm in the remote woods of Washington's Olympic Peninsula; twelve miles from a small logging community and fifty miles from the nearest significant town—and lacking a car much of the time. We had neither electricity nor telephone until after I had left for college. My high school graduating class numbered six, one boy. All of this had a definite impact on my politics, not to mention my personality or lack of one.

Both of my parents were Communists—my father, notoriously so. As noted above, his background as a major Western Washington organizer of the CIO logger's union, the IWA, made it very difficult for him to hold a job because of blacklisting, and, although we lived within eyesight of Canada, he was never able to go North for work, because, as a naturalized citizen, he wouldn't have been allowed back into this country. (This happened to some of his close comrades.)

During the time I was becoming vaguely aware of politics, my father was expelled from the CP (and my mother was effectively as well) for his "premature" anti-Browderism and generally disrespectful attitude towards party leadership. However, CP efforts to implement their normal shunning practices were ineffective because of my parents' solid relationships in their community and with the numerous CP/CIO working-class leftists in the area. In the late 40s, well after the disputed party policy had changed and my father's major antagonist had been discredited for cooperating

3

with the state in the Washington Smith Act trials,[1] the Washington CP begrudgingly recognized that his expulsion had been a mistake. In the early 50s, as I neared high school age, both my father and my mother were asked to rejoin the party and they did. Nevertheless, his politics, and those of the large local CP branch, were always suspect in the view of the Washington district leadership—pro-Chinese, ultra-left, and most important and relevant, "anti-leadership."

I want to spend some time on my father's background since it was a major influence—although I resisted it frequently during my early years in the CP, thinking that I knew better. Before getting further into this subject, I'd note that my sister and I weren't pushed towards left politics by our parents. In fact, we were pretty much oblivious to its impact on our family life during the very repressive period when we were young. I have some memories of confrontations with various scab-type reactionaries, usually drunk, from the period. My father expertly navigated them—something I still marvel at. However, my first confrontation with politics wasn't until the fifth grade when an older girl, whose mother was a rabid local patriot and anti-communist, called me a "stuffed-shirt Bolshevik." I hadn't any idea what a Bolshevik was, and I most certainly wasn't one—unfortunately, the stuffed shirt charge was a good fit. My parents, particularly my father, were very amused, and after that we regularly discussed political issues, although regrettably these were never adequately focused on my father's extensive past experiences.

He was born in Scotland in a large poor Scottish/Norwegian family that was in the process of emigrating to the US. The earliest years of his life were spent in Scotland with his mother while his father and older brothers were living and working on Vashon Island in Washington State. I'm not sure of the exact details, but a few years after emigrating to this country my father quit school and went to work with his four older brothers as an itinerant logger, seaman, apple picker, etc. Over the next few years, logging and shipping out were punctuated with periods of riding the rails, sometimes evading (and sometimes seeking out) the hospitality of small-town jails across the country.

He was the classic red-card-carrying Wobbly and was increasingly active in the logging and maritime sections of that fading organization during the post-WWI years. As was the case with many Northwest Wobblies, he got involved in the CP organizing efforts in the woods in the later 20s, both with the Trade Union Educational League and Trade Union Unity League, and he eventually joined the party. This logically led to the CIO organizing of the International Woodworkers of America (IWA) in the early 30s. The IWA was a dual union challenge to the Carpenters Union's logging affiliate, the Lumber and Sawmill Workers (LSW), which had rejected the industrial union model and refused to even attempt to organize the vast majority of loggers.

My father was a good organizer and quickly rose to a leadership position as the IWA supplanted the LSW. He became the IWA vice president for Western Washington, the center of the industry at the time. His approach to his role was significantly different from the current practices. Following IWW tradition, he advocated a regular rotation of union leadership and limiting functionaries' pay to what the average workers in the industry made. He kept his caulk shoes in the office and I'm not sure he ever completely stopped working in the industry, at least part-time. Both he and my mother specifically opposed the adoption of the union shop and dues check-off agreements with the major logging companies. Their support for such principles led to some charges of anarchism.

In any case, my father's stay in union leadership was relatively short. He quit the job when the Communist-led IWA adopted the general CIO priority on institutionalized contract unionism with no-strike provisions and recognition of employers' property rights. After leaving his union position and returning to sporadic work in the woods, he continued to stress the importance of job action to get more control over the work process and to resist any institutionalizing or stabilizing of the relation with the employers. At times, during my teens and through college, I worked on a few logging jobs with him and saw these approaches in action.

My father had only just returned to work in the woods when I was born in the late 30s. His replacements in the union leadership were less disruptive CP functionaries who were easily sucked into the general "unity against fascism"/no-strike pledges of the WWII period. It was a crew that was not anxious to hitch rides on logging railroad speeders to remote logging camps to convince skeptical loggers that they deserved the dues that supported them. Both of my parents viewed this crowd as largely "piecards"[2] and were critical of their reliance on political maneuvering combined with heavy drinking and partying at conventions and conferences that were purportedly focused on electing "solid trade union guys" and passing "correct" political resolutions—that weren't supported or understood by actual loggers.

My father was past military age and the draft when WWII started. However, as an experienced seaman, he joined the Merchant Marine and spent the war in the New Guinea area. Eventually he was court-martialed, an interesting story that I won't get into, except to say that it embodied his hostile/skeptical attitude towards established authority dating back to his IWW days.

I remember him saying frequently: think for yourself; don't get too enthused about any individual leaders; it's more important to question leadership than to applaud it. This iconoclastic stance dominated his entire second stay in the CP and didn't end until his death in 1968. I remember thinking often that he might have been going too far, but in light of all that's happened in the half-century since he died, his position stands up better than my own.

## A Rough Chronology of My Politics and Work

From 1955–61, I worked during summers at a variety of logging jobs. At one point, I dropped out of college and worked in a logging camp for the better part of a year. Some of these work experiences were with my father – most were not. I left for college in 1957 (Reed College in Portland). Joined the CP in Washington in 1958. Transferred to the CP in Oregon in 1958. Organized a CP youth branch in Oregon in 1960. Dropped out of college in 1960. Organized a coming out party for Gus Hall[1] in Oregon in either 61 or 62, during which I became known locally in Portland as a Communist. Was elected Oregon District Organizer in 1962. Went to work as a Teamster truck driver, 1961–65. Quit job and went to "secret" International commie leadership school in Canada in 1965 (approximately twelve in attendance). Expelled from "secret" school in Canada by the Mounties, 1966. Placed on CP payroll, elected to CP national committee, assigned to Oregon temporarily. Was publicly named as Communist in closed HUAC testimony by informer Russ Kreuger. This led to extensive publicity (e.g., *Time* magazine), 1966–1967. Was selected as political action director for the CP and assigned to NCNP [National Conference for New Politics][2] in Chicago in the summer of 1967 . In the fall and winter of 1967 I moved between Portland, Chicago, and New York, assigned to developing an external political challenge to the 1968 Democratic Convention. In the late winter and spring of 1968, I was in Chicago working with Tom Hayden and Rennie Davis on various aspects of 1968 convention preparation, which ended badly in a disastrous planning meeting that May. My factional work in and around the CP was in full flower in this period as attention swung to the summer 1968 CP Convention. (I've detailed this convention elsewhere, see "More on the CP and Me," esp. pages 11–13) The "success" of my faction at the CP convention was quickly followed by the disastrous impact of Czechoslovakia;[3] my paid party position and political action assignment were summarily removed and I was offered the choice of returning to Oregon without a job or income or moving to Birmingham, Alabama as a public Communist without a job or income. During this period my father was dying and my first marriage was ending, so I went home to Oregon, expecting to be leaving the party and organizing the thirty or so communists in the Portland CP youth branch into something better approximating a communist grouping. I received a request from some remaining close CP comrades to come and work on Charlene Mitchell's presidential campaign – paid – which I did for a few weeks until relations with the party completely degenerated. I left the campaign in Chicago in the fall of 68 and returned to Oregon to enjoy the New York State unemployment benefits that were the unexpected fringe benefit of CP employment. I assumed that I was out of the CP since I had written a formal resignation from the CP National Committee. Much to my surprise, early in 1969 I was summoned back to NYC for a party 'trial' to determine if my resignation from the national committee should be "accepted" or if I should be "expelled" (I've described that Kafkaesque episode a bit more below in "More on the CP and Me," esp. pages 15–16). During the spring and summer of 1969, I was involved in developing a communist organization out of the few dozen members of the Oregon CP who had left with me. The grouping was loosely affiliated with the MDS [Movement for a Democratic Society] offshoot of SDS*, and was allied with the leadership of the RYM II faction of SDS.[4] In the fall of 1969 I moved to Chicago and lived and worked there until 2000.

The Sojourner Truth Organization (STO)* was formed as a Chicago collective in December 1969 and functioned, more or less, until about 1983-84. It varied in size from a handful to a few dozen comrades through three major splits. After the mid-70s it had functioning sections in half a dozen cities outside of Chicago. From roughly 1985 to 1994, Janeen and I were not in any political grouping. Our continuing public activity was centered around

Janeen's efforts to develop a popular music infrastructure incorporating punk and outlaw country and the substantial left printing of C & D Print Shop that we operated.

From the mid–80s, we had some contact with punk anti-fascism, the Twin Cities Baldies, Love and Rage*, etc. from the growing class struggle anarchist/left communist milieu. This relationship became much more significant around 1995, when we began working closely with Chicago anarchists associated with the Chicago Autonomous Zone.[5] Much of the initial focus of this work was around the protest and counter-convention to the 1996 Democratic Convention in Chicago, but it quickly expanded to include involvement in post-Seattle anti-globalization activity and, most important, a variety of work with Chicago ARA* that continued up to and after our move from Chicago.

Since 2001, Janeen and I have lived back out in the woods in the same house where I spent the first eighteen years of my life. But now, we have electricity and a phone … most of the time.

## More on the CP and Me
## July 2021

What follows are truncated memories from my political past—undoubtedly softened and rounded off by the passage of time, which also conveniently limits any contrary narratives. It's only an attempt to situate some of my early political views in relation to my rapid rise and fall in the Communist Party USA (CPUSA) between 1967 and 1969 and is abstracted from a good deal of the politics I was involved in at the time. This was quite a chaotic period, filled with actions, encounters, meetings, and events that are difficult to remember in their actual sequence. Keeping that in mind, I remain quite certain about the major turning points.

Some background: Since early 1966 I had been an open CP member and the paid organizational secretary for Oregon. In mid-1967 I was assigned to national political action work with a general responsibility for contact with the New Left, particularly SDS (Students for a Democratic Society), but also CORE (Congress of Racial Equality), SNCC (Student Nonviolent Coordinating Committee), and the NSM (Northern Student Movement). My party background and the experience in Oregon had led me to a "left" criticism of party policy and structure. However, for reasons that aren't worth detailing here, from the early 60s through much of 1967 I was also somewhat of a protégé of the national head honcho, Gus Hall.[1] During that period, Hall was concerned with developing a personal support base among the more active and radical young people who were beginning to join the CP in substantial numbers; he frequently bloviated about the need to renovate the party, develop a more aggressive and radical approach to political work, and eliminate the "dead wood" in the existing national leadership.

More background: the party had been essentially illegal during most of the 50s and early 60s, with its political leadership either in jail or operating semi-underground. Not to mention that in the decade beginning with the Stalin renunciation* and encompassing the development of the Sino-Soviet split, quite a few of the leadership had died and a number of others had splintered in various factional directions.

In any case, the party had taken some initial controlled steps towards election of a new leadership in a strange semi-legal/semi-public partial convention in 1966 where many of the delegates didn't know who was there and what, if anything, they represented—not to mention what was at issue when the heavily managed elections were held (this led to some funny stuff not relevant to this particular story).

In any case, the party scheduled a full convention for early 1968 to elect a new leadership and adopt a new strategic program. The dissident grouping I was a part of had great expectations. Hall prompted me to write up my positions and criticisms in a "strategy document" for the pre-Convention discussion. He understood I would criticize reformist and economist stage theories and the trade unionist limitations of the CP's so-called "anti-monopoly coalition" strategy—the "strategy" that was the basis of a garbage CP "Draft Program" that was up for adoption at the time. However, the political content overlapped with issues that I had been raising to various national leftists in preliminary discussions about forming a substantive revolutionary left movement/organization from the ingredients that were emerging in that political moment. Of course, building a revamped radical left tendency that would incorporate substantial New Left groupings as well as a range of party dissidents would have been a classic example of factionalism. However, notwithstanding the evidence that it went counter to the main thrusts of Moscow-aligned politics and, in retrospect, was never within the realm of possibility, in my fever dreams I (and a few others) saw this all as a reasonable path towards a new radical political alignment.

I wrote a document sometime in later 1967 and circulated it to a few dissident comrades in the CP as well as some outside leftists (I'd be embarrassed to provide names). I also gave it to Hall and he asked me to pass it on to Henry Winston, the party chairman. Winston had been blinded in prison and needed a reader, so this was hardly a casual request. Initially, I got some fragmentary and perfunctory reactions from both Hall and Winston indicating, at least, that they considered my arguments a legitimate part of the pre-Convention discussion.

This brings us to an enlarged National Committee meeting in the fall of 67. There had been some sharp debate and discussion concerning different estimates of the radicalization of the Black Liberation Movement. Based on our experiences of the immediate past period, our left grouping argued that effective popular unity had to be anti-capitalist, not "anti-monopoly." This crystallized some strategic divisions with sufficient clarity that I had begun lobbying the left faction to identify circumstances under which we would leave the party in an organized way.

A number of us were ignoring the rote speeches at an enlarged ceremonial post-meeting event, when Jim Jackson, a legacy Black leader on the downside of senility in our estimation, began a long diatribe against the petty bourgeois "infection of our party" which needed to be purged. It amounted to an extended riff on the first sentence of my draft which he asserted had demeaned hundreds of thousands of working-class militants who had died for the struggle, by suggesting that the revolutionary movement was in a crisis. Filled with rhetoric like, "Who is this scum that views the historic accomplishments of socialism as reversible?"[2] Since my draft had not been circulated, only a handful of people knew that I was the intended target. There was no opportunity to challenge or discuss Jackson's nonsense, although some party stalwarts, like San Francisco Longshore hero Archie Brown, were provided an opportunity to pile on with the predictable themes.

Realizing that this could only have happened with the active intervention of Hall and Winston, I decided to quit more or less on the spot and prepared for the Port Authority bus station and a long trip back to Portland. Half a dozen comrades located me and made a big push to change my mind. They argued that we were likely to win major changes at the upcoming party Convention and that the assignment to develop a challenge to the Democratic National Convention (DNC)[3] was still operative. I began pushing to clarify what changes would constitute a sufficient reason to remain.

Through the winter/early spring of 67–68 there was a lot to do around the DNC that kept me in Chicago—away from CP intrigues and in extensive contact with a range of other leftists. I had already concluded that my trajectory was probably out of the party when I asked to have my piece circulated as an aspect of the pre-Convention discussion. That was denied, and I was told to summarize my points in a thousand words or less and to defer all decisions about circulation and discussion to the current party structures. Then Hall and the Secretariat announced that the upcoming Convention would not include new elections to the leadership and the adoption of a new program. Instead, it would be another "special" convention, limited to a discussion of policy for the 68 election and to setting guidelines for the production of another draft program revision.

In my view it was already clear that the party was not going to be transformed. However, we achieved a number of political and organizational victories at the Convention. Most notably, we stopped Hall's attempt to run for president on a CP ticket after he had announced publicly (*New York Times*) that he was running and that he planned to have the party lay out some hundreds of thousands in the attempt. At the time this was quite a coup although it doesn't seem so much now. We also got the previous draft program completely rejected—although like Phoenix it rose from the ashes a few months later. There were also a number of other "victories"— the specifics of which have faded in my memory, but the essential point is that none of this occurred because we had majority support; it all flowed from our asserted willingness to go "public" with our differences, potentially undermining Hall's status as "leader" with the Soviets.

Then comes the French General Strike and, most important, the Soviet crushing of the Prague Spring.[4] Suddenly confused and demoralized liberals became iron fists of the Rebellion in Party rhetoric, while at the same time our political alternatives, particularly the DNC protests, were immolating. So it was clear that while the prospects for a productive struggle within the party were essentially imaginary, unfortunately the non-party alternatives were also in big trouble.

As it became clear that there was going to be no significant discussion in the CP, I began to modify what I had written to address new developments and a broader audience. This produced the changed intellectual points of reference in the second version, the most striking being the replacement of André Gorz and Lelio Basso with Althusser.*

Following the CP Convention my role in the DNC saga had come to an ignominious end, and Hall told me that I no longer had a national assignment and would be taken off the CP payroll. I was given the choice of going back to Portland or to Alabama as a public communist without a job. I chose Portland and became the first (only) person to draw unemployment compensation from New York with the Communist Party as the employer of record.

In this period, the fossilized old-line party began a counterattack that centered around sanctions against those who had publicly opposed the emerging official line on Czechoslovakia. I was among the dozen or so that were so sanctioned at the next-to-last national meeting that I attended. Following that meeting a group of us pulled together the major dissidents to decide what we were doing. Almost everyone who attended is dead now so I'm fairly comfortable with indicating some things about the participants. In attendance were the leaders of the New York and Southern California Districts, the current and subsequent editor of the West Coast paper, the 68 presidential candidate, the head of International Publishers, a previous editor of the *Daily Worker*, and half a dozen younger members of the Central Committee—most of them Black.

The discussion quickly reached a number of impasses that made it clear that while there was little disagreement about the disastrous situation in the party, no organized split was possible. I'd locate four general reasons, all of which I still believe had some merit. First, a number of older comrades who had gone through the splits of 56–60 argued that nothing could be won without a systematic and persuasive critique of Soviet Marxism. Second, that same group could not be persuaded that there was enough political agreement between the dissidents. Third, it was generally felt that there was insufficient experience and agreement in the general left to provide a viable initial base. And fourth, the substantial minority of Black participants indicated their first alternative to the CP would be a Black Nationalist communist formation—particularly since the CP had reluctantly fielded a Black presidential candidate and that campaign still had some months to go.

I went back to Portland, intending to quit the party as soon as alternatives could be developed. I was put under a lot of pressure to defer the decision and eventually was hired to work with the presidential candidate. I set up some functions with New Left contacts—including participating in an SDS National Council meeting in Boulder, Colorado. I also met with a lot of hostility from party structures in Minnesota, Michigan, and Washington that was clearly nationally stimulated. Finally, I had organized a non-public meeting of the candidate with the Chicago SDS national staff collective and the Chicago Union of Organizers when the Chicago CP demanded that their functionaries be allowed to participate. I had gotten the meeting by promising that this would not happen.

In any case, I canceled the meeting and quit the campaign and the party. I got on a bus with my suitcase and the FBI captured my underwear in Omaha as I slept … A fitting end to an inspiring story.

I can't remember my resignation letter, but I must have written one because some months after returning to Portland and organizing a substantial communist grouping outside of the party, I received a strange request/demand from the CP: I was instructed to return to New York for a national committee trial that would determine whether to accept my resignation or to expel me. Something along the lines of "no one leaves the party." So I went back for my trial. It was a full-day affair where I argued I should be expelled against a strange leadership argument that greatly exercised the hacks that "my resignation should be accepted." I lost that final vote 52 to 48—so I guess that I resigned from the party rather than being properly expelled.

The two documents eventually worked their way into the various versions of the STO Party Pamphlet where they remain to entertain the enlightened.[5]

## More on STO and After
## August 2021

By the end of the seventies a succession of STO* industrial concentrations[1]—from International Harvester's Tractor Works to
GM's Electromotive, with dozens in between—had culminated in
losing struggles against plant closures. It was evident to most of us
that the political momentum of capital in its core areas was no longer producing larger and more strategically located oppositional
movements with increased militancy and radicalism, as it had in
the previous decade. The trends were particularly dispiriting for
workplace organizing. Decreasingly frequent examples of class
militancy and self-organization were increasingly associated with
tactical and strategic defeats that didn't provide a promising terrain
for the future growth of a culture and community of class struggle.

Initially, most of us saw these changes as part of a tactical ruling-
class move "South" in response to a sharpened class struggle, a
move that didn't challenge our working assumption that a "class
against class" polarization would shortly re-emerge—although
perhaps with a modified geography. Our first attempts at adjustment through slight shifts in our orientation and through "working harder" mainly resulted in accelerating organizational splits
and "burnouts" of good comrades. It was increasingly evident that
we were dealing with processes that raised questions about some
basic assumptions about the trajectory of capitalism. By the end
of the period, most of us realized that our organizational future
would be short without significant modifications to our approach,
and that the success of such modifications would probably depend
on changes in objective circumstances that were well beyond our
political influence.

During this period, the Nixon "opening" to China, followed
shortly thereafter by the end of actually existing socialism,[2] had

combined with the neo-colonialist response to national liberation to prompt our awareness of the significance of capitalism as
a "world system" with no outside. We noted the increasing diver-
gence in capital and labor flows from classical imperialist patterns,
the emergence of a potential alternative capitalist hegemon (first …
Japan), the growth of transnational corporations and cartels that
could operate outside of and frequently challenge capitalist nation-
state and sub-state governing formations, and the emergence of the
"Third World" within the "First" (see Hardt and Negri 2003).

Around the same time, we had become aware of the crisis perspective of the *Grundrisse*'s "Chapter on Machinery" (Marx 1939,
esp. 690–95) and its relevance to the impact of technological development on the factory system and the industrial labor process.
This was a framework for looking at capitalist politics in terms of
a conflict or tension between the socio-economic trajectory of an
increasingly transnational capitalism and the nation-state–based
political structures that had jurisdiction over the "laws and bodies
of armed men,"[3] that are the essence of the capitalist state and that
provide the apparatuses that maintain its legitimacy. Out of this,
some tentative discussions of the contradictions between state
structures and the global pursuit of profit and rent—major themes
in my current writing—came into view.

For a short period, revisiting the issue of the "system" was part
of STO's effort to retain organizational cohesion by emphasizing
theoretical development and building a "tendency" around our
strategic approach. However, we realized that "tendency building" with autonomous communist politics is a difficult project
when your activity has not produced many tangible results, and
we always saw the priority on "theory" as a temporary phase from
which a clearer and more firmly based set of practical priorities
for political work would have to emerge. In any case, it was clear
that our "growth" in this period was moving the organization in
an increasingly academic and elitist direction—developing a cadre
convinced of their superior capacity to "think," with a political
practice that was becoming less coherent and consistent … but

mostly just less.[4]

Some additional factors underlay the political discussions of the early 80s. Sustaining a working-class political collective with real collective practice that could attract and incorporate cadre who were willing to assume substantial political and legal risks was a greater priority for some of us than others. Janeen and I were in the camp that wanted to develop a real organization, rather than a distribution mechanism to promote the output of a circle of intellectuals. While no one openly disagreed with our general stance, concrete actions to implement it were less important for those inclined towards the "Facing Reality,"* Jamesian attitude that the class struggle would produce the organizational forms it needed.

Much of the public face of the organization during this period centered on our positions on white supremacy, working-class autonomy, and revolutionary organization. At the time, most of these topics could be approached relatively openly, although issues of economic survival imposed some limits. However, even in this early period there were some limiting factors at play that originated from the objective difficulties of combining "legal" and "illegal" work within the same organizational structure. These factors became increasingly important and have some relevance to what was written and openly discussed in that period—and what was not. I will touch on this factor again—after some more context has been developed.

STO always explicitly considered itself to be a local adjunct of an international struggle and openly attempted to develop relations with the domestic and international "Movements of 68"[5] that were doing work similar to ours—although perhaps to better effect. It is not so widely understood that our work also included persistent attempts to maintain and develop relations of solidarity and joint work with anti-imperialist revolutionary nationalist groupings in this country and throughout the world—attempts that frequently were not open. Despite serious practical reservations and important political differences with some of these movements, our estimate was that they were more likely to challenge capital than anything developing from our independent efforts. As the conditions for, and the outcomes of, our own work deteriorated, this view became stronger within STO.

Developing political relationships with the Black, Puerto Rican, Native, and Chicano movements and organizations in this country, and providing political and material support for insurgent struggles in the Caribbean, Southern Africa, Ireland, Iran, etc., was a major element in the life of the organization and placed increasing demands on our resources. As I said above, in the political circumstances of the early 80s there were good reasons to regard support for these movements as a more significant contribution to the overall revolutionary process—at least for a time—than our increasingly frustrated attempts to implement "our own" work and organizational development.

In STO, Janeen and I supported these priorities, along with Ken Lawrence and a clear majority of the organization. There were significant differences that had played a role, for example in the 1978 MAL split.[6] Noel Ignatiev also had differences. However, even these oppositions shared significant agreements with the general estimate and approach. In any case, a good deal of the political life of the organization concerned these issues at a moment when many of the groupings we worked with were increasingly embracing some variant of armed struggle—up to and including placing a priority on clandestine military operations.

During the same period, we were reorienting our approach to working-class "base-building" to emphasize a more "interventionist" approach to emerging episodes and arenas of class struggle. This had two features. The first stressed building the organizational and ideological capacity to intervene at points of class confrontation from the "outside." This contrasted with our previous approach to workplace organizing that emphasized autonomous internal development and "self-organization." The second feature prioritized a confrontational approach to the capitalist state and its policies. It was focused on countering policing policies and was specifically oriented against military production and imperialist intervention. In both issue areas we attempted to build militant rapid deployment combat organizations (some termed them "macho assholist") that were broader and less ideologically coherent than the pre-party forms that we had been working within. However, they were narrower and more ideologically coherent—also far more militant and more conducive to tactics that went beyond legal protest—than the workplace groups we had been attempting to build. This approach incorporated features of the "fronts," affinity groups, and "columns" that were being experimented with by radicals elsewhere in the world. In retrospect, it is questionable whether such tactical/organizational questions should have dominated our discussions at the expense of a more fundamental strategic focus on changes in transnational capitalism. Nevertheless, they were much more central to our political trajectory than the preliminary arguments about the trajectory of global capital and the issues of cyclical and secular crisis* that emerged in STO for a brief moment at the beginning of this period.

In any case, we made a series of efforts in the mass militant arena that included some radical innovations in anti-military and anti-fascist work, as well as some non-traditional strike support. We also, for the first time, expended a substantial effort on non-intellectual cadre development—on "training." However, given the contemporary political circumstances, it rapidly became apparent that we were taking excessive risks for questionable rewards and the likelihood was that we would not be able to survive very long. At the same time, risks taken in this arena were clearly jeopardizing our capacity to carry out the more specific quasi-military support activities for actual participants in efforts to develop Protracted People's War[7] in this country and internationally. These also were becoming increasingly risky and repression-prone. I assume it is evident why public theoretical/strategic discussion would play a decreasing role in such conditions—and it certainly did. I hope this helps explain why STO and its major remnants essentially dropped serious open discussion of some approaches to struggle and organization that look so promising in retrospect. We recognized the lack and some discussion continued, but it was not widely generalized.

Let me go back for a moment to those discussions that did happen so that the ramifications of the debate are clearer. At the beginning of the period of re-evaluation, Noel and Ken and most other STO members argued that the lull of the past decade was temporary and localized and that we should expect a more classical "class against class" polarization to reassert itself in the near future. They regarded my approach to the likely trajectory of capital and the future terrain for class struggle as a rejection of basic Marxist premises that exaggerated the issues of working-class marginalization and precarity and implicitly downgraded the centrality of white supremacy. Only a few in STO agreed with my views on these issues with even minimal conviction. Consequently, discussion of them evaporated quickly with few traces and was replaced by the re-evaluations of political approach indicated above, and by the re-examination of the potentials for fascism initiated with Ken's work on Pierce and the National Alliance,* and by the Greensboro Affair.*

During this period, any attempt to focus STO on differences about the conception of capitalism would have immediately polarized it along fault lines that would have guaranteed its quick disintegration—possibly I should say *quicker* disintegration. While STO also had internal differences on how to deal with the other issues, they came down along different lines and the relative size and strength of the camps were very different. Consequently, we pursued an approach to re-evaluation that didn't put the viability of the organization in immediate jeopardy. Perhaps ending STO a few years earlier wouldn't have been such a bad thing. However, it would have entailed abandoning some major obligations to the broader revolutionary movement at a moment when there had been a sharp acceleration of organized state repression against the leading elements of those forces—a moment when a substantial number of individuals and groupings that we considered to be comrades were being jailed or forced underground.

There were many mistakes involved in this process, and I was guilty of a major one that I completely failed to recognize and understand at the time. While some, notably Noel, persisted in the hope that a "class against class" struggle would reassert itself, I hung on to a different hope—that the national liberation struggle of oppressed peoples against the imperialist metropolis (Protracted People's War) would lead to a revolutionary social bloc that challenged global capital. This strategic assumption/estimate, combined with the organizational inertia generated from the "solidarity" features of our practical political work, produced a specific approach to risks and benefits. This in turn generated its own momentum that increasingly preempted serious consideration of alternatives, many of which may have better fit the problems and possibilities of the moment. It also produced some writing on my part that I now see as quite flawed.

However, along with this mea culpa, I should say that—although I wish it weren't true—I still think that none of the alternatives that were available in the period would have made STO any more likely to survive the twin collapses of "actually existing socialism"* and radical anti-imperialist national liberation that marked the period.

We were not oblivious to the dangers of the course we took—having seen them play out first-hand in other countries and with other groupings. Politically, the priorities a few of us chose led to an effective subordination of our strategic and tactical priorities to those of political and social forces with which we had important differences—differences that grew over time. Organizationally, it supported a trajectory towards centralization, militarization, and clandestinity, and heavily de-emphasized open political debate. In retrospect it's a bit hard to understand, but once taken, the path was very difficult to modify, much less reverse. For a substantial period there were always some promising struggles and movements to work with, even as the general hollowness, futility, and corruption of the politics we were linked with was becoming increasingly apparent. That we survived more or less intact personally and

23

politically is a historical accident, but we're happy about it.

Things began to change in the early 90s. A radical activist anti-fascist youth constituency with significant class struggle anarchist segments had begun to emerge, and we began to orient back towards some of the possibilities for radical mass struggle that we had considered and then abandoned a dozen years before. These new potentials, and the culture of resistance in which they were embedded, emphasized opposition to democratic electoral reformism, support for the Zapatista insurgency in Chiapas and no-border agitation, and, more centrally, anti-globalization (Seattle) and anti-fascism (Anti-Racist Action).* Of course, this was more than a quarter century after we might have passed ourselves off as young, and our role was essentially supportive, not participative. This provided some real limitations, but we did our best to help develop organized collective approaches to radical political work—"at a distance from the state," as Badiou says.*

From that point to now I have written a lot—perhaps too much. Some of it goes over old ground and some makes arguments that I couldn't make earlier. All of it is part of an attempt to contribute to the development of a radical politics that is organizationally and ideologically competent. It may be a bit redundant, but to fill out the narrative a bit further, I'm adding an overview of what I have written about over the years.

Before 1967, my focus was on what might be called left (CPUSA) rectification—a doomed effort to resurrect an organized revolutionary core from the CP legacy ingredients at hand that would challenge the dominant myopic right-wing sectarianism and shed some substantial layers of incompetence. I didn't write much that is still available during that period, but there were some feeble attempts to integrate the approach of Marx's 1844 fragments[8] into the prevalent conceptions of class exploitation. I picked up some initial Gramscian* views when the material became available in English, but these didn't really become apparent until the end of this period. Unfortunately, looking back, it seems to me that I basically accepted an improved version of the existing Stalin/

Plekhanov*orthodoxy with a slightly more radical assessment of political forces and potentials. In short, it wasn't that much of a break with Gus Hall's mantra: "the line was basically correct; its implementation was at fault."

Around 1967, my political stance began to undergo significant changes—something that happened widely in that period. I was unable to accept the official version of either side of the Sino-Soviet split, although I found the "bombard the party headquarters"* side of the Cultural Revolution* attractive. I was increasingly skeptical of my earlier assumptions that the specific politics of the CPUSA might be uniquely bad or that other international segments of official communism might provide a substantive alternative. I became convinced the basic strategic premise of a two-step revolutionary process based on the unionized sector of the working class was illusory, and started to argue that the only conceivable revolution in the Lockean Heartland* must be anti-capitalist from the inception, that its mass vanguard* in this country would be the Black and Brown working classes, and that its political/strategic orientation would be extra-parliamentary and armed. These politics dominated my last couple of highly factional years in the CP and continued through the initial STO period. They are reflected in the split documents from the CP and in the STO Party Pamphlet (STO 1969) and various other things I wrote for STO in the early/mid-70s.

Around 1980 a few of us in and around STO began responding to what we can see in retrospect were important developments in the national and international political context. We sensed that there were some important changes that impacted the flexibility of capitalism and the terms of class struggle, but at the time our understanding did not extend beyond the realization that our section of the left had to do things quite differently and that some fundamental reorientations might be needed. The fact was that the combination of the crushing of the radical possibilities of the Cultural Revolution, the disintegration of the radical "Movements of 68," the consolidation of a neo-colonial response to national liberation, and the palpable rot of Soviet Marxism and its state required a basic rethinking of revolution. Our political circumstances made it increasingly difficult to publicly argue our changing positions, so there is not much that was written down during that period. However, some of the changes are fairly evident from the changed approaches to political work that I have indicated above.

By the time of the Soviet collapse and the Bush Sr. episode, most of our earlier political reference points were essentially memories, dead and gone, but some new possibilities were emerging in the form of a growing anarchist/punk youth culture and community with substantial anti-state, pro–working class components that were increasingly differentiated from individualistic anarchism. We gradually reoriented to this potential, more or less deliberately, through some relationships with Love and Rage* and the initial anti-fascist/anti-racist groupings in the Midwest, and through our connections with portions of the Midwest punk milieu. By the middle of the 90s, this orientation had led to a substantial involvement in the anarchist-organized 1996 Democratic Counter-Convention protest. This extended quickly to a continuing involvement with ARA*, primarily in Chicago, and to participation in the activities and groupings in the radical anti-globalization struggles begun by the watershed struggle in Seattle.

From this point, starting with the piece I wrote on the Seattle action and the *Confronting Fascism* book with Sakai and Xtn (Hamerquist and Sakai 2002), I began to devote more time to writing. Learning how to manage a computer—more or less—contributed to this process, as did retiring and moving out to the woods. I might mention that 9/11 did slow everything down for a couple of years when we put some intensive efforts into an assortment of doomed local ecological efforts that I'll leave unelaborated.

In any case, although this may be repetitive, we want it understood that from the late 90s to the present, most of what we have done and written should be seen in the context of promoting the formation of a defined radical activist tendency with the capacity to think and act collectively. There's still a ways to go, but then we're not dead yet.

# I. ORGANIZATION

**Thoughts about Organization
late 2000**

*This essay was originally an email to a comrade responding to a discussion paper proposing a militant anarchist organization in Chicago. The paper circulated within and around ARA\*, and the discussions around it eventually led to the creation of the BRICK Collective, which affiliated with the short-lived Federation of Revolutionary Anarchist Collectives.*[1]

I like the paper and hope to be included in whatever develops out of it. This is a response to four points and some related issues. Hopefully, the criticisms and differences won't overshadow my general agreement.

It is impossible to spend much time in the movement without encountering opportunistic attempts to incorporate local projects and key organizers into some kind of structure designed to maximize some grouping's regional and national influence rather than to improve the work and develop a shared politics. There is a healthy aversion to such organizational initiatives, particularly when they come with politics, stated and/or implicit, that aren't fully accepted. The more disciplined and centralized such a project appears to be the greater and more reasonable the reluctance to get involved, particularly for experienced activists who are fairly confident of their own politics. But this concern, despite its general validity, does not seem to me to apply to the situation that exists here—one that is unnecessarily disorganized, atomized, and fragmented despite substantial political agreement and important shared experiences. Certainly, it does not explain or justify the reluctance to commit to efforts to improve the situation such as is represented by the paper.

I would like more clarity about the sort of organization that is under consideration. This absence of clarity allows skeptics to read the proposal as a projected solution to all organizational needs, something which it cannot and should not attempt to be. There is a range of organizational needs that could never be handled with one solution. We need organization to improve and generalize debate and discussion. We need organization to implement political and military self-defense. We need to link up the ingredients of an alternative cultural bloc ... organization. We need an array of new political and cultural organizing initiatives and a qualitative strengthening of those that exist ... organization. We need to develop a street force that can remove some of the ad hoc character from current activity without sacrificing its spontaneity. All of these involve arenas of autonomous organization with unique self-determined internal dynamics, not something possible within the usual thinking-head/acting-body, vanguard/mass dichotomies.* In fact, however, all of these areas could benefit from an organization, and possibly more than one, that is able to think out the issues, clarify some alternatives, and take practical steps necessary to test its political conclusions; an organization of conscious revolutionaries committed to the development of a coherent collective revolutionary project.

I think this is the type of organization that the paper envisions, but I'm not totally sure. It never says this in so many words. This unnecessarily clouds or leaves open important problems in the relationships between the proposed organization and other organizations, movements, and political individuals. There is no discussion of the tension between individual autonomy and collective politics. A whole range of unanswered questions remain—who would be organized into the group and how? How would the work relate to the general movement? I have some opinions on these points that will emerge later.

I understand why many militants are suspicious of all proposals for a revolutionary cadre organization and have some agreement with their position. However, the alternative perspective is that various islands of organization should "naturally" coalesce "from below," and this, in my opinion, is nothing more than a pious wish. Every one of us knows from experience that radical political activity contains as much impetus towards fragmentation as towards unity, and that when "the people are united," despite the slogan, they still are regularly defeated. Even when unity of a sort is attained more or less spontaneously it doesn't necessarily lead to a viable strategy, reasonable priorities, and a careful use of resources. It seldom even leads to a sense of a common enemy that is sufficient to be the basis for sustained joint action. Add to this the fact that we have an active and organized enemy with lots of resources available to see to it that "logical" and "natural" unification is always either diverted or aborted.

So here are my four points. I confess to no reason for their order. First, the issue of the initial political agreement, "unity"; second, the federation/confederation issue; third, the issue of discipline and of the relationship between majority positions and dissenting minorities, including individuals; and finally, what I'll call the issue of authenticity. (After the points will be my usual meandering conclusion).

### "Unity"

I disagree with the weight the paper puts on initial political agreement, points of unity, and that sort of thing. I am more interested in clarity than unity, initially and ultimately. Frequently, the best approach to clarity is to understand the elements of strategic disunity. One thing that is certain is that political positions change. Sometimes this is a change towards a more revolutionary stance, but often it is quite the opposite. There is always a good possibility that political positions arrived at through a more or less intellectual process—as contrasted with a more organic process involving collective activity as well as discussion and debate—will not be implemented when the implementation proves to be both hard and risky.

In our conditions, three "initial agreements" are required. Despite their vagueness, they point to real political tendencies in our movement and would draw some fairly clear lines. First, we want people who aren't reformists and whose orientation is to fight the system. We all know activists who are moving towards one or another version of the politics of the possible, based on various allegedly realpolitik considerations. This is not generally a reversible process. Much grief will result from trying to incorporate such people into an organization that aims at revolution. Second, we want people who believe that revolution must be achieved through the development and exercise of popular power and who understand that political work must embody and develop this power as a practical content, not just an ultimate goal. A number of political tendencies have such a limited and skewed view of popular revolutionary potentials in this country that they are destined to remain trapped in either subcultural utopianism or clandestine adventures ... perhaps both. Finally, we want people who are willing to subject their ideas and activity to collective discussion and decision-making. Individualism elevated to a purportedly anarchist political perspective has always been a factor in this section of the movement. This individualism is often expressed through a proprietary approach towards particular areas of work and extreme defensiveness on some political questions, which combine to make collective work difficult if not impossible. An initial commitment to collective work and discussion is an important separation from these politics.

Obviously, huge differences can and will exist among people who might share these general agreements. It also will never be easy to judge whether these agreements are solid and not pro forma. In the beginning we will be heavily dependent on the way prospective members define their own politics, but many of them will not have clearly and independently thought them out. There is no magical way to determine whether people's actual positions are the same as those that they are comfortable expressing, or whether their actions will conform to either. Furthermore, collectivity, the last of the three points mentioned above, requires a good deal of space and time, and some joint activity, before abstract agreement on the need for collective work will be implemented in actual political projects.


## Confederation/Federation

I'm baffled by the federation/confederation debate among anarchists, unless it is just a surrogate for differences about discipline and decision-making. I'm not persuaded by either of these alternatives and don't find the arguments between them to be productive. I understand that the emphasis of the arguments for a confederative structure is to develop more genuine participation and actual democratic decision-making, while the arguments for federation may place more emphasis on political coherence and unity. However, no structural arrangement can guarantee either of these results. Each of these particular arrangements could easily lead to results quite different and even in contradiction with its supposed virtues.

It is a little bizarre that anarchism, which views itself as universal and internationalist, should put the most immediate, local, and parochial concerns and issues in a privileged position. The overemphasis on the local and immediate side of things that follows from the confederation emphasis on "from below" can lead to an artificial restriction of debate and discussion. The concept of local is infinitely reducible, so that we may never be able to realistically evaluate actual political alternatives without stepping on one or another set of semi-sacrosanct toes. As an example of the potential problems, consider if local work was reflected by the B. Dominick (2000) piece in *Arsenal* #2.[2] Should such local work have a privileged position in any organizational structure? Should the mere fact that this work was local prevent a clear consideration of whether it was reformist or whether it had any redeeming revolutionary significance at all? This would certainly be putting unwarranted weight on what currently exists rather than on what should exist.

I understand that Love and Rage (L&R)* is seen as the archetype of federated organization. My experience with that group was minimal and from the outside. However, it was certainly enough for me to question the linkage between federation and political coherence. L&R substituted a formal, common-denominator unity for actual political content and the process of debate and discussion that is essential to it. This muddied up all sorts of major differences and distinctions to maintain a superficial facade of unity while extending organizational hegemony as far as possible. Anybody and everybody's priorities were formally acknowledged and then conveniently ignored unless they fit with the fad of the moment. The fate of the group was completely predictable.

The issues of organizational discipline versus individual autonomy and of the relationship between majority and minority positions will still be there whether the organizational structure is centralized, federated, or confederated—and whether it is local or international. Let me move to that point in terms of the proposal.

### Discipline and Autonomy

I think that a revolutionary organization that does not expect minorities to accept majority decisions on basic issues and that does not collectively evaluate everyone's political work is an organization that will quickly become an ex-organization or an organization of ex-revolutionaries. This said, a number of clarifications and elaborations are needed. Not all issues are basic ones, and attempts to impose majority positions across the board are stupid. Indeed, I think that majority positions should only be obligatory on minorities in extreme circumstances. Minorities should not be expected to abandon their positions or to cease arguing for them both internally and externally. At times external debate might be curtailed for security reasons, but the reasons for such a limitation must be clear and compelling. Obviously, this debate has the potential to undermine political work, but without it much more

34

is undermined. Ongoing debate is the only way to keep alive the actual political alternatives in a situation. Without it, the terms for evaluating work are lost and the critical essence of the organization will be eliminated.

Beyond this, so long as the majority positions are clear and understood, there are important areas of work where individual and group autonomy should be respected for practical reasons even when this means implementing minority positions. For example, you almost never want a situation where an organizational majority that includes a minority of women is imposing its positions on how to organize among women on an organizational minority that includes a majority of women. Similar arguments extend to a number of other points. On a more tactical level, it is seldom smart, although it is sometimes necessary, to impose a position that is opposed by the majority of those directly involved in the area of work.

Finally, on a range of questions, including some of the most basic points of theory and analysis (what's a revolution? who's a revolutionary?) there is no reason to even aim at unity and/or division into majority and minority. What is important is to encourage and broaden individual initiative in order to sharpen and generalize discussion and debate, clarifying real alternatives and clarifying the criteria for their evaluation. These are issues that should never be "closed."

*Authenticity*

We live and work in the context of an historical struggle against capitalist social relations and institutions, a struggle that, unfortunately, has been more successful in transmogrifying capital than in building a revolutionary alternative to it. This struggle is a tremendous (and tremendously flawed) history full of self-sacrifice and heroism as well as stupidity, mistakes, and crimes—a history that can illuminate questions and problems, but that has not and will not provide us with answers to the pressing political questions. I don't see any left tendency, specifically including any variant of anarchism, that would have led to a substantially different historical outcome, if it only had been more widely adopted. And we cannot forget that it is never just an accident when some positions are adopted and others are not. I think that self-defined anarchists include the same essential range of politics, good and bad, as does the general left (although the relative emphasis in the mix may vary).

If we are looking to create a revolutionary perspective, the problems and the possibilities must be found in the entirety of the tradition of which we are a part, however reluctantly. I think that it is a fundamental problem to look for a viable perspective for today in some segment of this tradition or in the positions taken by some set of historical figures, as if it is something to discover. Instead, we have to realize that this perspective is not there to discover, it must be created out of the ingredients that exist—one of which is our collective history—through an effort of will and analysis. I place great stock in the conception of radical self-sufficiency, but we have a complicated set of tasks and it is certainly prudent to avoid wasting or discarding some important resources. I'm hopeful you can figure out what this means.

I have been involved in various attempts to resurrect an authentic "Leninist" or "Communist" position. These were, and I am convinced will always be, a waste of time and energy. I believe the same will be the case with attempts to consolidate the authentic anarchist position, as is the intent of one strand of the paper's argument. All sorts of time will go into worthless discussions about who and what is actually, genuinely anarchist. So, on the issue of "planting the flag, a black one of course." The red flag is weighted down with a tremendous historical burden of error and crime, but one that I believe is proportional to its relative, if horribly flawed, "success." The paper tends to see all this burden as the inevitable outcome of M-L political philosophy and strategy, and even as its intended result. Soviet Russia is seen as the embodiment of the vision of Marx's *Manifesto* and Lenin's *State and Revolution*.[3] When the paper is stretched to its Manichean limits, the communist movement is seen as a self-conscious attempt to impose a new, but still capitalist, rule over mass movements of revolutionary people. I disagree with this position and see my own completely M-L politics as a sufficient refutation of it. Even if this isn't accepted, which it probably shouldn't be, I think that any serious revolutionary organization should keep such issues open for discussion and debate between different interpretations of historical fact and different theoretical approaches.

As a substitute for dealing with some real questions and disagreements, the paper advances the model of Michigan's Active Transformation as one that they would replicate here.[4] I would like Active Transformation to be as good as possible and have been impressed with what little I know about it. However, it is not likely that they have solved the main questions of revolutionary organization in their few months of existence, and if they have the paper should tell us a good deal more about it.

Rather than this overly general argument by example I would like some treatment of how the proposal would impact on issues we know about. I'm thinking about Anti-Racist Action in particular. In the discussions of this organizational initiative, the question of ARA has come up a number of times, and yet at other points where it is certainly relevant it remains strangely outside the discussion. ARA is an important organizing project and a number of important and difficult political questions are being raised in and about it. I'm raising a few of them, not only because the issues are pressing, but also because they are conspicuously not treated in the paper.

Anti-fascist work that is militant and radical has demonstrated a spontaneous potential over time and in a number of different areas of the country. In many cases, including Chicago ARA, this leads to an organization that amounts to a core group with a fluctuating periphery—at times the periphery is only a handful beyond the core group, but at other times it far outnumbers that group. The core group is not a formally constituted leadership, but a largely self-selected and co-opting de facto leadership. The leadership has two potentially contradictory functions: raising the general level of understanding and participation of the entire group, and making decisions on issues that are not fully understood and reasonably cannot be fully discussed in the entire group. Participation vs. efficiency (which sometimes means security) is a dilemma not at all limited to ARA. Since ARA's leadership is anarchist rather than Leninist, the tilt is probably towards full participation, but real security concerns are a factor limiting and conditioning participation that anarchists have to take into account ... and do. In my view, it's not possible to see ARA as *the* revolutionary organization, without undermining its ability to grow and develop and/or messing up on important issues that require serious discussion, internal security, and substantial preparation.

Butch Lee has raised "jumping off the cliff" as a political category.[5] ARA's political work inevitably raises potentials to jump off the cliff. Much of ARA's floating membership is only theoretically aware of these potentials and neither can nor would be willing to fully participate in discussions where such issues are on the table. Nevertheless, they can be seriously affected by the outcome of the discussions. I think that as a general rule, such discussions should involve participants beyond those who are caught up in the organizational momentum of an area of work and should involve a reasonable mix of alternative propensities. This best guarantees (although all such guarantees are suspect) consideration of all sides of the issue.

## Revolutionary Organization:
## A Contribution to the Discussion
## January 2007

*This piece was written in response to a paper presented in an early phase of the Kasama project, a communist organizing project active from approximately 2007 to 2013 that centered on a website for sharing ideas. It was heavily influenced by Maoism and sought to constitute a militant communist pole in North America. Kasama began as a website to discuss a document by Mike Ely (2007) called Nine Letters to Our Comrades, which critiqued the Revolutionary Communist Party (USA), which Ely and several others in the Kasama scene had recently split from. Later on, a loose association was formed around the website to explore an organized implementation of its ideas.*

A revolutionary subject committed to the necessity of a transformed society and prefiguring its possibility emerges through a process of separation from capitalist society, rejecting its limits and commands in daily life. Popular resistance to the coercion of the capitalist state and refusal of its hegemonic dominance foreshadow an alternative way of living and working. This can be manifested through a range of forms—mass strikes, soviets or councils, liberated zones, people's armies, even political parties. For anarchists, this developing popular autonomy is defined not only by its break with official society, but also by democratic and participatory social practices and institutions that break with external regulation by self-appointed or delegated "leaderships"—"condescending saviors."* Clearly, this is at odds with the prevailing M-L conception of the relationship of vanguard parties to mass movements.

Keeping Communists from screwing up the movement is a real enough problem, but it shouldn't obscure the importance for revolutionaries to be organized in a disciplined structure that is separate from mass movements and institutions. I don't accept all of the main propositions of *What is to Be Done* (Lenin 1902), but I do accept the necessity for an organization of "professional" revolutionaries. Anarchists generally recoil from this notion, seeing it as opposed to their priority on autonomy and opposition to hierarchy.

There are two issues: the first is the relationship between revolutionary organization and mass/class movements; the second is the relationship between majorities and minorities, the individual and the collective, and leaderships and memberships within revolutionary organizations. They are related, but not identical. The first will always be difficult but, if technocratic and militaristic approaches are rejected, it can be worked through productively. The second issue also has major problems to which anarchists add one that is quite unnecessary by conflating autonomy, a social break with the dominant system, with individualism, a prominent aspect of that same system.

Revolution will be a collective process. It will develop out of collective projects implemented through the pooling of scarce human resources. This process will self-destruct if it cannot prioritize some estimates and approaches over others; especially when all alternatives are seriously held and there is no previously agreed upon way to determine which will prove to be the most productive.

In my experience, anarchists are hard pressed to discuss their political work critically and are wary to the point of being hostile to any process that might result in one area of work being prioritized over another. They are unwilling to collectivize an estimate of political conditions if it means everyone's ideas are open to discussion and criticism but will not end up with equal validity. They find it difficult to deal with destructive tendencies in their own social and political culture. They don't take responsibility for evaluating major strategic initiatives that encounter obstacles—e.g., the anti-globalization movement after Genoa*—or political developments that dramatically alter the context for work—e.g., 9/11 and the War on Terror. These factors combine to create an amorphous anarchist milieu where major issues are determined according to what feels comfortable, what people want to do, what makes them happy, what is not too difficult or too dangerous—as if questions of revolution were individual lifestyle choices between fads and hobbies.

The lack of strong and disciplined revolutionary organizations is a particular problem when mass struggles are in a period of retreat and retrenchment, and when state repression is increasing … a period like the present. Without revolutionary organization, the gains in militancy and understanding from periods of insurgency are quickly eroded and may increase fragmentation, cynicism, and defeatism. With it, there is some possibility to generalize lessons and ensure that everything doesn't have to be learned again from scratch.

## Am I for Seizing the State?
## October 2009

*The following was an email sent to comrades in response to a discussion about the importance of the Russian revolutionary experience and the suggestion that Hamerquist was in favor of seizing state power as a revolutionary strategy.*

These remarks imply some differences that I don't want to pass over.

I, in agreement with Alain Badiou,* understand the "Russian Experience" to include the Chinese revolutionary process up through the dispersal of the remnants of the Cultural Revolution.* At discrete moments this experience dramatically unlocked the "possibility of possibility" (also Badiou) for tens of millions. In a more extended and demoralizing process, it suppressed and repressed everything it appeared to promise—also for tens of millions of people. For revolutionaries, this is a historical (and philosophical) fact of enormous magnitude. I don't believe that your politics, nor any revolutionary's, can or do escape this fact.

Contemporary anarchism is heavily defined by its negative critique and moralistic condemnation of the Russian Experience. This provides the content for your second paraphrase ... "Hamerquist is still for the seizure of state power." Not true! I would change one word, add another and remove yet another—further, I believe most Leninists would as well. I am for smashing, not seizing, the capitalist state. I am not for some generic state power. I believe that power must be exercised by any post-revolutionary order, just as it will be exercised by any revolutionary movement, but that it is crucial that this must not consolidate a new state defined, again utilizing Badiou, as a "system of constraints that limit the possibility of possibilities." (2010, 243). Your position, and that of anarchists in general, is that the Russian Experience demonstrates that "smashing" will inevitably become "seizing" and lead to the reinstitution of state power over the working classes. I respect the argument and know the history that supports it but question its "inevitablism," as the Maoists say—and, probably more importantly, the viability of any alternative anarchist perspective.

## Thoughts on Naomi Klein
## April 2008

*This was written as an email to Tom Hanley, a former prison education instructor, who asked for Hamerquist's opinion of the popular Canadian author Naomi Klein, and specifically of ideas put forth in her 2007 book* The Shock Doctrine: The Rise of Disaster Capitalism.

I've been reading Klein with my usual cynical bias. Given the unadulterated crap that passes for left political and social analysis, I hesitate to be too critical of her more skillfully adulterated output. But it's only a momentary hesitation. The surface distinctiveness stemming from Klein's straightforward hostility to US power obscures, but does not eliminate, the underlying similarity between her analysis and liberal reformism. She is a non-US left-liberal "third way" advocate who looks better by not being home grown—but probably isn't. There is a reason why she is welcome on Bill Maher's show and why the well-intentioned Cusack family bases a movie on her work.[1] She challenges, but not too much.

Of course, nothing but good can come out of the journalistic muckraking aspect of her book. It is good to see the two Friedmans[2] linked and MKUltra tied to structural adjustment.[3] It is good to see an approach which begins with the assumption that this country is on the wrong side of virtually every issue in which right and wrong play a role. But the analysis is terrible, unsupportable, and eventually will prove to be very vulnerable to counterattack by overt supporters of the current economic and political powers that be. I'll only make a few points, all of which you should feel free to challenge, because—as in too many cases recently—I wouldn't mind being wrong.

Contrary to Klein (2007), the issue is capitalism, not "shock capitalism" or "disaster capitalism"; the issue is capitalist ideology, not a bad "Chicago School"* neoliberal trend versus a good "Cambridge School" neo-Keynesianism.* Her essential argument is that a certain economic doctrine has captured state power and economic hegemony and has seduced ruling elites to the extent that the ruling strata of the ruling class is operating out of the most narrow conceptions of its economic and political self-interest. This is not unfamiliar. It has roots in the "cowboys vs Yankees" analysis of the mid-period in SDS,* not to mention in the Comintern* conception of fascism and the anti-fascist united front.

It has always been difficult for the left to understand that capital rules through force *and* through hegemony—through repression *and* through concession, through incarceration *and* incorporation—and that it utilizes both tactics simultaneously, although not according to a preconceived plan. Klein follows the dominant tendency in only seeing the repression as intrinsically capitalist, and actually removing the concession element into a dream world where it becomes a popular basis for further struggle, not a substitute for it. I've written a lot on this and don't want to pursue the points unless you do. I would just point out that during the gestation period for her "counter-revolution" in the late 50s and early 60s, there was a clear coexistence between "shock" and Keynesianism (Klein 2007, 444). Everything depended on the concrete circumstances. LBJ[4] was certainly a Keynesian and hardly a Friedman supporter—viz. war on poverty, Medicare—however he freely utilized the equally rotten University of Chicago Sociology Department and popped the Dominican Republic and signed off on COINTELPRO* without a qualm.[5] Under Carter, at the same time as support for Pinochet and the Southern Cone military actions was going unquestioned,[6] Andy Young was abandoning Rhodesia and accommodating with ZANU.* I could do a lot more along these lines.

The point is: whenever capitalist power is seen in terms of exclusive tactics, reformist results are virtually inevitable. In one case, it is because a "good" capitalism (Keynesian) is posited as a non-revolutionary alternative. In the other, it is because a limited tactical flexibility in rule is transmogrified into an endless potential for gradual improvements.

The worst part of the book is the final section, which attempts to cobble together the ingredients of some sort of popular counter-hegemonic coalition out of a range of forces covering the gamut from liberatory anti-capitalist revolution through various reform-ist/reactionary populisms to fascism. This is the essential danger with Klein's picture of the ascendancy of neoliberalism as a "counter-revolution." Its other side is that the most motley array of political oppositions—Chávez, Hezbollah, Putin—are assigned an essentially "progressive" coloration.[7]

I want to say only a brief word on the treatment's economic determinism. Klein explains ruling-class policy virtually exclusively in terms of cupidity—maximizing returns for the elite. This is the basis for the ascendancy of the Chicago School and the explanation of the course of recent history. Strangely, much of the left, and I would assume Klein as well, share in a privileged ruling-class background and education, but have no real difficulty seeing themselves as motivated by things beyond the wallet. What's the evidence that the balance of their social strata can't or doesn't? This gets to a disagreement that I have with Klein—and Chomsky and most of the left. They see a ruling class, but not really any potential for a categorical class opponent to it. Thus, everything reduces to a type of conspiracy where all ruling-class professions about fighting a real enemy are seen as fabrications intended to divert the majority of us from their incredible hoggishness at the trough.

Pretty feeble effort but maybe it will provoke you.

## On the Relevance of Old Debates
## August 2011

*This was originally posted as a comment on* Khukuri Theory, *a militant communist blog whose subtitle and perspective was, "toward radical reconception of revolutionary theory." The website was closely related to the Kasama Project\* and took its name from a machete-like knife popular in the Himalayas, in a nod to the Maoist movement active in Nepal in the 2000s. Hamerquist's comment was in reply to a piece titled "Marxism or Anarchism or —?" by John Steele, published on August 1, 2011.[1]*

I think this is a useful contribution to the Marxism v. Anarchism discussion. I have also found this discussion to be frustrating and unproductive and would like to see it develop in a different way.

Some reconsideration of political issues from 1917–23 Russia, or Spain in the mid-30s—perhaps even a new look at what Marx thought about India (and why not Ireland as well?)—might help clarify enduring questions about the state, about capitalist development, about the prospects for and the tasks of a revolutionary insurgency. Virtually no one enters the movement knowing this history and its implications, and no section of the movement has developed a politics that makes this knowledge unnecessary. However, if the discussion is to be productive, it should be kept in mind that even where those questions still have relevance, it's within a drastically changed context and with a radically new content. None of the competing historic answers should be enshrined as revolutionary first principles and looked to for guidance for revolutionary work in the present. When they are debated abstractly—and particularly when this takes on a moralistic character—the resulting discussion is a bad basis for making organizational demarcations and drawing ideological lines.

And there are important political demarcations that are needed—between revolution and reform, between communist and populist, between participant and observer—demarcations that are essential for the development of a viable anti-capitalist strategy and a real collective practice. A revolutionary left must confront these to develop its ideological and organizational distinctiveness. But from the first steps of such a process, it will be evident that there are self-defined anarchists and self-defined Marxists on every side of all dividing issues. This reality will never be rectified by any discovery of a purer anarchism or any "corrected" view of Marx or Marxism, and such efforts should not distract us from what is really important.

Rather than debates over the conception and definition of the "state," we should begin from the contradictions currently affecting the capitalist state formations that are impacting our lives; rather than reruns of century-old debates over mass autonomy and the development of a revolutionary subjectivity, how about focusing on understanding and relating to the mass insurgencies that are appearing and, too often, imploding on all sides today?

**Marx and Revolutionary Politics**
**October 2011**

*The following was sent to an email list of comrades, including both Marxists and anarchists. It was written in response to discussion on John Steele's "Why is Badiou of political value?," a post on the Khukuri Theory blog (see previous editorial note or Glossary).*

It is completely possible to be a dedicated and competent revolutionary and know nothing of Marx. It is completely possible to be a well-read Marxist and know nothing of revolutionary politics. At this time I would have trouble formulating a political position without reference to some elements of Marx, although this has definitely not always been the case—notably during the extended decades when I was part of a Marxist-Leninist organization.

Personally, I think that all revolutionaries can benefit substantially from an engagement with Marx—if the engagement is critical, if all assumptions are open for discussion, if no important questions are seen as settled. But these are huge "ifs." Frequently, circumstances push the engagement into much less productive forms. Sometimes this is academia, but more pertinent for us is the discourse that emerges from polar opposite implementations of a common, false assumption that it is crucially important to identify a "true" Marx or Marxism. On the one side: the limitations of revolutionary collectives that substitute "knowing Marxism" for serious thinking, finding in it a basket of timeless maxims and injunctions and seeing their implementation as revolutionary politics. On the other side: the limitations of the anarchist attitude that this or that is all that "Marxism"—and by inference Marx—actually is, without clarifying a different approach to a revolutionary praxis.

C's initial intervention was in response to a *Khukuri* piece by John Steele (2011b) a couple of months ago. The following excerpt from John's argument says much of what I think about this topic and it's where I'd take up the current discussion:

Why is Marx of political value? First a point of clarification on the sort of politics I mean: the politics—to say it very broadly and for the moment without further elaboration—of human emancipation. Given that this is our politics, or our broad political aim, then what is of political value can be characterized, equally broadly, as what conduces to, or what is helpful in working toward this aim. (Obviously this will be relative to historical situation.) So, Marx is of political value if his works conduce toward this, and for quite a bit of the last hundred and fifty years he's been thought, on a very broad scale, to be valuable in precisely this way. Now of course a lot of the finding-Marx-of-political-value during this period was built upon an understanding of Marx as the creator of a science of society and a metaphysic of history which limned a sure course of development and eventual victory—a thesis, and an understanding of Marx, which I reject, as I'm sure do most here. That was *a* Marx, and it's a Marx which has lost the political value it may once have had, but this is not the only Marx. (Steele 2011b; emphasis in original)

I don't accept the notion that this "scientific Marx" is the only Marx because it is the variant that has been so dominant in the movements and formations that adopt the label. Nor do I fully accept the alternate view that there is another Marx, a "true Marx," that has been obscured by this dominant tendency for well over a century. The basic critique of the first part of this is straightforward. Official Marxism, including its pre- and anti-Soviet manifestations, has increasingly lost connection with a "politics ... of human emancipation." Its organized participants largely fail to realize that this is the essential point of the revolutionary process, not just some ultimate objective, and they persist in a project whose main product is anti-communists and anti-communism. Those participants with higher expectations are rapidly disabused of them and launched towards cynicism.

The dominant tendencies in official Marxism, both social dem-ocratic and M-L, have been directly complicit in expansions and reconfigurations of human servitude and oppression—and this, in my opinion, is established beyond any need for further debate. It might be argued that official Marxism has assisted in the devel-opment of some social preconditions for communism—but this is debatable. I agree with C that all equivocations on these points, any clutching at balancing estimates—Stalin was "70% right" (or 0.7% right for that matter), or Soviet Russia "defeated fascism after all"—should be taken at their worst reading: as reactionary apologetics.

Nevertheless, I think it is a mistake to look at this situation and conclude that Marx is the cause of, and fully responsible for, all variants of rotten Marxism. This is not to deny that there is a clear line of connection between them and that Marx who clearly pres-ents major portions of his theory as "a science of society" in ways that do imply they are keys to "a sure course of development and eventual victory." However, a line of connection, while certainly an area for criticism, is not the same as a line of causality. There is plenty of material in Marx that shows he would hardly see what has been presented in his name as part of the transition from the realm of necessity to the realm of freedom.[1]

It is beyond pathetic that some M-L grouplets still hang on to this stuff and call it Marxism. However, even laying them aside there is still a broad Marxist current, including social democratic elements and anti-Soviet tendencies on the left, with determin-ist, reformist, and state-centered political perspectives that they ground firmly in Marx—and with ample textual justification. I'd like to believe this could somehow be reduced to a falsification of a completely contrary worldview, but it really cannot be.

While I think the reality of a different Marx should be accepted by anarchists, unless they are willing to argue concretely that it is an illusion, I don't think it is productive for dissident Marxists—like me and some others here on this list—to try to excavate a different Marxist system, a "true" interpretation that falsifies what has been advanced in his name. This is not to deny that major elements of official Marxism-Leninism were conscious falsifications of both Marx and Lenin. Soviet Communism suppressed major works of both when they didn't fit with the diamat doctrine.[2] I could give a long list, but I've done it elsewhere. I can personally testify to the active discouragement of any actual engagement with Marx's *Capital* in that framework, and even Althusser refers critically to the boundaries of M-L orthodoxy as "slight idiosyncrasies in … using the Famous Quotations" (1969, 27).

Both C and M have argued, following the 11th Thesis on Feuerbach,[3] that the self-conception of Marxism creates a unique obligation that it be judged—accepted or rejected—as a social movement and a distinctive praxis, not as a set of theoretical propositions. I might quibble. This is hardly less appropriate for other revolutionary perspectives; notably those emerging from anarchism. And while I see that they accept this position, I doubt that they advance it with similar intensity. Then, in my view, official Marxism-Leninism always rejected the 11th Thesis, in line with Althusser, who says, "It was, *and always will be*, only a short step from here to theoretical pragmatism" (1969, 28; emphasis in original). But that stuff doesn't go very far.

I do agree that Marxism should be judged as a praxis, and that the judgment is necessarily harsh. I find it important to work through how I, and people I have some respect for, accepted things that are unacceptable—but approach the questions with the primary goal of a better understanding, not a separation of good from evil. For me and possibly some others, it is very important to deal with these issues because we were active participants on the wrong side of them. The matter is essentially different for those who are attracted to Marx for political and intellectual reasons. Their positions can be treated on their specific merits outside of any of the problems with a political tradition that they have no responsibility for. This is no different than recognizing that anarchists don't have to be defined through denunciations of John Zerzan* and Ted Kaczynski, or to take responsibility for every ex-anarchist that has become a liberal dilettante.

## IWW, Base Building, Reformism
## 2009

*The following was sent as an email to comrades. It was most directly in response to one person's positions (identified below as N), though it speaks to the work and perspectives of the broader group. The two areas of work most directly commented on are: first, contemporary organizing in the Industrial Workers of the World (IWW)\*, most notably the efforts to gain legal recognition at Jimmy John's restaurants in Minnesota; and second, the work to repeal the anti-immigrant Arizona state law known as SB1070, specifically with an organization called the Repeal Coalition.[1]*

This essay continues discussions about the reform/revolution issue. The primary focus is on some questions around workplace organizing, immigration, and fascism through which I expand on what kinds of actions move us toward revolutionary potential while avoiding the traps of reformism. We start with some direct initial questions raised by N: "What is base-building?", "Why do you think Repeal is reformist?", and "What ought communists do tomorrow … ?" My response won't be so direct. I want to sidle around some of the points before actually attempting to begin a response to the questions themselves.

I think it is crucial to realize that the actual historical experience of "socialism," augmented and flavored by its interpretation and socialization through bourgeois filters, bears major responsibility for the current separation between the notion of communism and the existing mass movements and popular attitudes. The reality is that what was "won" historically turned out to be very distant from, and even opposed to, what was fought for—so distant that masses of people have to be re-convinced that fundamental answers to their wants and needs are possible outcomes of their own initiatives and struggles. This is manifested in protests against "pessimism" that tend towards exercises in left positive thinking and probably result in increased support for pretentious academic dilettantism. The same reality should also lead those anarchists who believe it is self-evident that the Russian and Chinese experiences were essentially coups and putsches aiming at different forms of capitalism to take another look at the terms and assumptions of their argument.

I've found it useful to look at the changes over the past century in class struggle revolutionaries' view of working-class movements and struggles and their place in them. Consider the attitudes expressed in Haywood's address to the IWW founding convention[2] or in William Trautmann's essay "Why Strikes Are Lost! How to Win!" (1912). What is striking is the harshness and immediacy of the view of the class contradiction—the extent to which the mass struggle is seen as directly related to the revolutionary objective and vice versa. For example, a common theme was that any term contract with an employer that obstructs practical solidarity with other workers' struggles—and they all do—amounts to "scabbing on the class." This stands in contrast to current IWW struggles for contracts, struggles that sometimes emphasize NLRB recognition procedures, still further limiting worker participation and encouraging passivity.

History has shown that there are some problems with the maximalist attitudes of the early IWW, but far more important contemporary limitations follow from their opposite, from radicals' capitulation to the lack of working-class self-confidence and autonomy, and their subsequent failure to orient towards reestablishing the connection between revolutionary objectives and the struggles of the day. This capitulation is expressed and justified in the crudest terms in that incredible statement, "I don't care about struggle, I care about winning." Winning what?

A growing oppositional mass consciousness and culture provides a necessary continuity in the development of a categorical radical alternative. This is as much a part of the revolutionary process as the moment of sharp qualitative break with official routine and the assault on established power. This counter-hegemonic pressure cannot be identified with or against any specific reform goal or any particular method of struggle. As I argued above, both the sense of revolutionary immediacy and the cumulative historical tradition of class autonomy were drained from the class struggle by the implosions of the nominally successful seizures of power in Russia and then China. However, whatever the causes of the current situation, every radical perspective must be evaluated and should evaluate itself according to how its work contributes to advancing these revolutionary preconditions. This is a wordier way of restating a point that I made in the previous discussion of the border issue—if the communists aren't organizing around the most fundamental aspects of class solidarity, who is?

I'd like to look a little further at some related issues that can be seen in the same historical experiences related to the formation of the IWW (not so coincidentally, also at the time of the 1905 Russian Revolution). Consider the IWW's reformulation of a now famous slogan from the Knights of Labor. Originally the slogan was "an injury to one should be the concern of all." It was changed to the more familiar "an injury to one is an injury to all." Of course, there are many ways that this change represented an advance. It confronts the distinctions of craft, industry, job classification, employment status, and ultimately nationality, and asserts a commonality of interests and a common enemy. This had a basically positive significance at that historical moment and in many ways it still does. But there is a weakness, too—maybe falseness is what I mean rather than weakness. What was dropped in the change from the Knight's version was the ethical imperative, the "should" and "ought," that was a major part of the original. Most supporters of the new formulation probably assumed this imperative, but the failure to state it then has some relationship to an increasing failure to act on it now.

The new language posits a commonality of the individual and sectoral interests in the working class that allows them to be aggregated into a universal class interest. However, this imputed class "interest" does not accurately describe real relationships in the structure of capitalist domination. Injuries to some workers can and often do translate into real benefits for other workers. This reality was certainly seen by the radicals in the IWW. It was the substance of their argument against narrow trade unionism. What was—and still is—less evident were the reversed implications of this reality. To be a little clearer, if the slogan is formulated in a different, but logically consistent, way, it might be restated as—"a benefit for one is a benefit for all"—and this is far from being nec- essarily true. However, its essential validity has become an opera- tive assumption for a good deal of left organizing among workers, which sees virtually all partial victories for class fractions as a net gain in a process of accumulating a countervailing class power. Even when these "victories" are tied to a zero-sum process that joins all working class fractions, winners as well as losers, in sub- ordination to capital by buttressing the "competition among the workers" on which capitalist power relies.

The posited common interest that workers have in collectively redressing these "injuries" is only an aggregation of separate inter- ests, each of which have been decisively shaped by a capitalist con- text which privileges atomistic consumption, not cooperation, sol- idarity, and collectivity. Looking at this issue a bit more abstractly (if such is possible), this concept of "injury" bleeds over into a con- ception of "victim" and indirectly delineates a status of non-injured and non-victimized which tends to become a regulatory standard for labor within capital. This contributes to a reformist focus on notions of "bad" capitalism that distract from the Marxist concep- tion that all capitalism is "the appropriation of alien labor without exchange, but with the semblance of exchange" (Marx 1939, 509). In the Marxist conception, one which I believe is widely shared by class struggle anarchism, it is the wage relationship itself, not its abuse, which is the actual injury.

Once the conception of workers as an "interest" within capital is accepted, the class struggle becomes more of a mechanism to distribute material benefits according to definitions and priorities largely defined by capital, a process that is basically hostile to the emergence of the collective solidarity that might present a more fundamental challenge to capital. In my opinion, this conception of a working class defined by "interests" developed within the framework of their subordination to capital tends towards populism, not revolutionary, liberatory communism.

A passage from Scott Nappalos's recent blog post "Direct Action? Who Cares!" helps to illustrate my point:

> The groups are basically the same—well organized, serious, etc. Let's say they both succeed. All things being equal, the group that gets a contract without a no-strike clause will probably come out with less other gains. The group with the no-strike clause will probably have a contract with more other gains. That is to say, the no-strike clause is worth money. Refusing it will come at a cost; accepting it will come with benefits. (Nappalos 2011).

From the classic IWW perspective, the mere fact of a contractualized agreement amounts to an implicit "no-strike" clause. All labor contracts intend to prevent interruption of work during their term, ruling out the "legal" potential to use strike action on issues beyond the wages and conditions of specific bargaining units. This is the case irrespective of whether or not the contracts have explicit no-strike language. So, this passage refers to something beyond that, to a contract that contains a more explicit no-strike obligation, "illegalizing" withholding labor in response to issues within the bargaining units during the term of a contract.

This leads me to question his assertion that a no-strike clause "will come with benefits." In what framework or what sense is this the case? I think that this calculus implies acceptance of the hegemony of capital. These terms: "benefits," "gains," not to mention "succeed" (which N also uses) only make sense within the logic of labor's subordination to capital. In what larger sense is any contract provision that trades off the ability to act collectively in exchange for marginal improvements in certain wages and certain conditions a "benefit"? Can a bribe intended to disorganize be transformed into a benefit which contributes to solidarity?

Perhaps sometimes, but not typically I think.

To expand further these concepts of how reformism appears and what it looks like to reject the legitimacy of capitalism, one can compare the left and right approaches to the border and immigration. My criticism of many left positions, including N's previous arguments on the border issue, is their failure to see that the right is increasingly presenting a clear and fundamental challenge to the existing social structure, while the left confines its activity to easily digested reforms within the framework of capitalist legitimacy.

I will limit what I cover here to the question concerning whether some radical elements of this movement are organizing in terms of "various forms of dual power."[3] There is a good deal of imprecision about this term: dual power. Strictly speaking, it refers to a defined political situation, a very temporary and very unstable equilibrium where neither of two antagonistic political forces possesses the hegemonic authority to successfully assert their political and military power. The term also has a related but much more general usage as a characteristic of radical political strategies that emphasize the importance of a categorical break with institutional legitimacy and the development of counter-institutions capable of exercising power in more and more significant areas prior to a direct challenge to state power. Frequently, this strategy emphasizes the prefigurative aspect of this counter-hegemonic strategy.

It is the second of these conceptions, a strategic orientation towards building elements of a dual power, that is relevant to this discussion. I assume that it's clear that I do not think neo-fascism is close to creating a dual power situation in the US Southwest. More importantly, neither do the neo-fascists and other reactionaries. However, it seems clear to me that this growing section of the anti-immigrant forces quite consciously rejects the legitimacy of the existing government structures, including those segments of them that share similar politics on the immigration issue, and does not have a perspective of "capturing" them. Instead, they are considering various mechanisms to implement their position that involve dual power conceptions—political secession, private militias, and resilient communities. They are developing a social analysis around the "country-class/political-class" axis that has a counter-hegemonic character. And they are also increasingly concerned with developing movement organizations and forms of struggle that prefigure a very different future society.

With these distinctions about reform in mind, we can turn to addressing the questions framing this piece. First, "base building": this is a term that can mean many things, a few of which are innocuous and a few that, in my opinion, are noxious. If communism is the self-abolition of the working class, communists must either be a part of that working class or—even if they confine themselves to the role of "recognize and record"*—they will find it difficult to say "no" to the role of "condescending saviors."* This is assuming, perhaps unwisely, that they are not actively trying to accept that role. Of course, it is important that communist cadre be located so that the needs and grievances of working people are also theirs, and that they are in a position where the risks and benefits that face communist activism are not grossly different from those that impact normal working-class people. This is a reasonable part of helping the organizing process of a class that must make its own revolution, a process which always involves a degree of confrontation with what exists politically. However, it does not involve an intervention that attempts to manipulate political agreement and support in a manner that does not treat working people as the actual subject of their own lives.

N says, "We want to build a base for communist ideas and we want more communist cadre." I agree, but a sentence that contains both "base" and "build," doesn't necessarily constitute a base-building perspective. In normal left conversation, base building refers to a process of linking a mass constituency to an "appropriate" leadership. The process may rely on spontaneity in practice, but the essential concept is a mechanistic, social engineering one. There may be some capitulation to what allegedly "is," where communists function as liberals and become cheerleaders, but the main characteristic is the attempt to coalesce an active body—the base—around a thinking head*—the builders. This is a process in which communists typically become manipulators and bureaucrats and whatever it is that they "build," it is not a good base for "communist ideas" and it seldom results in "communist cadre." It is normally the case that bases built in this way either function more as anchors or become someone else's base.

There is also a strong sense that base building is an essential prelude to real struggle, something that must be accomplished to some extent before much else can be done—a necessary stage, but one with no clear metrics. Thus, it diverts from obligations to intervene in existing conjunctures: moving quickly with the resources at hand to emerging fault lines that are frequently time-sensitive. What communists have to offer is a set of ideas, a willingness to think critically, and a commitment to purposive collective action. This has very little to do with base building, although if presented and implemented adequately, it can be a big contributor to building a movement. You see the dualism. Base: fixed, static, heavily defensive, open to incremental change at best. Movement: dynamic, flexible, offensive, open to transformative qualitative change.

The next question asks: "Why do you think Repeal is reformist?" Although I never stated that Repeal is reformist, I have questions about it: why was this approach of "Repeal" to the issue selected—if it was selected in a conscious way—and how is it being implemented? This is not primarily because of its focus on a limited reform demand within a parliamentary/legal arena where revolutionary methods and objectives are a poor fit, although that is certainly a factor. I don't believe that relating to reforms or to legal, even parliamentary/electoral, methods of struggle is inherently reformist. The issue is always how the stated objectives relate to real, mass needs and how the forms of struggle attack fault lines of capitalist power. It will always be the case that reforms that correspond to needs will elicit reformers to organize them—reformers who don't regard a label of reformist as a criticism as I hope that we all do. My first questions would be whether the communists in the Repeal movement maintain a critical distance from this tendency—a precondition for communist activity in my opinion—or whether they present themselves as a "better" leadership of the reform struggle—a first step towards the abyss, also in my opinion.

My second question would be one of how the specifically communist obligations in this struggle are presented and implemented. In my opinion, there are two aspects that are particularly important: first, sharpening the antagonism and divide between what is "right" from an internationalist working-class perspective on this issue, and the entire range of capitalist responses, those that would incorporate and defuse it as well as those that would crush and illegalize it; second, on an issue that is so intractable for capital, the focus should be on where the break is clearest and most categorical, with the most radical and militant expressions—not the broadest ones with the best potential of "success."

I wouldn't want to say much more without knowing at least a little more. I'm going to conclude with some reactions to your position on current communist priorities, elements of which I'm citing below:

> It would really help to talk more about what communists ought to do tomorrow. ...

> We are unlikely to make a decisive intervention to the border issue. I think we are even less likely to see a revolutionary situation. So we need subsidiary goals—in my opinion, our goal should be to come away with more and better cadre.[4]

I think the question of what communists ought to do tomorrow is crucial. There is a remarkable lack of "talk" about this problem—as if there is really nothing to talk about. Rather than clarifying the revolutionary implications of the needs and potentials manifest in working-class life, considering both its features of accommodation and of resistance, the emphasis typically comes down heavily on a more efficient pursuit of questionable intermediate objectives that are not subjected to critical scrutiny. In terms of the Repeal work, although the same point could be made more generally, I would be greatly encouraged just to see more attempts to pose certain central questions—recognizing that mistaken answers would still remain to be considered.

To say the least, a decisive intervention on the border issue in the sense of eliminating borders is "unlikely." If you agree the underlying border issue is internationalist working-class solidarity, it is closely tied to the general question of revolution, and we are far from that. However, I don't know what is meant by "decisive." I think it quite possible that a communist intervention on the border issue could crystallize a number of possibilities and cause a rupture with a prevalent pattern of incrementalist, social democratic political work.

Finally, I completely agree that one major goal in this area, and all others, is to come away with "more and better cadre." I would put this in the framework of the intermediate organization since I think the notion of cadre is not only of an aggregation of individuals whose politics have broken with capital, but of a collectivity of such individuals with the intellectual and moral capacity to critically implement an oppositional strategy. The intermediate organization, then, consists of those who are reclaiming the understanding that the immediate conflict is inseparable from the ultimate goal; that struggle contains its own rewards; and that revolutionary politics is a vocation.

## On Shop Floor Organizing
## January 2010

*This and the following piece were written as personal emails to Scott Nicholas Nappalos, an active workplace organizer and anarchist theorist who has been heavily involved in the IWW\* as well as various North American anarchist organizational formations.*

I'm assuming that you appreciate the level of initial agreement I have with the approach to contract unionism and the emphasis on direct action in what you've sent me, so I won't mention those points. I also won't make other points on the topic that I might—most of them based on experiences of people who were much better at workplace organizing than I. Instead, I will start with a criticism, since that may be as much as you want to hear.

First, on the organizing context …

The first sentence assumes this perspective will be implemented "free of the restraints of labor law," etc. No, it won't. It is one thing to choose to challenge these factors, it is quite another to believe you can transcend them. This is an example of the document's evasion of the reality of this organizing. What it proposes as the very initial steps of a perspective are, in fact, always illegitimate, and quite often also illegal. They are actions that will get you, and perhaps others, fired or more. At least this is the case without precautionary steps that I don't see indicated. In fact, such precautions run counter to the unquestioned premise of the document, that these initial organizing steps can—and indeed must—be done openly and "democratically." In my mind, this is completely utopian; as is the further assumption that these initial direct actions will lead to cumulative successes and eventually result in "large-scale industrial actions." This is a substitution of hope for reason. This may happen once in a hundred attempts, and in the interim a good number of organizers will have slunk back off to academia.

63

So what I see is a failure to realize that this is a serious struggle with employers and supervisory staff prepared—in fact, incentivized—to nip problems in the bud, disciplining participants and eliminating ringleaders. Unless adequate care is taken, this quickly leads to situations where the organizer is asking, explicitly or implicitly, that other workers fight and risk their jobs for hers. One thing that I learned from my father, an expert IWW and CIO (IWA) working-class organizer, was "don't make yourself the issue."

In all important situations, the most aware and experienced workers will understand these points and will never trust those who don't. Particularly when they are foolish college kids who have more and different options than those they are organizing to risk their jobs.

Secondly, on the understanding of immediate goals ...

Since it is foolish to assume that these shop-floor direct actions will generally lead to clear and tangible victories, even small ones, it is important to have organizers understand and be oriented towards capitalizing on other benefits of collective action—towards making the class line clearer and more categorical and, particularly, building on the expanded awareness that other workers will fight and sacrifice, even when the likelihood of direct benefits is small— that there is way more to one's co-workers than has been assumed in the routine of work. This is what is really essential to working-class "confidence."

Third: The importance of the organizer developing some initial credentials is not stressed. Just being an advocate of militant direct action is not credential enough. Organizers must also understand the job and be able to do the work and, particularly, must not function so that they increase the workload of other workers. They must also be recognized as people who actually care about the problems of other workers and are willing to provide some tangible help and collective support even when it doesn't provide immediate political rewards.

You can probably see where I'm going here. Much more emphasis must be put on covert organizing and implementing clearly "illegitimate" actions without merely piling up some martyrs. This makes the issues of organizational structure and democratic decision-making much less simple. The question of moving beyond the shop-floor issues is also not just one of scale, but also of locus, and while there are negatives in raising other arenas of struggle, this can often have a much more significant impact on consciousness and "confidence" than what shop-floor direction is possible and meaningful.

Enough for now.

## Comments on "Strategy & Struggle"
## February 2010

*The following was a response to a 2009 workplace organizing proposal titled "Strategy and Struggle: Anarcho-syndicalism in the 21st Century," written by a grouping within the Brighton Solidarity Federation, an anarcho-syndicalist organization in the UK. (The original document can be read here: http://libcom. org/library/strategy-struggle-anarcho-syndicalism-21st-century.) Hamerquist circulated this to comrades doing similar work in the US and was also in direct discussion with the document's authors. The proposal was not adopted by the majority organization, in favor of the more traditional syndicalist strategies similar to those Hamerquist applauds the authors for turning away from. All references in this essay are to the document in question (Brighton Solidarity Federation 2009).*

"... in the middle of the fight, we learn how we must fight."
—Rosa Luxemburg 1918

The document invokes Luxemburg's* beautiful and essentially true statement as a counter to the mechanical anarcho-syndicalism that "saw building the union as 'building the new society in the shell of the old'."

She provides no blueprint and leaves some gaps, but Luxemburg's recognition of the creative potential of mass class struggle, and of the fact that the organized structures and institutions developed in periods of relative stability will always provide some limits on these potentials, are vital—and cautionary—insights. I do think more note should be taken of the elements of ambiguity and the whiff of workerist determinism in Luxemburg's approach. Who is the "we" that learns how to fight in mass upsurges—is it all participants in struggle, or those who are already oriented to "fight" but don't know quite how to go about it? We can never forget that even fundamental fights teach contradictory lessons, some of which will work against that fight that is necessary to ultimately "win."

The classical syndicalist argument is frequently combined with proposals for some form of limited revolutionary intervention to transform class collaborationist unions into class struggle unions—or to replace the former with the latter. The document presents a general response to all such approaches, emphasizing that the character of mass permanent organizations (unions and social democratic parties) is always basically a result of the level of class struggle, not a cause of it nor an independent variable impacting it.

So what limits does this put on the range of left organizing perspectives that are premised on a radicalizing intervention in the union structure and/or the construction of "class struggle" unions to replace collaborationist ones or to function in what are characterized, often misleadingly, as "unorganized" situations? Actually, quite narrow ones, the document argues:

> Reforming the trade unions would be a waste of time, because the very level of self-organisation required to force such reforms would render the reforms themselves redundant, since we'd already be doing the things independently we were lobbying to be allowed to do.

That is, radical politics should aim to relate directly to the class struggle rather than presenting an intermediary step of essentially parliamentary maneuver that is restricted to a hostile terrain in which class collaboration is an institutionalized assumption.

This conclusion—that, with episodic exceptions, unions are "permanent mass" organizations that persist through cycles of the class struggle and normally reflect the class compromises characteristic of periods of lull—is argued at length:

> We therefore recognise that neither trade unions or so-called mass workers' parties are revolutionary organisations. In the case of trade unions, their structural role as

representatives of labour power within capitalism compels them to offer disciplined workforces to the employers.

If they cannot offer the promise of industrial peace, they are in no position to negotiate. Such social partnership is inherent to the idea of mass, permanent workers representation, de-linked from class struggle.

Exactly right, in my opinion.

They go on to say, "Consequently, we hold that not only are permanent mass organisations not revolutionary, but that in the final analysis they are *counter-revolutionary* institutions" (emphasis in original). This sounds a bit absolutist, but later sections of the argument clarify the issues in a reasonable way: "revolutionary unions are necessarily non-permanent products of struggle, and attempts to maintain them beyond the struggle of which they are an expression will see them lapse into a counter-revolutionary role."

This brings us to the alternatives confronting typical libertarian radical workplace organizing strategies. The dilemma for such strategies is that

internal democracy in a mass organisation when the majority of workers are not pro-revolutionary means the [revolutionary anarcho-syndicalist] organisation has to sacrifice either internal democracy [in the mass organization] or its revolutionary principles—either way breaking with anarcho-syndicalism.

Perhaps "defer" or "subordinate" would be less loaded replacements for "sacrifice," but the point would still hold.

I'd like to raise some more practical issues: what is at issue here is a strategic question, not a tactical one. On a tactical level, there can be any of hundreds of situations where it makes some organizing sense to "participate" in one way or another in a union or in an essentially trade unionist framework. In my experience, this has often happened where the union structure inserts itself between workers and capitalists in order to defuse or attenuate grievances. Quite often, in union-organized situations this involves manipulations of legal liability issues, refusals to contest injunctions or restraining orders, threats to deny representation to troublemakers, and just plain pork chop incompetence. It often makes sense to confront this by taking over union offices, shouting down representatives, demanding direct meetings accessible to normal workers, etc. And essentially, every time it is done with some success, it will lead to calls to kick out the leadership, run a reform slate, or bring in a replacement, "better" union, a "class struggle" union.

On the other hand, the promised benefits from having more access to elected or appointed union functionaries, including those who openly express their essential agreement with the mass grievances, seldom materialize. Not that these folks are necessarily hypocrites, although that is hardly unusual, but their role is virtually always shaped by various perceived possibilities to change the union leadership or its policies—or even to change unions—possibilities which are infinite in number, but generally will have little impact outside of a general insurgency. And if there is such an insurgency, it is always best to relate to it directly and not interpose a process of protracted parliamentary struggle which will quickly exhaust elements of spontaneous radicalism, leaving a residue of back-biting careerism that helps drown any of the sense of collective strength and potential that initially characterized the upsurge.

Of course, in most present-day workplaces there is no union organization at all, and these issues typically emerge in a slightly different way as "left" elements of union organizing initiatives attempt to shape struggles to conform to the legal requirements of gaining representation. This is only a different manifestation of acquiescence to the rule of capital that also underlies left union reform initiatives. In this case, the immediate impact of byzantine legalistic procedures generally allows even less space for militancy and direct participation of workplace militants, and the longer range perspective involves a demoralizing prospect of certifying a union in order to develop some kind of a challenge to its collaborationist structures and leadership, which then will have to be similarly challenged, and so on *ad infinitum*.

Ultimately—and maybe not so ultimately—the question that must be posed is whether there is any advantage whatsoever to having "leftists" or "radicals" presenting the face of the union to workers. I think not, not even when they are actually in leading positions in the union ... and I can think of some very concrete disadvantages.

Laying aside some situations where there is overt corruption, I'm also dubious about any advantage for workers in having leftists present the face of the union to the bosses. And even in such cases, it is usually true that honest militants will do as well as, if not better than, leftists. So I'm beyond skeptical of any strategic potentials from any variant of working within this structure.

Don't want to spend much time on it ... but it is *not* my experience—or that of many others who have done this work—that workers in this country spontaneously turn towards unions when they become active. Not any more than they turn towards the Democratic Party or some church organization. This is hardly surprising since, in this country as opposed to many others, unions are typically not voluntary organizations. Workers are enrolled semi-automatically through an agreement between the union structure and the management, which then checks off dues just like it withholds taxes. (Actually, when workers become militant, they are more likely to turn towards the classical sabot than "their" union. This also has its problems but they are not for this discussion.)

There is generally a collective understanding from the outset of struggle that not much will be forthcoming from the union— and where it doesn't already exist, such an understanding will be quickly developed. This is a lesson that sticks among workers, although it is quickly forgotten by leftists. When struggles develop, the participants look for help where they can get it. Frequently, one of the grievances with the union structure and leadership is that it passively or actively discourages such help and solidarity.

The document says later, "'Building the union' per se literally makes no sense, and represents a fetishism of form that forgets that the form can only ever be an expression of content, of class struggle."

This is clearly true. We attempt to organize within the context of the class struggle, and the particular level that struggle is at determines much of what is possible organizationally. But, although it is true, it is not sufficient, because it still looks to me like it contains too great an emphasis on conceptualizing political issues and options within the context of alternative forms of organization.

Whether or not this is a valid criticism of this document, it is likely to be an appropriate one for various leftists involved in these discussions. I think this because it is common to reduce the collective experiences and common understandings that develop out of struggle to issues of organizational structure and function. But what is significant in mass participation in class struggle is not so much the organized forms that it can assume, as it is the transformed understanding of power relationships and of the possibility for a social group to both do the right thing and do it in ways that expand human potentials and relationships. An experience of collective struggle and the ways in which it is thought and acted on by newly empowered individuals cannot—or, at least, should not—be reduced and distilled into an organizational product. Other elements of culture and consciousness, other forms of expanding the arena of cooperation, are at least as important as its organizational character, its organizational continuity, and its organizational stability. In fact, these equally important elements are frequently either lost or transformed into something substantially less when the attempt is made to capture them in an organizational form.

## Discussion with Comrade on "Strategy and Struggle" February 2010

*Like the text "On Shop Floor Organizing," this is an excerpt from an email Hamerquist sent to Scott Nicholas Nappalos. It continues the discussion of the "Strategy and Struggle" essay by a section of Brighton Solidarity Federation (2009) addressed in the previous essay, "Comments on 'Strategy and Struggle'."*

You raise an interesting point concerning the contradictions involved in developing sufficient organizational continuity and stability to implement a plan of work without fetishizing any particular organizational form or any particular work content (e.g., revolutionary propaganda). Using the categories of the Brighton document, these issues will probably appear in both minority permanent organizations—revolutionary collectives—and mass permanent organizations—trade unions and parliamentary parties. However, our main concern is with them in minority permanent organizations—and specifically those that are "pro-revolutionary" in the Brighton terminology.

While they are always combined in reality, it is helpful to conceptually distinguish the form and structure of any revolutionary organization from the radicalizing experiences of collective struggle and mutual cooperation which are the foundational elements of the revolutionary movements it hopes to help build. The organizational element to one degree or another still contains the inequalities of a division of labor and the institutionalized elements of hierarchy that flow from it. This is not the case with the fragmentary manifestations of self-organization and self-discipline. These imply an essential equality between individuals, a content that embodies Badiou's notion ("people think; people are capable of truth" [1999]) and cuts across distinctions between "members" and non-members, "leaders" and rank-and-file. It is easy to kill the second element (which should be the primary focus) in misdirected attempts to preserve and extend an organizational structure. Of course, if matters are left to the sort of individualized autonomy which ends in movement entropy, this element can be lost as well. (I should probably avoid analogies from high school physics.)

The pressing issues concern what revolutionaries should do now in order to clarify and maximize future possibilities. I want to be quite clear that I don't feel that I have anything approaching satisfactory answers in this area—certainly no models that have "worked." Instead, I have some appreciation of what is unlikely to work and some ideas about projects that might be attempted. Assuming, of course, that such projects will be treated in a consciously experimental fashion, keeping the alternatives that are being preempted or rejected in collective view and including intermediate objectives with sufficiently clear metrics to allow the work to be reassessed and, if needed, reoriented in a conscious, collective, and timely way.

The fact that this discussion of options and priorities for political work is happening to the extent that it is points to the emergence of a political subjectivity able to choose from among alternative possibilities—some incompatible with each other and some not so much. Actually, it would be more accurate to say there are fragments of such a subjectivity which largely exist outside of working-class conditions and external to what there is of a class struggle. This is a subjectivity that is not sufficiently collective and is far too socially distant from the problems it hopes to address, limiting our collective capacities to determine "what is" and evaluate "what is to be done?"

In our wing of the movement these limitations are more likely to promote political timidity and vacillation than vanguardism and self-appointed leaderships. This gives us a certain degree of inoculation against forming cults or neo-religious formations around an omniscient leader or a revealed scripture, but probably makes us more subject to a less noxious variant of messianism in which political work is viewed as "teaching" and we define ourselves as the "teachers." This quickly raises Marx's question in the Theses on Feuerbach, "Who will educate the educator?"[1] Our first organizational steps should try to move beyond these pedagogical illusions by linking these fragments into a collective subject that is part of its social base and in a real position to help the development of increasingly self-conscious struggles and movements.

I'm concerned with two tasks: first, developing the organized character of the existing subjectivity as an initial base of political activity; second, working out the organizational approaches best suited to the areas of work being considered in this discussion. I would tend to see this as a linked process of transition in which the initial organized groups develop the possibility and terms for their supersession by a more competent class force—the elements of which will be defined through their implementation of the second task. I will try to take this bargain-basement Hegelianism out of the realm of gibberish in the rest of this.

There is one central problem that we've encountered in communist organizations that placed a high premium on theoretical discussion and agreement—on "centralism" and, more importantly, on "unity," on conscious adherence to an elaborated set of common principles and estimates. We have found that this idealized unity is unlikely to survive in a real struggle situation when ideas begin to have consequences. To put it differently, it is not nearly so certain that unity will develop through collective struggle, as it is that any latent disunity will emerge and crystallize as the struggle raises the potential costs for the participants. A very developed political "agreement" can quickly dissolve if a political position incurs risks and sacrifices, so it is important to ensure that the initial cadre grouping develops its positions in a manner that includes an actual commitment to "construct acts to the end"*—a posture that is more ethical stance than intellectual agreement. In fact, this commitment is more significant than a high degree of intellectual agreement until the latter has been tested in some meaningful way. When the point of action is reached, and that should be early in the process in my opinion, it is most important to draw organizational

74

lines so that those militants who will fight are included and those who just talk a good fight are always challenged.

When the primary purpose is collective action, unity (in the sense of agreement among the core cadre) is less important than clarity about essential options. And this clarity can and probably should include actual poles of disagreement within the collective, since that is the best guarantee that there will be known alternatives to the chosen initiatives. Of course, any level of basic disagreement exacerbates conflicts and contradictions around issues of discipline and implementation, but there is really no possibility to avoid these and it is best to confront them openly. What must be stressed is that all work—and all lack of work—must be subject to collective evaluation. This demand, again in my experience, is a much more likely source of what you call "fundamental contradictions ... [that] paralyze an organization," than clear political differences over stance.

This leads to the need for other organizational forms to take advantage of the possibilities for a more organic revolutionary development, something similar to what you have characterized as "intermediary organizations of militants," when we're dealing with workplace organizing. But, I think, probably also in a number of other areas, the most productive organizational form is probably going to be some intermediary, interventionist organization of militants, not tied to specific workplaces, but capable of relating to such issues; not premised on a high level of intellectual understanding and prior political agreement, but sharing a collective understanding that it is important to "think"; not afraid to take risks, but understanding the differences between politics and theater.

## Angst
## June 2018

*The following emerged from a personal discussion between Hamerquist and a long-time friend and comrade. It later became the version below, which was sent to a larger email list of comrades. Note that the ellipses do not indicate elisions but were present in the original.*

I haven't written much lately … partly for personal reasons. I'm old and my head and hands find it increasingly difficult to combine chainsawing and wood-splitting with thinking about politics and manipulating a keyboard. However, there are some more general reasons for my silence that others may share to some extent. We're at a political moment that is disorienting. Experiences that should strengthen us do the opposite. Opportunities and potentials explode on the scene only to disintegrate almost as quickly as they arise … generally leading to increased demoralization rather than providing the foundation for new initiatives. And such initiatives, to the extent they attempt to develop functional and resilient structures on a left mass or left cadre basis, start too small and tend to quickly get smaller—fragmenting and imploding over dismayingly similar conflicts—typically routine dilemmas and disruptions that we should have learned how to deal with, but quite apparently haven't. And this all happens when a number of features of the objective conditions appear to favor the emergence of a generalized opposition to established power.

It's not much of a comfort, but these problems aren't unique to our sector of the left, to this part of the world, or to this period of history. If I had the energy to look it up, this is where I'd insert the well-worn Gramsci* quote about the characteristics of a period where the old is dying but the new is not ready to be born.[1] Not that such observations provide much comfort either.

For some decades we have lived through a period in which capital's global *triumph* also marked the beginning of its secular crisis.* The ruling class's chronic and expanding difficulties in maintaining capital's productivity and profitability interact with growing fault lines in its political legitimacy and effective power … shredding the pretensions that capitalism marks the end of history that were widespread not so long ago. Our dilemma … or one of them … is that this underlying crisis doesn't develop uniformly. It passes through rough cycles, and we are at a relatively bad point in the latest of these in which capital is achieving some adaptive successes. One of the benefits of being quite old is that I have lived through a number of such cycles, including the end days of the one that initiated in an earlier period of capitalism—the Depression of the 30s. Hopefully I've maintained sufficient political awareness to provide some context and perspective for the current left malaise.

If we take 1935, 1968, and 2009 as points of significant breaks in capital's evolutionary stability—a rough periodization that I know doesn't apply uniformly across the global terrain, although it works for most of the capitalist core—they start from sharp breaks with political routine characterized by a flowering of radical possibility. Elements of creative, spontaneous struggle appear everywhere and look to be inexorable. What previously seemed utopian or even impossible becomes a basis for live action on a mass level—mass action that includes widespread epistemological breaks* that appear to foreshadow the emergence of a mass revolutionary subjectivity. Experience indicates that every cycle of crisis and the explosion of political possibility that accompanies it leads to an adaptive response of capital on both the level of profit (the economic) and that of power (the state). For example, the emerging conflict between nationalism and globalism—too simple a dichotomy, I know—is both an index of crisis and a path towards a possible capitalist recovery. The juxtaposition of an autonomous fascism with new forms of globalized social democracy should be understood in the same vein in my opinion.

Failures to adequately understand these circumstances promote some distinct left responses and an assortment of illusions. One rests on the expectation that the dramatic changes of the moment of crisis are linear and incremental—and will define the political context for an extended period, if not permanently. A possible implication of this view—familiar in our tendency—is to limit our role to facilitating the mass process and, above all, to avoid becoming an obstacle to them—even as such processes begin to lose their oppositional potential. An alternative approach of others on the left sees the transformed political scene as the long-delayed fruits and validation of past labor and takes steps to implement a claim on organizational leadership. In the process, the politics of the "vanguard" become either irrelevant or, more frequently, indistinguishable from those of overt reformists. The best that can be said about such positions is that they fail to recognize major characteristics of these cycles of struggle.

Unfortunately, moments of general insurgency tend to be short lived, and like the initial burst of popping popcorn, they are followed by increasingly sporadic and incomplete explosions of the lagging kernels. This process creates some forks in the road for radicals, where diminishing grouplets search for better outcomes from fewer struggle opportunities while attempting to survive as groups and individuals. This frequently contains a tinge of desperation and results in a moralistic, exhortative approach to political work that is not sustainable with normal-assed people. At the same time, an increasing fraction of the momentarily-radicalized lapse into cynicism or accommodations to some variant of reformist politics—which itself is often only a stepping stone to cynicism and passivity. As the reality of a mass epistemological break with established politics recedes into nostalgic memories and overly hopeful estimates of current forces, we quickly find ourselves in a period which the jaded among us call a "lull"—sometimes not very helpfully. I think it's useful to think about what can and should be done in such a lull—particularly if it can be kept in mind that no lulls will be permanent.

I want to raise two related responsibilities and opportunities: first, it's important to use the opportunity to collectively think about our circumstances; and second, this collective thinking should never lose focus on the potential for the radically changed circumstances that will certainly materialize. Sooner, I think, rather than later. Just a few words on both points:

I emphasize the importance of combining attempts to develop a radical, collective will with an organized approach to developing capacities to think *collectively*—involving exchanges of estimates and hypotheses between positions that don't agree and don't necessarily look to reach agreement: exchanges designed to expand critical participation in the discussion rather than to gain adherents to some version of the truth; exchanges that aren't subordinated to organizational empire-building or distorted by assumptions that the relevant questions are self-evident and that adequate answers are close at hand.

My initial assumption is that the general instability of the situation—the "flailing and churning"[2] within capitalist power and the diverse questioning of its legitimacy and permanence—will turn out to be decisive. However, that is certainly open to question and challenge, and I recognize that history is not clearly on my side … While this assumption is in some tension with the need for clear and critical political discussion that is not weighed down with a lot of preconceptions, I think it is vitally important to focus on the circumstances, objective and subjective, that raise possibilities for breaks, "events,"* qualitative changes in context, and that one proposes approaches to deal with the possibilities that these will create.

## Recent Thoughts on Insurrectionism
## October 2021

*The following was part of an email exchange regarding how revolutionaries should relate to institutionalized protest movements and organizations, with a particular focus on the legacy of the Black struggle in the US. Some introductory and other material was removed for clarity, and some Wohlleben quotes refer to private communications with him.*

Z's recent email says:

> The desire for inclusion and that for a new society is the main contradiction and in certain moments/course of struggle it makes itself evident and sharpens. For me at least, rad-liberal historians like Hinton[1] refuse to see these seeds and grapple with them. I doubt the Hintons of the world would look at certain moments, even the Montgomery bus boycott, as striving for something more than inclusion and rights. As revolutionaries our task is different—it's to study and see these seeds and to do our best to be involved in developing them.

> Yes, there are social groupings whose framework/horizon is social democracy and they have some programs that we would be highly critical of but I never want to dismiss the larger numbers of people who want a more liberatory society and are drawn to them. We just don't know what large numbers of people are capable of.

STO* had an early split over its majority's allegedly utopian preoccupation with revolutionary "seeds of socialism." I won't burden anyone with the metallurgical metaphor that was advanced as the alternative. I had Z's position in that debate, and it is where I am still. I'd like to contrast this position to one recently put forward by Adrian Wohlleben in a piece titled, "Memes Without End" (2021).

He capsulizes his position as the need to "propagate memes across" social movements, to "place them into *flight*," and to "open the vortex, extend the meme, to the point of ungovernability" (Wohlleben 2021, emphasis in original). I agree with some aspects of Wohlleben's argument on a tactical level and in certain circumstances, as I'm sure Z does as well. However, I think their positions are incompatible on a strategic level, although I'm not assuming either of them would agree with me.

I'm sure that we all share the objective of a mass, anti-capitalist, emancipatory movement based in a self-conscious working class. In that framework, I certainly agree with Wohlleben's first priority, "propagating ungovernable moments," although more clarity about how to sustain them would be useful. However, I'm not taken with his second concept. Rather than looking to "disperse" social movements, I think these have to be approached as complex and contradictory political conjunctures where Z's revolutionary "seeds" are potentially either developed or destroyed.

Wohlleben speaks of a singular "social movement apparatus." I assume that it is primarily this apparatus that Wohlleben believes should be dispersed, disrupted, and put to flight as a part of "propagating ungovernable moments" in the mass struggle. Let me start again by acknowledging some agreement, particularly when the ubiquitous NGO institutional complex with its 12.5-million-employee solution to grad student precarity is considered as a part of the social movement apparatus. I'll attempt to keep such possible agreements in mind as I raise questions about the following passages from Wohlleben (2021):

> To the extent that the real movement signals an exit from the apparatus of classical politics, we might be tempted to speak here of an "anti-movement" or a movement of "antipolitics." However, the negativity of such formulations would be misleading. What is in question is a positive liberation of conflictual action from established rules

and customs, a departure from the constituent logocen-
tric "game" in which politics discovers its consistency in
discourse, opinions and ideological programs, and the
replacement of this game by another.

And:

We must neither abandon nor embrace social movements;
rather, we must explode their frame, cause them to break
away, force them to *encounter* their outside and keep
them in contact with it. In short, we must place them into
*flight*. What we want is both more and less than a social
movement: more antagonistic than an institutional framework will ever be able to express—more contagious, more
viral, more complex and capable of absorbing becomings,
mutations, self-destructions and rebirths of subjects, and
not simply "recognition" of their existing demands—but
also less than a social movement, since we don't always
want to have to "appear" to one another or to power as a
social entity, we don't want to play the games of language,
dialogue, critique and negotiation. We're tired of games
whose playing field is stacked against us from the start.

If a vanguardist advanced this strategic argument, the political
subject that would implement its programmatic priorities would
normally be clear, usually some variant of the "party." However,
when a horizontalist, anti-authoritarian, communist insurrectionist (I hope that doesn't mischaracterize Wohlleben) is involved, the
questions of who or what is the *"we"* and the *"us"*—the political
subject—are more elusive. I find no clarity about where and how
this revolutionary subject, the "we," originates and how it will consolidate and grow—or even if it sees its own growth as a legitimate
objective—in these passages. The relationship of this political
subject to the masses of working people is crucial in my opinion,
yet these excerpts leave some basic questions unanswered. In my
opinion, an important element of incompleteness lies in its misty

conception of the revolutionary subject.

Notwithstanding the perfunctory opening denial of any intention to "turn our backs" on movements, Wohlleben is oriented towards maintaining a qualitative political distance of the revolutionary cadre of militants from any prospective mass social base. This involves the militants assuming a negative posture towards most popular conceptions of needs and possibilities. I believe that whenever militants become politically visible in a form that has some political impact and popular legitimacy, a development that is essential to successfully implement any strategy, they will need to deal with the content and forms of the existing struggles against power and profit as they are understood on a mass level. I agree with Wohlleben that this will require a clear differentiation between real popular needs and desires and the various forms in which they are contained (and ultimately thwarted). However, this differentiation must recognize that the "social movement apparatus" is not really singular and it is more than an "apparatus." In fact, it is a complex and contradictory phenomenon with some elements which should be "exploded," but also with others that are the husks, or perhaps part of the substance, of Z's "seeds." Without a working project to sustain and develop such seeds, radical projects to transform rebelliousness into revolution will constantly need to start over again from scratch, as the tides of popular resistance movements ebb and flow.

The mass needs, desires, and potentials that are expressed through the social movement must be treated as more than "platforms" from which to continuously "break the frame" of the conflict. While there are moments that call for this approach, there are also moments where the priority should be to preserve and develop the cultural, political, and organizational elements of resistance to capital in an oppositional social bloc that prefigures a future dual power. This certainly includes propagating elements of ungovernability, but if this becomes primarily a critique of the political demands and organizational forms of the mass struggle, it risks positioning the most militant sectors of the struggle as opponents of material improvements in popular living and working conditions. Perhaps Wohlleben will see this as an unfair criticism, but I think that as struggles recede, the essentially negative posture of these excerpts—assuming they don't end in cynicism and abandonment of revolutionary work—will drift towards the 22nd thesis of Nechayev's revolutionary catechism.[2] And we don't want that.

> 22. The Society has no aim other than the complete liberation and happiness of the masses—i.e., of the people who live by manual labor. Convinced that their emancipation and the achievement of this happiness can only come about as a result of an all-destroying popular revolt, the Society will use all its resources and energy toward *increasing and intensifying the evils and miseries of the people until at last their patience is exhausted* and they are driven to a general uprising. (Nechayev 1869; emphasis added)

So how should we understand the "partisan memetics" that Wohlleben proposes? He speaks of "circulation of leading practices or gestures" by militants that have a "contagious" or "viral" quality such that they might open possibilities for mass direction. What are these gestures and how do they open possibilities? What is involved here beyond an academic version of the "front-liners" perspectives that prioritized the positions of the core of militants and emphasized their needs, desires, and inclinations? Wohlleben's stance might be contrasted with the ancient and much-abused maxim—"Serve the People"*—that I share with the Panthers (and some others). Is the position premised on the clandestinity and autonomy of the militant cadre that would perhaps follow a modified Bakuninism—"In the midst of the popular tempest, we must be the invisible pilots guiding the Revolution" (Bakunin 1870)? (We might remember that Bakunin's organization was illegal and underground by necessity, not tactical choice, in the "popular tempest" of those times. Other circumstances might have led him to take a more consistently anti-authoritarian and participatory, democratic approach.)

I realize that partisan memetics would probably reject any notion of "guiding the Revolution," but it does seem to position the militants as *"invisible pilots"*—pilots of obscure origins and, unfortunately, questionable competencies.

Some time back, I posted Jasper Bernes's essay "Revolutionary Motives" (2020) along with some of my tentative criticisms and agreements with it. Bernes claims that any approach to social revolution that involves revolutionary vanguardism will be counterproductive and ultimately counter-revolutionary. He divides vanguardism into "pastoral" (leading the working class, allegedly like Lenin) and "pedagogical" ("teaching" the masses, à la Gramsci and perhaps Facing Reality).* In distinction to conceptions of an organized collective leadership that relates organically to a mass social base, Bernes advances an alternative that he explicitly describes as "adventurist." In this approach, the cadre of revolutionary militants shouldn't attempt to function as a "vanguard." Instead, they will act according to their own strategic needs and inclinations, even though this may involve jumping into an abyss of uncertainty about the outcomes.

> Bad odds can be transformed into good ones if, by misapprehending the situation or ignoring the risks, some small group decides to go ahead anyway, creating felicitous conditions for everyone else. A leap into the void can make the ground appear, just as a refusal to leap can turn solid ground to thinnest air. (Bernes 2020)

I'm interested in whether Wohlleben agrees with this approach—partially or completely. If so, it's important to note that, as implied by the title of his essay, Bernes has added an element to the argument that, if valid, substantially impacts its potentials. This is his conception of proletarian "revolutionary motives" (which he alternatively terms "interests"). Without going into detail, I understand that Bernes sees these motives as a biopolitical reality of working-class life, elevating its "altruistic" features over "egoistic" ones, and potentially facilitating the transformation of mass resistances and rebellions into revolutions. For Bernes, these class motives are a more significant revolutionary factor than any type of purposive activity expressed through any form of political consciousness or organization.

Notwithstanding my differences with Bernes's approach to vanguardism, I think his conception of revolutionary motives/interests is useful, although I would understand them in terms of the Badiou*/Maoist notion of the communist invariant* where their limits are more clearly evident. However, at this point, I'm mainly concerned with Wohlleben's position and the extent to which he might share Bernes's position.

If Wohlleben agrees with Bernes's rejection of "vanguardism" and is also serious about rejecting any sectarian stance that would denounce them externally, more clarity is needed about the "circulation of leading practices or gestures" that he proposes. I think the tactical possibilities will fit into a relatively few general categories—perhaps even fewer if Bernes's blanket rejection of "pastoral" and "pedagogical" leadership is accepted rigorously. Such efforts might include actions that cause "material damage" to the system, actions that "refuse" the legitimacy of official authority, actions that "prefigure" social and cultural reorganizations beyond capitalism, and other "exemplary actions" that might arguably constitute an effective "propaganda of the deed." I see possibilities in all these areas, but I also see two related problems.

First, remember that Wohlleben's basic stance with respect to mass movements is to use them to spread "viral" content that "break[s] the frame." Problems will emerge with and out of the circulated "leading practices or gestures" that conflict with this overriding negative and critical role of the militants.[3] This conflict may be avoided or deferred, particularly when the tactical thrust is focused on challenges to the legitimacy of established power, but it will be harder to avoid where the goals are the development of the prefigurative potentials of any given arena of struggle or an effort to consolidate a social base. Of course, Wohlleben may reject any such intermediate objectives that don't promise to "break the frame" of the conflict. However, in my opinion, this will not be a sustainable stance over time and changing terrains of struggle. Consequently, to survive as an effective force, Wohlleben's tactics will have to assume, explicitly or not, that the social movement is more than its apparatus and its demands—and that those "seeds" of which we speak are also present and must be tended.

The second problem concerns variations in the general political climate. Wohlleben presents an approach that is fitted to times of radical upsurge—Bakunin's "popular tempests." While there are always such upsurges somewhere in the system, and eventually they may be expected anywhere, they aren't always present, and when they are present, they aren't always on the ascendency— and radicals are not always an effective part of them. Particularly when the struggle recedes and the "movement" grows increasingly fragmented and on the defensive, Wohlleben's approach will lose viability. Its benefits will decline while its costs will be more immediate and more damaging. This is not to mention the danger that as the general struggle loses momentum this posture will degenerate into self-caricaturing performative exercises.

Unfortunately, the widespread conception that exemplary actions outside of a contemporary mass context can provide political rewards years or decades in the future—à la Ali la Pointe in *The Battle of Algiers*[4]—rests on little but the "imbecilic optimism" that Gramsci located in social groups that have experienced the struggle primarily as an accumulation of defeats. As Luxemburg* pointed out (and Lenin as well), organized revolutionaries, whether in "parties" or not, "hidden pilots" or not, always tend to lag behind the radical possibilities of mass upsurges.[5] During those extraordinary moments when the entire movement is experiencing epistemological breaks,* exemplary action is the most effective, but that is when the movement itself is generating and diffusing "repeatable gestures" and "ungovernable moments." If organized militants are limited in what they can effectively teach the mass movement at this time, they are certainly offered a good opportunity to learn from it and perhaps help preserve its elements of break with capitalist power. Only if this learning process happens will it be possible to generalize a practical understanding of an extraordinary moment around which to consolidate an organized cadre committed to continuing action in less fortunate circumstances. This collective core of militant "pledged" cadre will need to have maintained and developed an organic connection to a mass base if it is to have sufficient resilience to take the optimum advantage of such changing circumstances.

Note: for better or worse, I have a good deal more to say on these topics. I'm ending here in the hopes of a broader discussion.

# II. EVENTS

## Three Points on Anti-Globalization Protests
## April 2000

Author's Note: The context for this piece was the protests against the IMF in Washington, DC, in April 2000, those against the WTO in Seattle in November 1999, and the schedule of planned protests of upcoming global capitalist meetings in Quebec City, Prague, and Genoa. The worst of the legalist/pacifist sectors that had been erased at Seattle were no longer real participants, and the banners of militant protest were headed by motley groupings termed DAN (Direct Action Network).[1]

Our contingent of ARA* activists and other Chicago anarchists hoped to participate in a way that helped cohere a black bloc grouping that was somewhat clear of the Seattle primitivists* and able to play an increasingly serious role in the anti-globalization movement—starting with Quebec. We were comically unable to accomplish this goal at this action—for reasons that illustrate some problems with anarchism.

I wrote this piece for discussion at an ARA meeting (US and Canada); however, I was sick and didn't attend so I'm not sure how the discussion went. However, the Quebec action was much less haphazard. There were still a range of major problems resulting from underestimating the forces we were up against, which emerged fully in the fiasco at Genoa* in the fall. Then, before these issues could be internalized, there was 9/11 and people got very scared.

*d.h., 2022*

Is there an emerging popular, spontaneous anti-capitalism, or are we taken in by superficial matters of stance and style? I think that there is something real here. The depth of alienation from and opposition to official society manifested in the Seattle-DC actions, while extremely contradictory and confused, cannot be reduced to either specific grievances against aspects of capitalism that are easily co-opted or to transitory cultural rebelliousness. Though this is encouraging, it is likely that these elements will be seriously eroded and might even disappear, if the political and organizational steps to consolidate and build on them are not taken. It is also clear that this is not a generalized phenomenon: its social base is limited, localized, and compartmentalized. Finally, there are serious weaknesses apparent both in tendencies towards messianic elitist fancies and in organizational self-indulgence.

My impression is that the b.b. [black bloc] is rapidly gaining support among the main force of activists. This is true with respect to political content, which increasingly is overtly anti-capitalist, and with respect to the tactical emphasis on militant and mobile street illegality. This is a superficial and subjective initial assessment, but it appears to be true despite the ideological barrage after Seattle, and despite DAN's efforts to administratively curb the b.b. for the DC action. This is an important issue and we should look at the evidence carefully. If true, this would be a development that has occurred more or less independently of any specific organizing by our folks ... indeed in spite of the lack of the same.

The mobilizations in Seattle and DC were not only occasions for these developing radical tendencies to express themselves; they also brought into view the techniques and frameworks for response. After DC, an attempt to defang the emerging b.b. anti-capitalism with a suffocating reformist embrace is replacing earlier attempts to isolate it as leftist craziness. It is certainly wise to proceed carefully when Michael Albert, the author of a near-hysterical criticism of the b.b. in Seattle, is brimming over with compliments and suggestions for it after DC.[2]

There are two major elements in the b.b. co-optation ploy. Both can be found in the Albert piece. First, there is the conception of the movement as an aggregation of disparate demands and their "constituencies." These, considered separately, are all partially resolvable through capitalist reform. More importantly, in many if not most instances, they can be put into conflict with each other. Second, there is the related attempt to confine the movement within the framework of capitalist legitimacy, parliamentarianism, legal protest, and pacifist civil disobedience. This is a framework where our major strengths, ones that can only develop out of categorical irreconcilability, will be lost.

It was clear that a major bloc of the participants in DC were concerned with capitalism as a system more than with any specific policies or aspects of capitalism. This is a major strength that must be built upon. If the "friendly" suggestions of Albert et al. are followed, the essentially reformist problematic of constituency-organizing will be strengthened to the detriment of the overall radical challenge to capitalism. Capital will continue to be able to play off one set of demands against others that are equally legitimate and pressing. Perhaps more important, organizing approaches that are really attempts to retain and strengthen relative advantages and privileges will be seen as important parts of the movement, rather than as dangers that actually raise the spectre of fascism more clearly than the potential of radical reform.

The "non-violence" of the Washington action, embodied in the four-point DAN "non-violence guidelines," was honored more in the breach than in the observance.[3] The essence of this position in general and of the DAN guidelines in specific is the notion that we must confine our activity within a neutral structure or it will lose its legitimacy. This structure always turns out to be nothing other than the institutionalized hegemony of capital. Thus, the conceptions of non-violence fit nicely with the conceptions of the aggregation of constituencies. Both would confine our actions totally within the terrain of reform. While in DC there were no "peace police" to speak of and no one got too upset with the militancy, nevertheless these issues have not gone away. It is still necessary to make a coherent political critique of the position that the movement should be confined within a non-violent, pacifist discipline. Until this is done we will have to begin from scratch on these issues over and over again in each new arena of action—

taking away valuable time and energy from actual organizing and demoralizing newly involved people.

What was the basis of the police response in Washington? It is not smart to think that the action was so strong that it imposed a certain response on the police, and it is unlikely that it was just an ad hoc adjustment to the situation as it developed. There have undoubtedly been counterinsurgency analyses of Seattle and of the movement that led to it. Given that this was an action taking place in the national capital and that there was lots of preparation time, we must assume that such analyses dictated the main form and content of the police response. The nature of the response, particularly on Sunday when the bulk of the protestors were present, provides evidence of this point.[4]

There were no pre-emptive actions against the b.b., although these were certainly well within the capacity of the police. The police policy towards the b.b. (on Sunday) was to avoid or minimize confrontations and limit arrests. (We must beware of letting the entire left's bizarre desire to be seen as victims of excessive police force obscure this essential reality.) This was the case even though the b.b. was almost the exclusive focus of police concern and even though it systematically and massively committed acts that are normally not tolerated. We can be absolutely certain that this tolerance would not have been the policy of choice of the DC police, nor will it be for any other local police force. The policy of restraint was determined elsewhere and the police on the scene were constrained to implement it.

There were a number of factors that could have contributed to this policy. This is an issue area where there are major policy differences in the ruling class, and there is no united opposition to disruptive protests so long as they are not too disruptive. Police forces in general often display and profess a fake helplessness for public relations reasons when it might increase their funding. The demonstration was militant and heavily illegal, but it was also contained within an inner and outer perimeter without challenge by any organized element including the b.b. The general atmosphere was one where the b.b. could not have been easily isolated from the DAN sections, and attempts to deal with it harshly could have backfired. Finally, it was significant that the action occurred on a Sunday, and the minimal disruption of work and commerce was more easily tolerated than would normally have been the case.

While some of these factors might have been involved, I think that we should seriously consider the possibility that the major determinant was the desire by policy makers above the DC police to get a handle on the makeup and politics of the b.b., in order to develop an adequate political/military response to it in the future. Of course, a major action like DC is hardly a laboratory situation, so it is likely that there was a policing cut-out—probably if the b.b. had escaped containment in organized strength. However, short of that, the decisive interests were in intelligence gathering and movement mapping to lay the groundwork for penetration: all from a counterinsurgency, low-intensity conflict perspective.

The most important element of our response, in my opinion, is to prepare for a systematic attempt to penetrate and determine the b.b. and its constituency by inserting credentialed active agents and, possibly, by developing pseudo gangs.* Given the loose and spontaneous nature of our movement, it is possible to predict some of the elements of such an approach. b.b. formations and supporters will spring up in a variety of surprising places advocating all sorts of politics, but most importantly ones that purport to be more militant and serious, going beyond mere vandalism and "pranks." Beginning to deal with such possibilities, in my opinion, is far more important than attacks on "police brutality" and much more prudent than assumptions of police incompetence and incapacity.

A final note on b.b. organization, or lack of it. In my view, the inadequacy of the prior preparation of the b.b. makes the successes of the day all the more striking. I suppose a consistent anarchist would think that the disorganization was responsible for the success, but I'm not buying it. No element of the b.b. took responsibility prior to the action for working out tactical options and clarifying logistics. There was no practical way for potential b.b. activists to meet up and work out anything approaching a coordinated plan, or even to find out the rudimentary facts about what was going on. There was no way, after the action, to begin a collective assessment of it. Possibly an indirect benefit of this is that it must dismay police attempts to penetrate the b.b., but unless it is remedied, it will be suicidal.

What is needed is a careful approach to key individuals and groups around the country to begin to establish a network capable of implementing a minimal level of self-protective security, of working out tactical possibilities in advance of national and regional actions, and of beginning the process of discussion and debate needed to project a comprehensive political project.

## Madison & Egypt
## April 2011

*This piece was originally a post on the blog* Khukuri Theory.[1] *Its target audience was North American revolutionaries trying to determine how to appropriately intervene in the gathering wave of unrest in 2011. Specifically, starting in February 2011, tens of thousands gathered in front of the Wisconsin State Capitol to protest the anti-union and austerity budget proposed by the recently elected Governor Scott Walker. The demonstrations were mirrored by similar actions in other Midwestern states; while they began to decline after a couple of months, as of June there were still as many as a thousand people involved. The subsequent four essays are rooted in this same period; these are a small sample of the writing, thinking, and discussing with militants Hamerquist engaged in during and immediately after this significant year of struggle.*

Various reports from Wisconsin and from similar activities in Ohio and Michigan note the contrast between the actual and potential energy of these mass mobilizations as well as their continuing commitment to objectives and approaches that can't maintain a minimal momentum, much less build on real possibilities that have emerged within the struggle. This can be demoralizing for radicals who, looking past their initial hopes, see narrow limits on the struggle that appear to be more restrictions on the movement's imagination than consequences of the response of the state or of capital—either repressive or incorporative.

This reaction is understandable, but the pessimism it supports is not really warranted and should not be allowed to contribute to radical inertia—perhaps inertness is a better word. These moments of explosive insurgency will always resurrect obstacles to their development that will have to be countered. But this shouldn't obscure the main point: that a mood of rebelliousness is emerging in new places, globally and in this country, and that it is showing evidence of a greater staying power.

But even if "Madison" falls short of Badiou's* description of the "event"* as "the sudden creation … of a myriad of new possibilities," (2012, 109) the changes in political context that it announces will positively impact the potentials for radical work. Tipping points in popular moods are hard to estimate, but it is still possible that we may discover proof from "Madison" that what we thought was impossible yesterday is here today.

I think it is helpful to look at Madison in terms of the Gramscian* notion of "contradictory consciousness," between workers' "practical transformations of the real world" and that which workers have "uncritically absorbed" from the world as it is (Gramsci 1971, 333)—recognizing that for Gramsci, as well as for us, "consciousness" in its usual meaning is too restrictive a framework for the actual topic.

Two things are important here, in my opinion. First, the changed conditions mean there are greater possibilities of success for critical challenges to that which is "uncritically absorbed," assuming the typical paternalistic left stupidities are avoided. Second, the possibilities for major innovative mass struggles to emerge quickly out of an apparently calm terrain have been demonstrated, and a further possibility, one that is rarer but more important, should also be recognized. This is the possibility for mass protest movements to move from a focus on a little more and a little better—on concessions and adjustments to power that are "reasonable"—to a stance of radical intransigence that might actually effect a "practical transformation of the real world" on a meaningful scale—an autotransformation. To illustrate this possibility, I'd cite the emergence of Black Power in the movement of the 60s. This transformed an important mass reform movement—one that was arguably on the cusp of a general reform victory—into a revolutionary challenge to existing power. Something similar, although perhaps not so basic, developed with the Seattle WTO action in 1999. (The contradictions and potentials for reversals in these challenges to power become evident soon enough, but that is for a different argument.)

I say autotransformation here (although the computer tells me it is not a real word) since the essential impetus towards transformation will only be discovered/created within the struggle. Revolutionaries who hope to play some role in expediting a difficult and far from automatic process must be a part of that struggle—oriented more to learn than to teach. This entails giving much more attention to making the ambiguous and amorphous "we," which is so often invoked in these discussions, into a larger and more coherent and cohesive element in the actual struggles.

Here I'd like to bridge over in an awkward way to the different struggles which are occurring more or less simultaneously and might be generically termed "Egypt." Obviously, there are important differences between "Egypt" and "Madison"—differences evident in the character and objectives of the struggles and, more dramatically, in the stakes that are involved for the participants. However, they certainly share one common thread—they are both maximal innovative actions that seem destined to produce tired, sick, minimal outcomes—at least in the short run.

I have some things to say on both what is distinctive and what is shared between these struggles that I will approach in a roundabout way. There are a number of arguments in Alain Badiou's article "The Universal Significance of Popular Uprisings" (2012) that I take issue with.[2] For one, we have his recurring image of "East" over "West"; for another, we have passages where I think Badiou oversimplifies and idealizes the Tunisian and Egyptian insurgencies—although I confess to wanting him to be closer to the actual truth than he probably is.

For an example of this last point, consider:

[In Tahrir Square] we find all sorts of people who make up a People, every word is heard, every suggestion examined, any difficulty treated for what it is. Next, [the uprising] overcomes all the substantial contradictions that the State claims to be its exclusive province, since it alone is able

to manage without ever surpassing them: between intellectuals and manual workers, between men and women,
between poor and rich, between Muslims and Copts,
between peasants and Cairo residents. (Badiou 2012, 111)

Despite the reservations, I very much like the way the essay
combines Badiou's conception of the characteristic features of
mass insurgency in this "intervallic period" with his notion of the
"communist idea"—or to be more accurate, with the implications
he draws from its current weakness as an underlying assumption
of the struggle.

Badiou argues here that we are in an extended historical inter-
val following the revolutionary sequence which was organized
around the theme of the "party/state." The party/state theme in
his view is exhausted and most attempts to revive it tend to be reactionary, but no alternative has yet emerged in the form of a mass
movement with a "shared idea." Consequently, when and where
the real and massive power of growing popular discontent emerges,
as in "Egypt," it is essentially negative (negative in a Hegelian*
sense, I would say).[3] Therefore, "the form of mass collective action
in an intervallic period is the riot."

Badiou is not hostile to the notion of riot. He advocates "empa-
thy" with the riot and stresses the essential productivity of its "negative power" (more Hegel?). But he argues that without the "shared
idea," which "explicitly presents itself as an alternative," the mass
collective action remains unable to fully reach its potential capacity,
"to solve insoluble problems without the assistance of the State."

This might be interpreted as something of a statement of
historical causality, where the "shared idea" is the cause and the
successful revolutionary movement the effect. Certainly, any such
position would be at odds with the excellent statement earlier in
the essay: "we should be the students of these movements, and not
their stupid professors" (Badiou 2012, 107).

How can notions of mass collective action and rioting coexist
in the same phrase? On reflection, I think the combination is pos-

sible when it is understood to involve the Gramscian contradictions that I mentioned above. Using such a framework, we might look for both the conservative elements that have been "uncritically absorbed" (more or less) in "Egypt" and "Madison," and the elements that point—even if just tentatively—towards "a practical transformation of the real world." We see this in both places, even though there is no coherent counter-hegemonic social force that is currently capable of playing a determinative role.

I see significant differences between "Egypt" and "Madison" on each side of this contradiction and think understanding these differences can help clarify unique problems and opportunities in each context. There is a good deal that can be said in this area but I want to focus on a couple of points regarding the "uncritically absorbed" obstacles to radical advance in the respective situations. In "Egypt," the essential element is a bourgeois conception of "democracy" encased in a refurbished populist nationalism. (Realize that this is not saying that such conceptions are uniformly accepted in a coherent form—just that they are firmly in place and their critique faces a hard road against significant opposition before it can hope to prevail.)

In "Madison," there is something a bit different, although equally bourgeois. I'd characterize it as an assumption of the moral rightness of an unequal status quo organized and expressed in various forms and layers of relative privilege. The revolutionary alternative "idea" for both "Egypt" and "Madison" must be radically egalitarian and internationalist, but the difference in context means it will emerge through distinctive processes and face different challenges.

But let's begin with a very basic similarity. Short of actual revolution, the global economic and political circumstances in which both develop offer little political and—perhaps more important—economic space for any major popular gains. Genuine national independence and autonomous development in postcolonial societies such as Egypt is not possible. The relative privileges of sectors of the metropolitan working classes will continue to erode, undermining the rotten political compacts in the imperial core despite any complaints of the benighted beneficiaries.

So to the distinctions. In "Egypt," the "uncritically absorbed" bourgeois liberty elements relate to "rights" and "freedoms" that have been denied for generations by corrupt, autocratic, post-nationalist states. Their essential absence meant there were few initial shock absorbers to deflect and delay insurgencies. With few buffers preventing them from moving quickly to challenge existing power, the movement quickly emerged as a "riot" when and where it encountered significant resistance. However, the lack of a broad experience with the essentially fraudulent nature of bourgeois rights also made the Egyptian movement susceptible to structural concessions and reformist tendencies that promise "democratic" solutions to real problems. As these approaches are shown to be bogus, or even just ineffective and the political and economic context means that this will not take that long—the element of "riot" will rapidly regenerate.

It remains to be seen how much momentum a regenerated movement can gain … and how quickly. The diverging responses to "concessions" from different class segments and the smarter ways that repressive tactics will be employed in future in "Egypt" will repeatedly "fork" the movement, as John Robb puts it (2007). And other centrifugal pressures, such as tendencies towards authoritarian warlordism, are likely to be exacerbated and to provide a new range of challenges that complicate the fundamental oppositions around the class question.

However, this all will involve an increased polarization and a much more categorical opposition that will have little tolerance for attempts to impose "national unity" by edict. Of course, attempts will still be made in this direction.

In "Madison," the "uncritically absorbed" elements were pastel versions of the palingenetic mythology that posits an increasing erosion of a democratic and representative social order that allegedly was a good place for the "middle class" in the not-so-distant past.[4] (I'm always amused at the aspects of those discussions which point to the "good" factory jobs with "living family wages and some benefits." I remember seeing those jobs in the context of William Blake's "Satanic Mills,"[5] as did many of those who lived hard and died early in their shadow. Perhaps we were just soft and privileged ... )

In any case, rather than advancing new progressive goals to be attained, "Madison" presents itself as a defensive struggle aimed at restoring an idealized past. This is heavily influenced by the widespread perception that, if the stakes of this struggle are raised significantly, a good deal more could be lost than what is already on the table. These features combine into a different, but equally significant, buffer against rapid radicalization of the movement. However, there is no easy way that its goals can be universalized in the ways that were (and still are) possible in Egypt. That would demand a more categorical break with sectoral interests, and it would require a posture that was not defensive.

Even when a general realization develops that no significant concessions are in the cards, in "Madison" this overwhelming emphasis on social strata that still have quite a bit more to lose will delay a real challenge to power. But this delay will not be indefinite. So while the insurgency in "Madison" might not have developed quite to Badiou's point of "riot"—to the undisguised relief of official society, including its component that is also out there "protesting"—the potential was and is there, quite close to the surface.

Along with the potential is the obligation on us to understand that, absent the semi-progressive clothing of oppressed people's anti-imperialist nationalism that exists in North Africa and the Middle East, "riot" in "Madison" raises a potential for large sections of the populist anger to take a xenophobic and quasi-fascist direction. When that happens, "riot" will certainly exhibit much more of a dual character, the "bad" side of which will contribute to elements of danger and fear of reaction/fascism that can be brokered into some degree of popular support for the global structures of repressive social democracy. Of course, it could also kill us in the process.

## Email on the Historical Situation
## October 2011

*This was written as an email to a comrade who was actively engaged in the Occupy movement—the protests and encampments inspired by New York's Occupy Wall Street (OWS)\*—in the Pacific Northwest. The main question at hand was how revolutionaries should intervene in a moment of tremendous mass militancy, but also tremendous political confusion.*

This is a beginning attempt to specify problems in a strategic context and involves hypotheses that cannot be confused with knowledge or truth. What's important, in my opinion, is to make these hypotheses clear enough so that they can be tested in the same process that evaluates their implementation ... How's that for clarity?

What's happening is global and systemic to capital. Crisis phenomena can and will appear anywhere in the system. Various likely common causes can be understood, but the characteristics and effects, the content and timing, of specific eruptions cannot be predicted. This dictates certain political approaches.

In the first place, it is important to always look at what is new—in this case, the newly emerged common causes. This means avoiding tendencies to forget them in a preoccupation with particular aspects of that history that "weighs like a nightmare on the brain."[1] So don't subordinate the new conditions and impacts of financial crisis to the circumstances and alignments that defined a pre-crisis equilibrium in specific areas (e.g., the function of white supremacy in US history). These should shape the lens through which we see politics, but they are not an unchanging given that sets the extent and limit of that politics.

In the second place, it is important to be in a position to be responsive to the fundamental unevenness that is inherent in the circumstances of sharp localized breaks rooted in globalized contradictions. We can't predict how or when possibilities will emerge and should be careful to avoid isolation, organizationally or politically. For instance, while it is important to develop specific initiatives and priorities, these cannot be taken as more than provisional and experimental. I'd worry about exaggerated emphases on the potentials of certain issues, arenas, and constituencies. It is not only possible, it is probable that unexpected developments will overwhelm such plans—so we shouldn't get too locked in.

There is an assumption in some quarters that the planning-significant outcome of these conditions will be the global collapse of capital and a centrifugal fragmentation with a variety of localized responses—most of them not liberatory. I think that a different outcome, although not one that is a clear alternative, should be seen as planning-significant. This points towards a new capitalist equilibrium: unstable, perhaps including a zone of chaos, and probably involving the collapse of the centrality and hegemony of the current capitalist nation-state formations. This is the terrain from which I see the emergence of global social democracy. Leaving aside for the moment the likelihood of this outcome in this country or elsewhere, there are a number of points about current approaches that are raised by its possibility.

First, and the reason why this is not a "clear alternative" to collapse, the social glue that binds this "social democracy" will not be the promise of more of a "people's capitalism"; it will be the cultivated fear of chaos and riot. Before any of the current episodes of protest get very far, they will confront this within the forces that are currently protesting, as a material basis for clinging to "order." This provides the added impetus to the arguments for "peaceful," "legal," and "responsible" protest within the opposition movements. Clearly, we must challenge this, but with the understanding that it has deeper roots than timidity and reformism. It will also divide the constituency of the movement sociologically as well as in terms of program and ideological orientation. Those who currently embrace radical stances may develop an unexpected reluctance about implementing them when they evaluate the stakes and risks; a reluctance that won't be so prevalent among the "less politically developed."

Second, and this gets to the question of specific demands, the politics of the protest have to become more concrete and specific as part of making its qualitative challenge to capital an organizable one. However, there should be no illusions that this can be formalized in more basic and "radical" reform demands that will play a definite "transitional" role in the process. Demands such as those of the Atlanta POC group,[2] which was presented as a non-discussed alternative to the confused, color-blind reformism that is certainly a big factor in the OWS movement, are postures that an incorporative social democratic policy of capital is very capable of assuming. Not to ignore the counter-pressures and the objective limitations, but significant ruling-class interest in "reforms" that choose labor mobility over nativism, soft policing over militarization, maintaining a social safety net over "austerity" and "fiscal responsibility," are not only possible, they are inevitable. Moreover, focusing on issues in this way offers up an expanded constituency for superficial, reformist promises—formal institutional changes giving the oppressed and repressed an expanded role in administering their essential subordination. These can become substitutes for substantial material benefits and, equally important, will provide roadblocks to the development of revolutionary intransigence.

Third, we can't depend on police repression to facilitate our strategic goals and help us make political points about system and state. When specific incidents of repression occur in certain areas, we should take full advantage, but we are dealing with an opposition that has a learning curve. The ruling class will make every effort not to utilize generalized repression in ways that expand opposition, and this will frequently override tendencies (on the part of the dominant contender within a particular sphere of operation or activity) to maximize the use of state power and force. This reality cannot be effectively countered with arguments about what happened at other times and in other places. It is also not smart to function in ways that premise expectations on the likelihood of a positive response to a repression that can be plausibly portrayed as a reaction to provocation … almost always a counterproductive situation.

The current movement is a spontaneous amalgamation that includes many levels and flavors of opportunism along with various dysfunctional radicalisms. It is overrun with a politics of theatrical posture that cannot sustain a mass protest in the inevitable political winter that is approaching. However, I think it is important not to organize as a left opposition to the de facto leadership—at least not mainly. Instead, we should look for ways to present a more active and imaginative pole of struggle against capital that stays connected to, but not confined by, the OWS phenomena—and that can benefit from the fact of OWS without getting crippled by its organization maintenance and its various dynamics of incestuous decline.

First, an important fact is that OWS tends to partially demonstrate the universality of the Arab Spring phenomena. Actions of handfuls in a few places can transform into actions of tens of thousands everywhere, and this can happen almost overnight. It can all reverse as well, and there are a number of very different possible trajectories that I don't mean to equate, but what I think is primary is that millions of people have learned this is possible—that it is a "platform," as John Robb says (2007)—and one that will be quickly activated whenever and wherever events call for it.

When the OWS, conceived generally, is in ascendency, it is a moving threat to capital—emerging everywhere seemingly out of nothing and much more than its known ingredients. But it quickly becomes a fixed and measurable point of stationary opposition—which still has possibilities but different ones and, I think, increasingly less strategically significant ones. It is at this point that the left should look to develop a much more mobile and flexible fight that can utilize a full range of real conditions and real circumstances rather than being confined and limited by a subset of them. That is almost criminally vague, and I will take some responsibility for trying to get more concrete—but here the best I can do is some disconnected ideas.

The central political issue/obstacle is the legitimacy of capital. This is something that is not susceptible to purely ideological or rhetorical expression; the challenge must be embodied in a politics and culture of resistance that understands and embraces its "illegality"—rather than its "democracy," or its "representative" character, or even its "militancy."

In the development of this requirement, political and ideological agreement—points of unity—become more than a little slippery. Positions will change rapidly, and the real divisions will emerge around who is willing to "construct acts to the end"*—perhaps more so than reaching a common understanding of either the "end" or of the current conjuncture. The grounds of left unity will be heavily moral: who will participate in decisions of the "what is to be done"[3] nature and be accountable to the others who have done so as well.

The issue of "riot" is/will be central. Perhaps it's unnecessarily pretentious to use Badiou*, but nevertheless, in the absence of a mass axiomatic conception of a global alternative, the popular breaks will take on the character of "riot."[4] The capacity of this issue to "fork" the movement is real—and, perhaps as another way of saying the same thing, the role it can play in the emergence of global social democracy is real as well. We must be very aware that such circumstances are more conducive to a variety of radical populisms than to communism.

Finally, what are the metrics? We have to judge this work by whether and how well it creates new communists and by the improvements in their capabilities. Of course, that's hardly different from the general case, but it's a good deal more possible and important to implement and evaluate in these conditions than in our "normal" ones.

## Initial Thoughts on Longview
## January 2012

*This piece was originally sent to an email list of comrades following a discussion about the militant struggle of International Longshore & Warehouse Union (ILWU) Local 21 in Longview, Washington that occurred at the beginning of September in 2011. The labor conflict centered on the automation of a grain terminal and the elimination of high-wage longshoreman jobs. Rank-and-file union members engaged in forceful picketing and alleged property destruction, captivating the attention of radicals both regionally and nationally. A number of the recipients of this email were actively involved in supporting the militant edge of the struggle against higher levels of union leadership who sought to pacify the rank and file and restore labor peace.*

I'd like to say a few things about the discussion of the Longview Longshore situation that was here a few days ago. In microcosm, and perhaps only fleetingly, the Longview situation poses the much discussed issue of the "encounter" between working-class people and the mass movement that has emerged in many historic situations: the Italian Hot Autumn,* May 68 in France,* the RUM movement in the US,[1] and in some ways the Cultural Revolution in China.* Like Lowell,[2] I think that such emerging working-class struggles, which have been largely absent in this country for decades, should be seen as priceless opportunities and major obligations, not as problems and diversions from other work that has more potential. And like Nick,[3] I'm reluctant to offer suggestions about complex struggles with real stakes and implications for others to implement.

However, the concerns that Nick raised must be confronted, as clearly and in as wide a circle of activists as possible, including the ILWU activists who are open to the discussion. It's important not to be seduced by any cheerleading rhetoric, including our own; to tell the truth as we understand it, even when it is painful; and to rely on and help develop the capacity of ordinary people to think about complicated alternatives and decide important questions.

But it is also possible to let our political concerns about sectoral interests and reformist perspectives overshadow what is new in the Longview situation. In my opinion, what is new there is the fact that a significant, compact group of working-class people have begun to fight. Actually fight: outside the framework of legality and propriety, as contrasted with the fake substitute for "fighting" provided by what is termed "bargaining" or "negotiating." When this break happens, ideas and relationships which were previously impossible begin to be reasonable and practical and begin to provide a basis for live action. But this doesn't happen in comfortable, incremental, irreversible steps forward, and it is seldom articulated clearly by those most deeply involved. The process can be clothed in objectless militancy, and/or reflexively assume the form of demands for sectoral advantage or maintenance of privileges. But at the same time, it can also manifest new understandings of equality, of justice, of social cooperation, and of the universal legitimacy of resistance to oppression, the axiomatic elements of the idea of communism. The contradictions can be evident at any level, including within the same individual.

These situations provide expanded possibilities for social polarization and confrontation—good problems for radicals. But there will not be a durable advance and real benefits for a revolutionary perspective unless radicals use the polarized situation to expedite the development of an organic connection with the conditions and circumstances of working-class life—and in that way limiting any possibilities to assume the "condescending savior"* role.

# Email on Longview
## May 2012

*This was posted to the same email list as the previous essay. It was a more extended analysis of the strategic and political significance of the struggle at the port of Longview. It mainly consists of a response to a draft essay by a comrade, P, who had been closely involved in organizing support for the militant rank-and-file activists in opposition to the union leadership attempting to tranquilize the struggle. It begins with a preface added by Hamerquist when it was circulated on the email list.*

I posted this in a brief note a few weeks ago:

> We've made some steps towards linking working-class needs and potentials with an embryonic revolutionary movement, but as a consequence the issues of reforms and reformism are presented in ways that can't be resolved rhetorically. We've made some steps towards becoming a fighting movement "outside the state,"* but as a consequence, the issues of militancy, illegality, "military" work, and state repression can't be treated as settled questions, and simplistic posturing has to be avoided.
>
> I intend to write some stuff on these questions in the near future—starting from some discussions with P and some others about the events around the Longview Longshore strike.

What follows is a quite messy start that begins from a narrow and inconclusive discussion of P's initial estimate of the Longview ILWU struggle and settlement that dates back a few months. I doubt that I'm familiar with all of the discussions on the topic. A lot has happened since last winter and without a specific effort it is quite possible that there won't be an adequate discussion of an important experience. This would be another sad example of our general problems in dealing with what is happening around us and what we are doing about it.

I'm essentially limiting this piece to the first of the two areas that I indicated above. The issues of militancy and opposition to the state will only enter in passing. This is not the best course. Extending and deepening the mass, working-class character of the movement neither can nor should be separated from the need to confront state power and authority. Not only are the issues tightly related, but the relationship is far from simple and straightforward and its main features can't be assumed. Beyond this, it will be clear that questions of militancy and illegality are a central part of the argument in P's draft and of some of the responses to it—including mine. However, the place of reform and reformism in an emerging insurgency raises its own questions, so, recognizing the limitations of the approach, I want to treat them separately, if only for the moment.

Most of this stays within the basic framework of an estimate of the Longview situation, but I do touch on some broader issues that I think are relevant. These include questions of changing class composition and its relationship to revolutionary subjectivity.

Finally, I hope to revisit some points about the "communist invariant."*

P,

This will more or less follow your draft. I expect that some points will be raised and then revisited. You write, "How does the struggle in Longview fit within the narrative of intransigence and militancy as the heart of the movement's strength?"

I think you should consider more carefully whether the lessons learned in Portland and Oakland actually do "fit" the struggle in Longview and, if so, how? I think both that the reform option might have significantly different characteristics and implications in that context and that some aspects of your narrative might apply to Longview in ways we wouldn't like all that much. You point to a "counterargument (against liberals and social democrats) … won in both debate and deed." I have some questions about what has been won and how conclusive the victory has been, not to mention whether it is wise to argue the point in public in quite this way. I would emphasize, although probably not in a generally circulated discussion, a different notion of what the militants in your area, considered as a bloc, have "won," stressing the fact that they have essentially won it in a struggle with themselves. The combination of cynicism and passivity embedded in our ordinary political routines has been disrupted, and some of us have learned that, as you say, it is the "moments" of "defiance of all institutions … [the] moments in which hundreds and thousands of 'apolitical' people have swelled the ranks of the movement … [that] have been our greatest strength." In my opinion, this growing collective self-consciousness, coming particularly out of Oakland and Portland, that what militants think—and what they do or fail to do—has real impacts and creates new possibilities as well as new obligations, will turn out to be a more meaningful advance than any defeat of liberal arguments—and, at least in the short run, this will be more meaningful than any concessions that can be wrung from capital or the state.

However, the core militants should take some care with this type of "victory"—it is subject to reversal and, as such, warrants the quotation marks. In fact, it's more of a "use it or lose it" situation: if the newly recognized capacities are not employed, they can rapidly wither into nostalgic memories; on the other hand, their careless use can permanently piss away opportunities. Most relevant to my main point, and I'll get back to this with more of an argument, it's not a victory that should be looked to as a stable platform for future advances—and particularly not in significantly different situations.

One recurring theme in what you write is that more militancy translates into broader support. We should certainly embrace every situation where this equation actually holds, but we should also be clear that this will not always be the case and that it is not a consequence that should be assumed as an element of every political initiative. So, I think that more care is necessary with formulations and examples like the following:

> When the movement defied the ILWU leadership nationally and marched on the Ports, in some locations engaging in hard blockades against workers trying to cross lines and fighting police to do so, we saw the movement's profile and popular support continue to rise.

This may have been partially true—at least temporarily—about Longview, but there is no guarantee of similar outcomes in the future ... and the future will certainly include situations where such relatively "good" outcomes are not likely, but where militancy and confrontation are still not only appropriate, but possibly obligatory for revolutionary activists. And, to repeat, it's always important to remember that many of these positive outcomes are reversible, sometimes quite quickly, and this can transform efforts to use them to boost morale into a sad parody with the opposite impacts. I don't know if you are in general agreement with these points, but if you are, they raise questions about the somewhat triumphalist tone in your opening section. I think a better opening would emphasize how the changed trajectory of Occupy* creates new possibilities for radical ideas and militant actions to have significant impact on increasingly significant elements of our circumstances—with Longview being a case study, although the situation is still developing, and the study requires continuing investigation and is not ready for any fixed verdicts.

At some point, hopefully sooner rather than later, serious radical movements must deal with the dilemmas of daily working-class life in a manner that begins to materialize actual alternatives to capitalism. In our corner of the left, this entails breaking down the various social barriers between radicals and the working class without adopting any condescending savior* approach or any other variation of substitutionism*—and while also avoiding classic reformism or a "serve the people"* populism. One significant advance in the Port Shutdowns[1] and the Longview situation is that you ("you" in the sense of a sector of the militants from Occupy) developed some capacity to function as a real factor on a central terrain of the class struggle, with all the limitations and possibilities that are associated with that terrain ... and this was not only as a "recorder"[2] or an external critic or confined within the limits of the "support" role. I think there is no doubt that this involvement was a determining factor in the ways the situation worked out. And, while it will never be conclusively demonstrated, and a lot of time could be wasted on the attempt, it appears to me that your intervention in Longview worked out generally for the better, even in the reform sense, than what would have been the case in its absence.

However, what this raises for me is the need for a different overview on the entire issue of victories and failures.

You emphasize the following passage in your argument:

Victory for Some a Victory for All

Seldom do our opponents cede concessions without forethought to their long-term implications. We need criteria for evaluating our "victories," worth, and pitfalls. Do they strengthen the sense of power and possibility for workers within or outside of the specific sector who will benefit from them? Do they level the field—create a greater equality within the class—or do they reinforce privileges and divisions within the class?

This raises two important questions, however they are both open to ambiguous and changing answers. You provide a representative set of these ambiguities yourself. We have "gains for workers in

Local 21" and "solidarity won the struggle" at some points. But at others there are different conclusions: "What initially appeared as a victory for Local 21 ... has now clearly become a defeat for everyone excepting the ILWU as an institution and EGT."[3] To me, this injects an unnecessary confusion that follows from looking at the struggle in two incompatible frameworks: one that is premised on an assessment of victories/defeats or gains/losses as essentially trade union outcomes with the implicit assumption that these are (necessary?) steps towards a revolutionary class confrontation; another that assesses whether significant characteristics of the struggle broke with the existing patterns and opened new possibilities, irrespective of whether they failed or succeeded in trade unionist terms. This second framework, I assume, is what is affirmed when you say, "Occupy did not come to this struggle with a narrow interest in supporting trade unionists in better contracts or wages for their ever-diminishing memberships." And that is the framework that I think is appropriate for us.

Think about the major episodes of class struggle: the revolutions and national liberations, the dual powers and general strikes. Not a single one of them could be regarded as an unambiguous victory—at least not when they are considered over any significant period of time—and some that we rightly believe hold out the best hope for the future look more like major defeats. The few weeks of the Paris Commune that ended with the slaughter of tens of thousands of the Parisian poor and working classes ... a victory or a massive failure? Or, perhaps it was a "victory" in that the true nature of capital was brought home when the direct casualties of class struggle escalated to the tens of thousands from a few here and a few there. Some screwed up insurrectionists and a fringe of Trotskyists might look at it this way—enough said.

Badiou* argues that we should evaluate major experiences of struggle as, "Beginnings [that] can, then, be measured by the rebeginnings they authorize" (2010, 219). And to look at this in terms of one of his major examples, the Paris Commune, we can find "rebeginnings" authorized by the Commune in virtually every major class struggle against capital that has followed it.

The question for us—and specifically for your review—is what rebeginnings, if any, do you see being authorized by Longview? I think your draft implies both too much pessimism and too much of a sort of dogged morale-building optimism to adequately answer this question. I'll try to make this a little less nonsensical as I stumble along.

The analyses from various leftist longshoremen that you've posted as background are unremittingly negative: the contract is a defeat, a "sellout"; the sacrifices made resulted in less than the status quo ante; the union structure demonstrated its total corruption; etc. While there is a large element of truth to all of this, it is almost certainly embedded in the trade union reform perspective that we know well, a perspective that leads inexorably away from confronting the class contradiction in actual situations and towards putting a priority on an "essential" initial step of successful union reform. To the extent that history should be our guide, this perspective maxes out with a different set of placeholders in the union institutional structure, who, sooner rather than later, are acting pretty much the same as those they have replaced.

In these trade unionist terms, militant actions can be supported as an organizing tactic, but only so long as they can be incorporated in the perspective of union reform. In even the best of such circumstances, a sustained direct challenge to capital will usually appear as premature. More typically, it will be regarded as counterproductive—with costs that will overbalance any benefits that might be gained. In my view, this highlights why it is more useful to look at the content of the struggle rather than its material outcomes—and, in particular, rather than those material outcomes that are measurable within the framework of trade unionism.

You provide a good example of an alternative way to place the issues: has the "sense of power and possibility for workers within or outside of the specific sector" been expanded? Although I don't have the facts that would be needed for a useful answer, I do think that just posing this question points to a better approach with more appropriate metrics, although they will be hard to quantify, than any quest for better contract language or the more radical and articulate professions of general support for class struggle and social unionism.

Let me say this in a slightly different way. It is common on the left to envision a revolutionary, working-class movement being formed from a process of incremental changes. In a typical version, these changes consist of those forced improvements in sectoral material conditions that are commonly termed "victories," although more sophisticated perspectives might use an alternative calculus based on incremental advances in popular consciousness that in turn are based on "lessons" that might conceivably be generalized from setbacks as well as "victories." But whatever the degree of sophistication, in my opinion, all attempts to premise a revolutionary strategy on such approaches are hamstrung by the essential ambiguity of conceptions of victories and defeats, gains and losses, often defined within the framework of capitalist hegemony.

We should guard against adopting a mode of discussion that gives away these points by reflexively slipping in the perspective of incremental advances and retreats when we know that our reality is filled with oppositions and contradictions that cut across and tear up these simple categories. This confounds the most diligent efforts to translate linear estimates of quantitative changes into a challenge to capital that, to be meaningful, must be qualitative—remember: "be his [sic] wages *high or low*."[4] Given the inherent contradictions in all attempts to apply reformist metrics to an estimation of revolutionary potentials, I think that you should focus more directly on those changes in class consciousness and the balance of class forces in Longview that might constitute something qualitative and point to something genuinely new.

I do see points where your draft presents a better framework of analysis that emphasizes the potential of a rupture with the terrain of encounters over the incremental and the various quantitative changes at the margins of the class struggle. Of course, this still leaves some persistent issues concerning reforms, reform motivations, and reformist perspectives, and I will touch on some of them below. However, in this more adequate framework such issues can be treated without such a heavily moralistic overhang, particularly if they are put in the context that your two previously mentioned questions suggest: Has the sense of power and of new possibilities been enlarged? Has the terrain of equality expanded and become more meaningful?

I know very little of the particulars of the Longview situation, but I think I can see some areas which are giving you more trouble than they should. Probably the most important concerns the significance of reforms and material gains for those working-class fragments that are relatively privileged and that already have substantially "more" than most working people—perhaps too much more in some ways of thinking. Here is how I look at that issue. Even high-paid, "privileged" workers and their families, such as the Longshore workers in Longview, have real and legitimate needs that are frustrated by capital. These might be less focused around the wage than for most other workers, but certainly they have needs for more collective time and more common space. My basic point would be that there are many types of "improvements," both perceived and substantive, that can make life within capitalism seem better at least temporarily, and while this commonly comes with some bad political baggage, there is no a priori moral reason not to view any of them as a "good"—even when they can't be shoehorned into someone's radical perspectives, including our own. Taken by themselves, they are unlikely to amount to significant steps towards revolution, but neither are they necessarily the building blocks of class collaboration or pro-capitalist reaction.

I'd like to put some of this in terms of what we do in the way of "political" work—if we are right to call it that—out here in the woods. Whatever our intentions, the more we get involved and the harder we work, the more we "win"—at least up to a point. And as part of what we win, there are a few people who get differential material benefits and there are a few who are persuaded that if we pursue a larger agenda of similar projects, we can have bigger victories—take over the Democratic Party, run "our own" candidates, elect "our" Public Land Commissioner. I smell reformism, as a sectarian Puerto Rican friend once commented.

Of course, we are quite aware that anything we "win" in this or that specific reform context always comes at the expense of similarly deserving, but perhaps less organized, constituencies in different reform contexts—and these may actually lose something that they currently have. Our truth is that more funding for salmon restoration means less funding for after-school programs, some restraints on Department of Natural Resources corruption and incompetence on State lands issues means more problems with DNR's regulation of private timber, etc. These multiple possibilities for incorporation and diversion, and for pitting different struggles for limited objectives against each other, always obstruct and deform the work.

To make the example more concrete: we spent a good deal of time this fall getting a log jam shifted to protect a neighbor's home from being flooded, without using the large, rock riprap that damages salmon habitat. It is the type of project that is unreasonably difficult, not so much due to ruling-class opposition as to the overlapping layers of bureaucratic incompetence and inertia. Getting it done was certainly seen as a good thing by the neighbors, but there is no doubt that it took resources that might have been used elsewhere with more beneficial social and environmental impacts. And there is no doubt that it provided tangible support for illusions about the potential of working through the system and was quickly put to that use by various functionaries who are always scouting around for ways to counter the widespread cynicism about their credibility, competence, and motivations.

Although the point shouldn't be exaggerated, such more or less apolitical efforts have a certain importance. There is more to social life and to politics than the reform/revolution dichotomy. What we are attempting to do, at its best, provides a form of collective self-organization that can help crystallize a broader notion of our side and a somewhat clearer picture of the other side—a more tangible sense of a "commons," including a physical and social space, a shared history, and an autonomous potential. This is all good stuff that implicitly contrasts potentials for social cooperation to the imprinted ideology of competition. It's light years from this to a revolutionary mass movement, but it's not irrelevant to the process.

I may be completely off base here, but I think that such an appreciation helps in the assessment of Longview. Even when workers who are already relatively privileged enter into struggle with definitions of interests that are far too narrow, they are not necessarily putting themselves on the wrong side of the class struggle. Though it is far from an unalloyed positive and always carries concrete problems that must be addressed, it is overwhelmingly preferable that people fight for perceived improvements and fight against losing them, at least if the alternative is that they remain passive and, at least implicitly, acquiescent in the existing state of affairs. At the very minimum, this engagement provides more concrete opportunities to critique the areas of privilege that buttress inequality, and more likelihood that the critique will find a receptive audience. And often, including in the struggle in Longview as I understand it, there are certain moments when mass initiatives expand the arena of collectivity and commons and result in political situations with potentials that go well beyond providing a better platform for a radical critique.

One possible response to the real problems with the Longview constituency and with the outcomes to that struggle is to argue for a changed strategic focus towards the more marginalized and oppressed sectors of the class. This is not a new idea; it was essentially Lenin's political response to the corruption and collapse of the Second International in the face of imperialist war. And I'm sure that we can agree that there are important new features in global capital that also point us in this direction. However, presuming that there are meaningful opportunities for such interventions, which is not always the case, it is an illusion to think that this changed focus magically solves the dilemmas of incremental reforms. Movements in this area are also immediately vulnerable to reformist distortions, although these might take different forms than among the "labor aristocracy." The way the limitations become evident might differ, but so long as the goal is "winning" within the framework of capital, the "winnings" of the precariat have no more inherent tendency towards revolution than the "winnings" of the labor aristocracy. It is not our experience that those who "have nothing," speaking metaphorically, want everything, while those who already have a little, only want a little more. And why anyone should expect anything different is beyond me.

Of course, I'm not arguing against a concentration on the issues and constituencies at the "bottom." I certainly recognize questions—and particularly the crucial question of equality—that can hardly be addressed without such a stance. However, the dilemmas of reforms and sectoral demands will still be there. So, I think that it is a real error to look at this (or any other) structural characteristic in the global division of labor for an objective index to revolutionary potential. This is a position that good people often include in a moralistic type of left "anti-imperialist" common sense, but without very clear arguments.

Longview is a political situation that is very prone to a type of reductionism that equates certain types of objective realities to certain social attitudes and performances. However, it is not the case that an outcome that objectively perpetuates or even extends a relatively privileged position is recognized as such by its objective beneficiaries, or that their ideas and actions are mechanically determined by their privileges, whether or not they recognize them.

I want to end this as I began it—with a self-referential excerpt. I was struck by the use of the term "communist invariant" in Bruno Bosteels' book on Badiou (2011), and think it is relevant to the discussion of how revolutionaries should relate to the potential and the reality of mass anti-capitalist insurgency. I posted this a little while ago on the concept:

> The communist invariant includes the concepts of equality and justice; the conception that resistance to oppres-

sion and rebelliousness is "right"; the intuition/convic-
tion that the experiences of cooperation in production
and social life generally point to a universal potential; and
the perception/intuition that people have the capacity to
think and to comprehend the truth of their situation and
its possibilities.

In my opinion, these relate to the elements of a dual consciousness that develop among participants in collective struggles, and
the more fundamental and widespread the struggle, the more
pronounced these elements become. They are ephemeral and
extremely resistant to being captured in any continuing organizational form—union, party, popular assembly—but they are both
the points of departure and those of arrival.

## Militancy After Occupy
## December 2012

*The following was an email reply sent over an email list of revo-
lutionaries across North America. The original post was by an
organizer for the Portland Action Lab (PAL), a grouping of activists in Portland, Oregon with the mission of coordinating large
street demonstrations. One such action was held on November 3,
2012, and was referred to as "N3." This demonstration effectively
closed the cycle of street militancy following Occupy\* the previous
fall. Notably, the police response with pepper spray demonstrated
the limits of what had become a standard practice of street marches
using reinforced banners to push against police lines.*

In this discussion, and in many others, the characterization of
tactical militancy as essentially symbolic and as a diversion from
more substantive matters is part of a criticism of a confrontational
approach towards the police. However, it also usually implies a
broader dismissal of the military side of the struggle—those elements and aspects that Gramsci\* would group in the "war of
maneuver"\*—as being irrelevant concerns for revolutionary
strategy in this country and others of its so-called "advanced" or
"developed" cohort. I don't agree with any of this for a range of
reasons and will get into a few of them here.

A good place to start is Steve Biko's observation that the most
important weapon in the hands of the oppressor is the mind of the
oppressed (paraphrased poorly).[1] In general, I don't think much of
Negri,\* but this is a point that (following Foucault) he also makes:

> The passage to the society of control does not in any way
> mean the end of discipline. In fact, the immanent exercise
> of discipline—that is, the self-disciplining of subjects, the
> incessant whisperings of disciplinary logics within subjec-
> tivities themselves—is extended even more generally in the
> society of control. (Hardt and Negri 2003, 330)

Look at this in terms of the police—broadly conceived as the immediate repressive apparatus of the capitalist state within more or less "normal" conditions. The police power normally is manifested as a limit, as a wall of impossibility for the movement. It is commonly accepted and obeyed without having to be employed because there appears to be no other rational option. In Badiou's* terminology, it manifests an "immeasurable" "excess" of power over and against a potentially rebellious population that is a part of the state of the situation in normal conditions (Badiou 2005, 146). The movement might aim to reform police power, but with the probable consequence of making it a more effective tool of domination in the (near) future. It might challenge it frontally, with the probable consequence of incurring tangible costs that will heavily overbalance largely intangible and very reversible benefits.

This real dilemma opens maneuvering room for the left reformist options, which at their best attempt to mobilize a majoritarian challenge to capitalist hegemony that can circumvent this police and military power until somehow it loses its efficacy. There are many reasons why such a challenge to capital holds very little promise. If it becomes the basis for a revolutionary strategy and does not quickly degrade into a thinly disguised reformism, the results will be disastrous for our side—unless capitalist state power self-destructs and shrinks to being the paper tiger* of the Maoists. And we should know from history, and from applying good sense to our current conditions, just how likely that is.

Of course, these reformist options are heavily infected by those "incessant whisperings of disciplinary logics within subjectivities themselves" that Negri raises. They provide the infected soil where Biko's paradox—of the "self-disciplining" of large majorities in the interests of the small minorities that oppress them—germinates dynamics like L describes in their PAL N3 context: "Many individuals and organizations ... managed to envision a situation in which marchers with banners were antagonizing the police ... [causing] the police ... violence."

No movement that aims for the revolutionary abolition of capital and class society can assume its own continuing "legality." How could it be otherwise when constituent struggles that are far more limited, even ones that are explicitly reformist—look at the dilemmas of the so-called secondary boycott—are already "illegal"? An oppositional movement that necessarily begins very small and that will remain an activated minority well into the future will certainly find difficulty handling this issue, but the point of departure should be that the "normal" operation of the police and legal structure is a significant part of capitalist power, and that it is no more "symbolic" to organize against its assertion of legitimacy and its exercise of authority than it is to organize against capitalist profit in a given worksite.

Of course, this is not an argument for frontal confrontations on military terrain against overwhelmingly superior forces. That is an approach that will be largely limited to symbolic struggles—and, at times, mere posturing and theatrics. It may produce a few exemplary actions when it goes beyond theater, but unfortunately these will come with the martyrs and with the *penitenti** following behind them—and we already have quite enough of both.

What is needed is mass struggle that—self-consciously, as far as possible—takes advantage of the political constraints on the repressive apparatus, using its institutional contradictions, rigidities, and brittleness to force it to reveal both its nature and its limits. For the existing left, more evidence of the pervasiveness and magnitude of repression should not be necessary, since we already tend towards a narcissistic exaggeration of the repression aimed at us. Far more important is developing a better understanding of the state's repressive capacity, including the limits and constraints on it, among newly activated forces. I'm not thinking here about liberals who may have vestigial illusions about "our" police, but rather about the popular class forces. These normally have few illusions about the social role of the police but lack confidence in their collective capacity to deal with it effectively. Experiences of mass struggle, where police lose their flexibility of operation and are forced to maneuver and adapt—even retreat—in response to a mixture of open, collective challenges and to calculated, collective evasions, can capsize deeply-rooted pessimism in masses of people about what is possible and can lead to a rapid expansion of the numbers and the organization of militants.

Badiou makes this point in a more philosophical context. I'll cite a couple of excerpted phrases from Bosteels's summary, and follow with a seat-of-the-pants explanation:

> The state's excessive power in fact only becomes visible as the result of an emergent political subject. When everything runs its course as usual, this excess remains invisible, even as … [it] secretly continues to serve an intimidating function.

And:

> Politics is … the art of the impossible. … This means … to give visibility to the excess of power in the normal state of affairs … [and it] involves a certain gamble, or wager, through which the state is forced to lay bare its inherently repressive nature … (Bosteels 2011, 30).

The element of confrontation with the excess power of the state is the condition for making it measurable: a finite obstacle, although undoubtedly still an imposing one. At the same time, such confrontations contain an element of risk, a "wager," as Badiou puts it, that is part of the process of creating a subjective counter-power from a largely divided and atomized—and thus passive—constituency of the oppressed and exploited. What emerges is a subject that is becoming aware of previously unacknowledged potentials, that can begin to measure ("count") its capacities, and that can actually contest and defend sites of struggle. This may be too vague—it looks that way as I read it over—but it explains to me how a point that may seem to be not just symbolic, but perhaps even trivial, can actually be quite important. Consider the case of the "sturdy banners" that L raises: "People and groups have successfully and without pepper spray used these sturdy banners in many actions and marches."

The police know that what is at stake here is their domination of the site of protest and they know that any loss of this domination will expand the arena of autonomy and disrupt the way they want to function in both tactical and strategic terms. That is why "sturdy banners" and associated matters "provoke" them. This police response is not spontaneous but planned and purposeful, and we will eventually find it detailed in some operational manuals. However, there are risks for the police inherent in any pattern of response, and this can provide some operational space for the movement.

Apparently, I'm at odds with a few others here who question L's category of "the institutionalized left." I like it, and would like to relate it to Badiou's concept of the "left":

> *Let's call 'the left' the set of parliamentary political personnel that proclaim that they are the only ones equipped to bear the general consequences of a singular political movement.* Or, in more contemporary terms, that they are the only ones able to provide "social movements" with a "political perspective." (Badiou 2010, 198; emphasis in original)

Badiou's use of the modifier "parliamentary" highlights two points: the defining strategic priority on work within capitalist party, union, and NGO institutional structures that are not sufficiently "at a distance from the state"* (Badiou 2010, 192); and political work implemented through proto-state organizational forms that have been exhausted in the past political sequence. This is a point he makes frequently in recent writing. For example:

> "Today" is the moment when we have to take up the challenge of thinking politics outside of its subjection to the state and outside of the framework of parties or of the party. (Ibid.)

Much of his more recent, brief book *The Rebirth of History: Times of Riots and Uprisings* (2012) is devoted to the more practical implications of these concepts as they apply to current conditions.

I think the notion of an institutionalized left conveys a problematic common characteristic of most left organizations. They find their answers to current questions in the past: past policies, past events, past debates, long-dead revolutions. And, not surprisingly, they are fractured in every conceivable way by their different answers to these questions from the past. It should surprise no one that this left finds it difficult to locate the political potentials that are new and unique, that they tend to gain influence as struggles wane and fall back into established routine.

Finally, and I know I have strayed a good way from the topic, there is an issue of how we see the time. Is it the closing moments of a period of capitalist disequilibrium that will be succeeded by a new cycle of capitalist stability, perhaps with some shifting of the deck chairs that requires a reworked plan for that "extended march through the institutions"?* Or are we in, as Badiou puts it, "Times of Riots and Uprisings"? We can't answer the question with certainty, but we can identify the answer we prefer and we can look for evidence and prepare to pursue its implications. It's possible these efforts will be disappointed, but that is a far better outcome than will result from the presumption that militancy and confrontation are always premature and that there should be no wagers on this sort of foolishness.

# III. ANTI-FASCISM

## Third Position
## May 2001

*This article appeared in the first issue of the Anti-Racist Action Research Bulletin in May of 2001 under the pseudonym R. Gibson. It deals with the question of "third position" fascism, which broadly refers to far-right tendencies that claim to be fundamentally different from traditional fascism. Some third position fascist tendencies claim to be anti-capitalist and distance themselves from white supremacy or antisemitism. Because of this, they at times seek connections to the left. It is notable to compare the trends examined here with those that emerged more recently in the Alt-Right. The questions and themes raised by Hamerquist here were later taken up in more detail in his essay "Fascism & Anti-Fascism" in the book* Confronting Fascism *(2002).*

Prior to a 1999 national meeting, ARA* was informed that the Church of the Creator knew some details of the time and place. The information was provided, indirectly, but probably deliberately, by the American Front, a part of the so-called "national revolutionary," "third position" wing of fascism.[1] So, what was happening here? Was it a little fascist joke ... was it some kind of COINTELPRO* police action ... or was it an example of the "beyond left and right" stance that is an element in third position politics? The answers are not clear. What is clear, however, is that ARA has got to pay specific attention to third position fascism.

Most anti-fascist research has concentrated on traditional white supremacists, Christian Identity,* and orthodox, Nazi-modeled fascist groups like the National Alliance.* This focus is understandable; such political movements have been the visible face of fascism in this country, even if not necessarily elsewhere in the world. However, if we look at fascism too narrowly, it becomes an easy target, easy to attack or to dismiss, at a time when we can't afford such a luxury. Fascism is a real and complex social movement, not a political pathology that is manipulated by one or another sector of the ruling class. A failure to come to grips with this reality will support some dangerously complacent assumptions about the course of our struggle.

What does it mean when fascists aren't pro-capitalist, but overtly pro–working class? What if they aren't reactionary but revolutionary? What if they claim to reject white supremacy and, in some cases, antisemitism? What if they claim to want to organize working people in a revolutionary assault on capitalism and attempt to develop alliances with the revolutionary left to accomplish this? All of these positions can be found in the third position tendency in the fascist movement.

The third position advocates for a racialist cultural nationalism, but it sharply separates itself from the dominant fascist tradition, arguing that Hitler, Franco, Mussolini, etc., were opportunists who sold out to capitalism. The position has roots in the radical "socialist" Strasser* tendency of the German Nazi movement, in similar elements of Italian and Spanish fascism, and in the Montonero wing of the Peronist movement in Argentina.[2] The third position is growing in this country and elsewhere in the world, partly out of the demoralization and fragmentation that has accompanied the collapse of the Eastern Bloc and partly out of the political weakness and lack of militancy of both the traditional left and the traditional right.

Determining the shape and direction of third position fascism is one major part of anti-fascist research. What is its political strategy and what are the contradictions within it? Is it getting a popular response? To what extent may it be state–influenced or manipulated? Has it had any success in its stated policy of developing working relations with anti-imperialist nationalists and popular mass movements against globalization and for "green" issues?

At least three points deserve immediate attention. First, third position groups project a planned and systematic infiltration of left organizations as well as radical popular movements. If this was just the information-gathering/disruption tactic which has been utilized by the Larouchies and Moonies in this country,[3] it could be dealt with as a variant of police infiltration. However, third position entryism raises problems beyond the security of our movement. Since third position politics have a substantial overlap with accepted left views on globalization, ecology, national liberation, and even working-class struggles, this infiltration could result in a catastrophic skewing of left political positions and the capture of some popular movements by forces that fundamentally oppose us. We can screw things up enough by ourselves without this help.

Second, third position politics have such an obvious potential to be disruptive and divisive in the fascist movement, not to mention in the left, that we must assume that these groupings are targets of state counterinsurgency programs. Some may even be state operations of the "pseudo gang"* variation.

Finally, and most importantly, we have to look at the implications of these third position politics for our radical anti-capitalist strategy. Do they constitute a real alternative to traditional racists and fascists? Do they have the potential of winning this competition? Can they successfully appeal to the same social base as we do, using some issues that we have seen as our own?

It is tempting to look at the third position as an invention of capitalist propaganda. Certainly, various liberal apologists for the system are attempting to use it as propaganda, with their groundless allegations of a convergence of "terrorists" of the left and right. State sponsorship of the third position could be a part of the reality, but that should be something to find out, not an assumption underlying the investigation. We must be careful not to limit ourselves to a search for evidence that the new fascism is just a cosmetic change, not so different from the old fascism, not so different from capitalist reaction, and in consequence, not such a serious challenge to us. We have to look at what is really happening and why it is happening. There are major political issues here. They go well beyond our need for enough information to develop a tactical response to the third position.

## Response to Bring the Ruckus: Four Points
## September 2008

*This essay was written in response to some internal discussions within Bring the Ruckus (BTR).[1] While he was never a member of BTR, Hamerquist uses four quotes from the BTR* Internal Discussion Bulletin *to structure his response. Some of the initial discussion is available in Dhondt and Olson (2008). The third and fourth quotes are from comments by Joel Olson.*

I was interested and encouraged by the Bring the Ruckus (BTR) discussion of fascism and would like to respond to some of the criticisms of my positions that it included.[2] I'm happy to see a critical discussion of these issues and hope that my continuing disagreements promote further exchanges without obscuring the substantial areas of agreement. I expect to be corrected if I misunderstand or distort arguments or concepts or in any way misrepresent the views that I don't accept. I'm a little embarrassed by how wordy my piece has become, particularly since it only covers a few of the issues.

To the extent that the discussion focuses on work priorities and current tactical possibilities for BTR, I don't have much to offer. I have argued for an emphasis on anti-fascist work at various times in the past, but it was related to the specific political circumstances. I don't believe that anti-fascist mass work should always be pivotal or that it has some revolutionary potential that can't be developed in other ways. It is not right to make a fetish of this area of work—nor of any other work for that matter.

That said, I do think that the contradictions and conflicts associated with the accelerating globalization of capital will make fascism increasingly relevant to every area of political activity. This calls for a serious treatment of neo-fascisms on a strategic and theoretical level that will undoubtedly include an increased prioritization of street-level anti-fascist organizing. However, in my opinion, this is neither the essence nor the extent of the issue.

I've loosely organized this piece in relation to four short citations from the BTR discussion. I deal with them in the order that they appeared in the material, making only minimal attempts to explore their interconnection and intending no ranking of their relative significance. I'm emphasizing passages that will sharpen differences, realizing that this doesn't take adequate account of other passages and arguments that temper and condition them.

### 1. "[Hamerquist's] argument that Black Nationalism could develop into fascism, for example, is not plausible."

The estimate of "Black Nationalism" and the consideration of the potential for fascist developments within the US Black population are distinct issues and should be kept that way: I neither argue nor believe that Black Nationalism will develop into fascism or that nationalist movements against imperialist oppression were seed beds for fascism. That position is part of left fatalism and pessimism which, more commonly, finds Stalin and the Soviet bloc, or whatever it is that China has become, to be the necessary culmination of the working-class communist movement.

The re-emergence of US Black Nationalism in the 60s, far from misdirecting the progressive movement in a reactionary direction, impelled a major breakthrough towards internationalism and solidarity with anti-capitalist and anti-imperialist struggles that were erupting around the world. The Black Nationalist movement shook the implicit assumption that the attitudes and activities of the white segment of the working class would be the decisive issues in the revolutionary process and transformed the US political movements of the period in an overwhelmingly positive fashion. The impact was not simply through quantitative, but rather qualitative, radicalizing. An important byproduct of the Black Nationalist emphasis on autonomy and self-determination was its challenge to the structures and attitudes within the left that replicated and reproduced capitalist hegemony.

However, the situation has obviously not remained static. As the trend towards capitalist globalization has accelerated, revolutionary nationalist anti-imperialism has become an increasingly hollow shell, and its potential as a vehicle of struggle against capitalist power is rapidly shrinking. It has been unable to effectively counter the neo-colonial response it has elicited from capital and has fractured into a demoralized constituency topped off with an array of warlords, factions, and elites competing for subordinate places at the capitalist table and/or initiating violent authoritarian projects with fascist implications. The partial victories that the revolutionary nationalist movement won, in fact and in perception, are emerging as obstacles to future struggles.

In my opinion, these are not just a collection of temporary setbacks that might be reversed. They are the consequences of the qualitatively changing terrain for class struggle and provide additional evidence of the need for changed categories of analysis and new revolutionary strategies. However, the fact remains that it is not Black Nationalism or revolutionary anti-imperialism that leads to fascism, but their failures!

The disintegration of revolutionary anti-imperialism, not its success, has contributed to the emergence of a cynical, alienated, and demoralized constituency for fascist movements among Black people in this country. I see ideological and organizational initiatives to mobilize this increasingly marginalized and declassed constituency in a fascist direction. The actual issue between myself and some of the BTR commentators is whether this particular potential for fascism is effectively negated by the unique history and institutional structure of Black oppression and white supremacy in this country. Clearly, we disagree on this estimate. I am quite willing to provide evidence and examples to support my view, but at this point it is probably enough to just note the disagreement.

The authors explicitly restrict their dismissal of the potential for non-white fascism to this country and discount the relevance of fascist political tendencies elsewhere in the post-colonial, non-white world—for example, in Africa, where many regimes and opposition movements clearly have fascist attributes. This is an important aspect of American exceptionalism that runs through the entire discussion. I find this stance increasingly problematic on most questions, including the future significance of the institution of white skin privilege, but will only touch on it in this piece.

Since the authors think that in the US "it is inevitable that any fascist program will be white supremacist," they focus on whether any non-white US fascist tendency might coalesce into a unified, and presumably white supremacist, fascist movement. This is an odd argument, long on assumptions and short on evidence, that doesn't deal with my actual position. Certainly, I think that unity between Black and "white" fascist tendencies is unlikely—though no more unlikely than unity between Black fascists and non-fascists. Accordingly, I agree that any conceivable mass fascist development in this country, including in the Black community, will probably "quickly turn murderous." I can't see how that makes it less important, "short-lived," or of merely "tactical" significance.[3]

As did Rosa Luxemburg*, I think that fascism is the "barbaric" response to the apparent triumph of capital on a world scale, a response that is increasingly unlikely to develop unified and coherent social movements embodied in relatively stable social orders. However, I don't think that the absence of such a unifying trajectory qualitatively limits the strategic importance of fascist movements, non-white or not.

2. *"Further, the cross-class alliance that makes up the 'White Race' has historically brought the white working class together with the ruling class, making a fascist anti-capitalist upsurge unlikely. That's why Germany gets the Brownshirts, but the US gets KKK."*

Before it is possible to argue from historical parallels—as this excerpt does—we must be sure both that the historical facts are accurately presented and that the social circumstances haven't qualitatively changed. I want to make a few comments here on the accuracy of the implied history, leaving aside most of the issues concerning the changing relevance of this history. I hope the narrow response does not obscure broader implications.

On the first sentence: this "white cross-class bloc" notion is overstated and too simplistic an explanation even for the past historical periods when it was a little more applicable. Beyond this, even without giving the complexities of actual history their proper weight, positing a general tendency for white workers to align with ruling-class interests in no way excludes the potential for significant fractures within the overall tendency. And when such polarizations occur, as they have and will, there is no inherent reason why one of the poles cannot be essentially fascist in character.

US history is complex and contradictory and the cross-class bringing "together" is much more conditional and tenuous than this passage suggests. There has always been white working-class resistance to such a class alliance, a resistance based on their contradictory collective experiences—as objects of capitalist exploitation and as subjects of significant, but insecure, political and economic privileges. This resistance has had reactionary outcomes, for example some aspects of the Civil War's outcome. It has also had more progressive outcomes, such as the eight-hour day movement and the industrial organizing campaign of the 30s. Many complex examples could be developed from more concrete historical examples: consider the white racist reaction to the threat of Black labor competition and the use of Black military units during major radical and anti-capitalist class confrontations, such as those of the Western Federation of Miners in northern Idaho and the failed steel organizing campaign following WWI.

On the second sentence: the sharp contrast implied by "Germany gets the Brownshirts, but the US gets KKK," is historically questionable. Prior to his primitivist* phase, John Zerzan (1993) wrote a piece on the post-WWI Indiana Klan that exuded surprise over the extent to which this Klan was radical and pro–

working class. Zerzan was clearly ignorant of the magnitude and militancy of the radicalism of the contemporary European fascists, which might have reduced his astonishment at finding similar attitudes in US reactionary movements. This passage from the BTR discussion makes the same mistake in the other direction. It pays too little attention to the elements of autonomy and radicalism that prevented the Indiana KKK—and will prevent modern reactionary groupings aiming at building a base among white workers—from always being pliable, dependably pro-capitalist, adjuncts of ruling-class power.

Historical patterns of rule and resistance can be correctly described—although I don't believe they have been in this instance—and an important issue remains concerning how, and to what extent, this history is relevant. What has happened does not always illuminate what can and will happen. I believe that the circumstances of class domination have changed qualitatively in this country and that the national cross-class alliances and accommodations that were important to capitalist hegemony are changing in character and significance. Capital has less reliance on the institutions and practices that have traditionally maintained political stability in the imperial center, notably including those involved in this particular, white privilege "cross-class alliance." Decisive ruling-class fractions in this country increasingly see its benefits as being outweighed by its costs, particularly the costs of diverting attention and resources from more urgent and bigger contemporary challenges to global capital.

*3. "What's the difference between fascism as a movement and in power? Hannah Arendt argues pretty convincingly (regarding nazism) that there really isn't one." … "Arendt argues that the Nazis and Stalin actually became more radical in power."*

So how does Stalin come into this discussion? I have some thoughts on how "actually existing socialism"* might be relevant to fascist potentials, but they don't support any minimalist view of the importance of fascism.

Laying that aside, the initial question is perplexing. The differences between fascism when it is a movement and when it is in control of a state seem obvious to me. They provide one overriding reason why it is important to confront fascism before it gains state power. In one case, you are competing for a constituency, ideologically and programmatically (and sometimes militarily), while contending with the reality of capitalist state power and cultural/ideological hegemony. In the other, you are attempting to overthrow a militarized state structure animated by a totalitarian ideology. An example of the difference: you don't wage a culture war against a fascist state unless you want to be dead, but this would normally be an essential part of the struggle against a fascist organizing thrust.

I suspect the real point here is not this question, but the notion that the Nazis became "more radical in power," minimizing the radical appeal of mass fascist movements prior to achieving power. Notwithstanding Arendt, I don't think this is the case. The issue comes down to what is meant by "radical." Arendt's conception of radicalism emphasizes the repression and regimentation that culminated in massive national, cultural, and racial genocide and world war. From this vantage point, the Hitler of *Mein Kampf* is less radical than Hitler in power (and Stalin may appear more radical than his Bolshevik predecessors).

However, without in any way questioning the radicalism of German state fascism, I can't adopt this analysis. Arendt discounts the crucial element: the anti-bourgeois and anti-capitalist aspects of totalitarian radicalism. When these are included, there is no way that Stalinism is more "radical" than revolutionary Russia and the Bolsheviks. More to the point, every previous fascist regime has moved away from the radical anti-bourgeois/anti-capitalist elements of the movement which brought it to power. In Germany these elements were very substantial and their influence was ended by the physical liquidation of a major section of the NSDAP a few months after the Nazi capture of the German state [the Night of the

Long Knives*]. There is no way that the NSDAP in power is more "radical" on these crucial issues without its substantial Strasser/ Röhm* wing—although it arguably might have been more reactionary and genocidal.[4]

This is an important point. The left has obvious and increasing difficulties articulating and organizing around a clear and consistent, liberatory, anti-capitalist alternative. The left's failures to develop a popular case for social revolution should provide a cautionary context for viewing the debates within modern fascist movements about the significance of the failure of Nazism to complete its "Second [anti-capitalist] Revolution." The danger in the way the question of "radicalism" is handled in this part of the BTR discussion is that it discounts the potential challenge from the non-state transnational fascist movements that we are likely to face, minimizing their ability to provide plausible ideological and programmatic alternatives for either Black or white working-class constituencies. I suspect that this attitude also questions the genuineness of neo-fascist radicalism, regarding it as more posture than principle. These attitudes rest on dangerous "history is on our side" assumptions and, particularly when the discussion is not limited artificially to this country, the absence of logical reasons and supporting evidence for such assumptions is almost equally evident.

*4. "As long as the white working class in the US has access to the state (such as via the herrenvolk democracy[5] before 1965 and through various white privileges today), it has no need to opt for fascism."*

Of course, I noticed the caveats that immediately follow this passage in the text. However, it is hard to take them seriously since they apply to eventualities that the authors have previously dismissed as remote possibilities in passages such as the following: "An American fascism, then, is a long-term prospect at best. There's a greater likelihood of the return of herrenvolk democracy and white standing in the US than there is of fascism." So, I will deal with the issues of estimate and analysis accepting this passage as it reads.

Before getting to my disagreements, I want to indicate my understanding of some ambiguous terms that are employed: "access," "state," "need," and "opt." I realize I could be wrong about the intended meanings, and it could make a difference.

I doubt that the authors view the US state as one where real power is shared between the working and capitalist classes. That is, I doubt that they believe that the US is not actually a class state. So, where this passage says "white working class ... access to the state," I'm reading it as meaning their access to the government. This reflects the language used at other points in the discussion. I also don't think that "access" is the best description for the relationship between white workers and the government. Perhaps "participation" would be more appropriate, particularly if it were understood that this participation is not formal, but part of an institutionalized process for distributing selective material concessions.

I'm reading the assertion that white workers will "have no need to opt for fascism" to mean that they will not choose this option under current or foreseeable conditions. I think the issue is not one of objective necessity, but of subjective inclination and volition. As I have said, fascism could only be a polarizing issue among these allegedly incorporated white workers, and they will not be opting for or against it as a unified subject with a common perception of *need*. White workers can provide an important terrain for fascist organizing initiatives even if these are selectively directed towards particular subgroups and only have potential to take root among minority fractions.

Continuing on the issue of terminology, I don't accept the repeated reference to the "white working class" as if it were a political subject, either one which is—or is not—potentially revolutionary. In fact, there is no white working class. The working class is multinational or transnational with a small and diminishing minority of privileged white (particularly white male) members.

Working class shouldn't be defined racially, ethnically, or in terms of relative privileges—although these factors must all be included in a concrete understanding of the US segment of the working class.

Beyond this, there are definite and growing problems in looking at class through the lens of nations and states. It is a short step from positing a nationally defined working class to accepting the limits of trade union reformism and parliamentary social democracy and reifying the most invidious "border fence" forms of "competition within the working class." The conception of a national US working class abstracts from the objective reality of massive and growing movements of workers across borders, and doesn't place proper priority on concrete steps to promote and develop working-class internationalism. (I believe that my position on this question is consistent with the white skin privilege analysis which the authors clearly hold. I doubt whether we will wind up with significant disagreements on this point.)

To clarify some differences with the approach taken in this citation, I want to locate the general argument of the authors in the array of left positions on fascism. Clearly, they reject conceptions of fascism that blur any distinction between it and capitalist repression. They appear to also reject more sophisticated variants of the same position that posit a capitalist tendency, preference, or "drive" towards fascism that is identified with the program of a particular ruling-class fraction.

This latter position has been the dominant left conception since fascism emerged as an ideology and mass movement, although it can be embodied in very different political approaches, from the most reformist popular front* stage strategies to the most sectarian "class against class" postures. The more or less official "communist" position has treated fascism as a capitalist policy option—a potential form of rule—often forgetting to add that the developed communist doctrine placed it as a policy of last resort, adopted out of strategic weakness where and when capitalism was in crisis and faced with a serious revolutionary working-class political challenge.

145

There are many features and problems with this position that don't require mention here, but one fact is relevant: they all regard the "option" for fascism, if it is taken, as an option taken by the ruling class, or some fraction of it, acting according to the array of ruling-class perceptions of what is required to maintain power. Disgruntled white workers might be involved as foot soldiers in a fascist organizing thrust, but it would not be their "option."

Apparently the authors are arguing that fascism has no potential within the ruling class because the viability of white supremacy makes it unnecessary and that any potential for a mass white autonomous fascist movement is ruled out by the persistence of the same system. (As mentioned above, a non-white potential base for fascism is also excluded—apparently as an article of faith in US exceptionalism.) In the mid–1970s, some of us in STO* agreed with the first proposition: so long as the institutions of white supremacy functioned within the working class, the ruling class would have no need to "opt" for fascism. The early STO position was rather quickly and summarily rejected. It presented an element of truth in an abstract and one-sided manner, treating fascism only as a secondary technique of capitalist rule, without recognizing its autonomous and radical side. This de-emphasized the potential for an autonomous fascist movement to impose itself on capitalism. More practically, it also de-emphasized the problems of working in conditions where such autonomous fascist movements existed and posed a real threat.

The position capsulized in this citation holds that the white section of the working class has no need to "opt" for fascism so long as it is privileged. This is significantly different from the early STO position because it implies that white workers understand and accept their privileges and will not see through or beyond them. STO regarded white privileges as real material benefits, but never discounted the potential for individual and collective repudiation of the system that generated them. We maintained that white workers should and could be organized to act in their class interests. White privileges didn't eliminate revolutionary potentials among white workers; they provided limits and barriers that had to be confronted if these potentials were to be realized.

However, if white workers have the potential to break with capital to the left, the possibility for them to break to the right can hardly be excluded. Indeed, since such a break to the right might simply be an extension of the ideology of white supremacy, it could be seen as relatively more likely.

There have been a number of revolutionary strategies that discount revolutionary potentials among white workers generally and view privileged white workers as ruling-class auxiliaries. Since its central point is that white workers are satisfied with their privileged position and that these privileges are stable, the BTR position leads in the same direction, although I presume that they would be reluctant to arrive at the same destination. However, the same estimate that minimizes the potential for a fascist movement among white workers actually applies even more against any potential for a liberatory revolutionary movement among them. Applying the logic underlying the simple argument presented in this citation ("access to the state … no need to opt for fascism") one might just as well say: access to the state … no need to opt for social revolution. Or: access to the state … no need to engage in class struggle. We know the political tendencies that have taken the white privilege concept to exactly these conclusions. I assume no one in BTR does or there would be more of you up here in the woods wondering what happened to the prairie fires.[6]

To get into these issues a bit deeper, the BTR selection maintains that white workers had access to the state (government) "via the herrenvolk democracy before 1965 and from various white privileges today." How valid is the concept of herrenvolk democracy? And what happened in 1965?

I have to admit the term "herrenvolk democracy" is new to me and I will rely completely on the definition that the authors provide: "In the US, the herrenvolk democracy (democracy for the master race, tyranny for everyone else) has historically performed the functions of a fascist state but with a democratic veneer." I think that this notion of "democracy for the master race, tyranny for everyone else" has only marginal applicability to the US. It's doubtful if it even applies to South Africa—perhaps it fits Rhodesia, pre-ZANU/Andy Young.*

Presumably the "master race" is white. Since the reference is to "master," we can overlook the fact that white women had minimal formal or substantive democratic access to government in the US until quite recently. In what sense, then, was there "democracy" for male white workers? My view has always been that the US is a bourgeois democracy; i.e., a system based on democracy for the bourgeoisie and something a bit different and decidedly less participatory or representative for everyone else, including in almost all cases white male workers. Possibly there were some localized situations where there was effectively "democracy" for all white males, maybe during the various genocidal operations against the native population. Normally, however, there was "bourgeois democracy," where white workers might be privileged with some minimal voice in their continued exploitation and some possibility to participate in the repression and oppression of people outside of their cohort, but little more.

Moving to the related second part of the phrase—"tyranny for everyone else"—I have to object again. I'm no fan of the constitutional parliamentary system anywhere, including in this country, but it did not and does not embody tyranny for all except white males. This is particularly the case if this tyranny is seen as the functional equivalent of a fascist state, as the authors maintain it should be. Fascist states are totalitarian and militarized and, while they may utilize a plebiscitary pseudo-democracy at times, they oppose parliamentarism. This is simply not an adequate or accurate picture of US society and history prior to 1965.

Then, what about 1965? I was alive then and more or less politically active. It wasn't a particularly calm period: there was the Malcolm X assassination, the Gulf of Tonkin escalation, the LA riots, the invasion of the Dominican Republic, various parliamentary gestures to the Black movement, the Civil Rights and

Voting Rights Bills. But I missed any watershed event that marked an epoch-changing passage from herrenvolk democracy to something else based on "various white privileges."[7]

I fear that the BTR authors must be looking at the extension of the franchise to Black people in the US South as the key change—although I'm ready to be corrected if this is mistaken. The Voting Rights Bill was a byproduct of a significant struggle, but at the time it had minimal importance other than providing some slight additional support for reformist perspectives in the movement. Its continuing impact has been ambiguous and in no way marks a change in methods of capitalist rule. To argue differently is to place far too much significance on the hollow, formal parliamentary aspects of bourgeois democracy. Exactly that which I fear was also done with the notion of "democracy for the master race" in the other half of the definition of herrenvolk democracy.

This BTR framework of analysis doesn't enlighten US history. While I can see some instances where it might apply, it is nowhere near an adequate explanation of the historical system of subordination and domination in this country. It doesn't help us understand southern and western populism, the New Deal, the Eight-Hour Day struggle, the Seattle General Strike, the racist socialist government in Milwaukee, etc.[8]

I question the relationship of institutionalized white skin privilege to the potential for fascism, as the issue is presented in the above citation and at other points in the BTR discussion. However, my differences probably go further than that. I think that it is necessary to generally reassess the role of institutionalized white skin privilege in US capitalism and to reevaluate the perspectives in which the concept is central. I will attempt to begin this in the remainder of this piece.

Since the concept of white skin privilege is part of a number of quite different strategies, not to mention much of the US left's conventional wisdom, some of which rejects a working-class perspective on capitalism and revolution, I want to be clear that the points I make are with reference to the strategic approach associated with STO. I believe BTR has a generally similar approach.

Historically, white skin privilege in the US functioned to incorporate white workers within the hegemony of capital by treating them as a privileged interest group even when this resulted in limitations on labor competition and kept short- and middle-term wages higher than they might otherwise have been. This institution was central to some aspects of the class struggle and the development of US capitalism that distinguished it from other capitalisms. With some notable and temporary exceptions, the US labor movement has been pro-capitalist, divided by internal competitions, and infected with a guild exclusivity to the point where it doesn't present even the most elementary alternative vision of society. There has been no labor party and no continuing social democratic tendency capable of contesting for control of the government or for basic structural reform.

On the other hand, there has been more social mobility in this country than in other capitalist countries. From before the Civil War almost to WWI, white workers could realistically expect to acquire property and possibly leverage themselves or their children out of the working class into the petty bourgeoisie or more. This potential provided a qualitative aspect to the privileges of white workers that augmented the quantitative advantages they also received.

For the better part of two centuries, the social base provided by white skin privilege was seen as crucial to long-term capitalist stability, and the ruling class made significant concessions to maintain it. These concessions were double-edged and complex. While there were economic costs involved in privileging white workers, there were benefits for capital as well. White labor mobility expedited the advance of Taylorism* and Fordism*, allowing, and even impelling US capitalism to develop labor productivity and extend its internal mass market more rapidly than its national competitors. This, in turn, increased its capacity to provide significant tangible differential benefits for white male workers and their families.

So long as capitalist development did not supersede the division of the world between oppressor and oppressed nations, and so long as "actually existing socialism"* provided some semi-plausible comprehensive alternative to it, this system worked fairly well in this country. However, it obviously was not the only way that capitalist societies, including this one, contained and incorporated the class struggle, and for some time it has not appeared to be any more viable than other methods. It seems to me that its unique role in this country depended on unique and, I believe, transitory and temporary features of national development.

Things have changed. Capitalist production is effectively globalized. It has no "outside." Maintaining political equilibrium in particular countries, including this one, is increasingly subordinated to requirements for profit maximization and political equilibrium in a capitalist world system, a system which is no longer in any sense "white" or even Euro-American. The loyalty of US white workers is no longer worth as much and less will be paid for it. The social democratic and "communist" challenges to global capitalism are increasingly defanged and incorporated, reducing the potential risks of incorporating potential challenges within the hegemonic framework of capital through social democratic parliamentarism. This further undermines any incentive for the ruling class to subsidize white supremacy.

These developments in the global capitalist system have not occurred without generating popular resistance that is increasingly costly to contain. There are other squeaky wheels for the concession/repression apparatus of capital—often ones that present much more pressing risks than any possible domestic white working-class insurgency. These challenges develop from the elements of secular crisis* in the system (the BTR discussion serves us poorly by avoiding this topic because it has been the site of so many left mistakes) and they have enlarged the terrain of operations and expedited the training of cadres for important neo-fascist movements which both directly and indirectly impact the politics of this country. Ruling-class segments are aware of these realities and ruling-class policy can best be understood as a response to them, rather than as a mindless demonstration of military force and financial cupidity encased in nostalgia for white power.

The concept of working-class white privilege has always been susceptible to a simplifying determinism which assumes that the reality of a privileged position will be automatically reflected in a consciousness of being privileged and in a sense of superiority and entitlement to such privileges that white workers will fight to protect. This mistaken view is present in parts of the BTR discussion. For example, "access" to government is translated too easily to support for government and the possibility of a felt "need" for basic change is eliminated by the fact, not the consciousness, of being privileged.

White workers can feel they are superior and thus deserving of privileges, but not recognize that they have them. It is not only possible, it is common to find that the recipients of privileges feel that they are actually the victims of discrimination, and that groups with greater access to government are more critical of it and cynical about it. Thus, the formula—privileged status equals cross-class alliance, equals support for one's own capitalism and ruling class—is frequently disrupted in real life.

White workers in this country are no longer going to be fully buffered from the impacts of international competition, and that is going to undermine their allegiance to the old system of rule. Whatever differential access white workers have to government, the benefits that result will be reduced. If the privileged sector thinks and feels left out and left behind—not so privileged and maybe even discriminated against—even when these may not be objectively true, it will shatter their compact with capital and open the potential for fascist developments as well as more hopeful challenges to the system.

The issue between me and BTR, I think, is whether we are facing such a tipping point in the struggle or whether it is only a remote future potential. I think the former. It seems that they are more concerned with the potential for the administrative resurrection of some reactionary white nationalist regime, which I can't see having any life outside of the fevered imagination of a Buchanan or Tancredo.[9] In any case, such a reactionary nightmare about a betrayed heroic and idyllic past would be the stuff of fascist movements. If it is viable, the commitment of white workers to the current system is not.

Apologies again for the wordiness and the lack of clarity.

## Email to K on Fascism
## 2009

*The following was a private email sent to the same mid-west com-*
*rade as another piece later in this volume titled, "Email to K on*
*the Iraq War."*

I want to limit this to the differences you raise with the approach to
fascism and to the working class in my latest rant. Sorry for the late
response. I was taken up with writing about Althusser. I'm sure
you agree with Janeen that Althusser is top priority, much more
important than fascism, the working class, and similar distractions.

I think you have a good point about my preoccupations with
radical fascist potentials. I've found myself wandering around the
internet looking for some evidence that National Bolsheviks and
National Revolutionaries actually exist and are capitalizing on all
of the opportunities that I see for them.[1] Not much luck so far. I
guess that should be seen as a good thing.

In any case, the main point is the one where we probably agree:
fascist movements in a variety of forms will become increasingly
important. Perhaps it is true that reactionary forms that are not
significant ideological challenges or potential competition for the
anti-capitalist base—although presenting serious dangers on other
levels—will continue to predominate. I agree with you that whatever emerges will mainly have to be dealt with as it actually is, not
as we (I) predict it might have been or might become. There are
a few points I would make about your references to al-Qaeda in
Iraq—but at another time.

However, we, the generic left, are so weak. We don't even do
a good job of misrepresenting our organic left constituency. It's
possible that our incompetence will continue to be subsidized by
the incompetence of the fascists, but it's a risky bet. I worry about
the likelihood that a clear evaluation of political trends will fall

victim to attempts to buttress competing left presuppositions and prejudices, allowing a charismatic fascist development with even the slightest flavor of radicalism to coalesce a mass populist and insurgent following very quickly after having germinated below our political radar. I'd be particularly concerned with the increasing potential for a dramatic event that could expand rapidly across national borders—a rhizomatic process as Negri* might say[2]—so watch out for marches on Rome and protect the German beer halls.[3] I know there is little point to getting obsessive with these potentials, but I don't want them to be forgotten.

Along the same lines, you speak of propaganda of the deed in terms of left approaches, and I agree with the sense of your remarks. However, I would also add that this is an approach that fascists can pursue as well, and one where they possess real advantages from their different risk/benefit collateral damages calculus. (At least I hope the left always maintains a qualitative distinction from fascism in its approach to these questions.) Consequently, the fascists will have few (or fewer) ideological qualms about manipulations of democratic decision-making and greater capacity to engage in a "strategy of tension" à la the Italian model of a few decades ago.[4]

So, this is the context in which I saw the discussion of the "British jobs for British Workers" wildcat strikes in Great Britain.[5] What is dismaying is the predictability of the left attitudes and interactions. If your group is on site with some influence, or if you can make it appear as if this is so, you defend the working-class bona fides of the workers, exaggerate the predictable incidents of spontaneous anti-fascism, and build a protective fence around the segment of the trade union structure which tolerates your hanging around. If your group is on the outside looking in, you do more or less the exact opposite. Neither is right. We should be trying to learn something—like, what the fascists are doing, and whether they are showing signs of developing the capability to do it better.

It's important to recognize from the outset that in an economic crisis a narrow, nationalist, essentially reactionary appeal to a privileged working class is the logical development both from and against reformist trade unionism. Such an incipient pro-fascist tendency will probably find a mass base, and, like it or not, we will be finding out what a "palingenetic radical populism"[6] looks like. If we pay attention, we might find opportunities to develop tactics and strategy with the potential to combat it without joining in the predictable collapse into popular front* hysteria.

I've rewritten the next section a number of times and still am not satisfied with it. It is roughly divided between some general arguments about how revolutionaries should approach the working class and more specific ones that focus on what differences might be dictated by the current crisis conditions. I doubt that you will be surprised by any of this. My hope is to move quickly beyond these first principles into more substantive discussion when, as I expect, we find we have no major initial differences—except, of course, on poor Lenin.

In any case, I said in the Akuno piece: "The left is going to have to organize itself, not the working class or the 'people.'"[7]

You responded: "What I think is missing from this approach is the fact that the Left (or more specifically the broadly militant anarchist movement/scene) has very little organic ties to working-class activity. This is a major problem; it breeds elitism and isolation. It also means that advanced actions can only go so far."

What you say is important and, I think, completely true. What I say is more of a throwaway line to irritate aspiring vanguardists … and is both ambiguous and very susceptible, as you point out in a kind way, to a particularly obnoxious substitutionist* inter- pretation. In short, both you and Kingsley,[8] who raised similar issues, are right to criticize my one-sided opposition to working- class "base building." My superficial and glib formulation allows for implications that I did not intend, but ones that, I agree, can be reasonably drawn from what I said. So, I welcome your correc- tions, and would like to center further discussion on how to orient towards a mass, working-class base, not on whether we should be making such an attempt.

It is certainly true that much of the left is caught in its own subculture and that this imposes strict limits on its ability to either understand or express the needs and desires of working people. You seem to think that my response to Akuno implies that I think that militancy and confrontational tactics by a better organized left might get around this lack of an organic connection to a social base. I can see how what I wrote might support this interpretation and want to clearly state that I did not intend it. In fact, I think that such an approach will lead to serious mistakes. Messianic political tendencies in an isolated left, rather than opening a path towards a general class confrontation and a revolutionary rupture, have frequently led to quite reactionary outcomes; e.g., Weather's arrogant attempts to implement its "which side are you on" approach to a revolutionary youth movement, or the primitivists'* view of wage labor as a morally flawed and corrupt choice which they have transcended.

What I meant by saying that the left should "organize itself" is that we cannot see ourselves as an already-enlightened general staff in possession of the *What is to Be Done* tablets and maybe the "Platform" scrolls[9]—needing only some linkage to a mass base to develop and orient our working-class army. I know that this has nothing to do with your personal positions, but you also know that there are some who think this way.

If anything, I'd place my own views at the opposite end of the spectrum from the positions that see the working class as passive potential for an external leadership. Particularly under current conditions, the class will develop its own forms of struggle and its own organic leaderships. We should not expect these to fall into a few predictable, linear, reformist tracks. They will embody the potential to explode, creating new institutions and radically transforming popular consciousness—and not always with the results we might, in our wisdom, prefer.

So, I meant the "organize itself" injunction in a different way: not as a call for a putschist action faction, but as a call to clarify our thinking and our forms of organization so that they can actually contribute to a combative social movement able to prefigure a genuine clash between civilizations. There's a mouthful.

This puts a priority on developing collective projects, clarifying what we want from them and which alternative possibilities they preempt. In my mind, the main weight of these projects has to involve a working-class orientation and constituency. This will be impossible with imaginary collectives that are essentially affinity groups of supportive and acritical friends enmeshed in an encapsulated and privileged subculture. Generalizing a popular consciousness of the necessity and possibility of a radical alternative to capitalism requires collectives in which individual priorities and approaches are subject to critical collective oversight and subordinate to collective decisions. That is not a situation that is widespread in the current left, and I meant to point to this problem with the "organize itself" injunction. I probably should have been more explicit.

The transformation of the insurgent and counter-hegemonic elements of a working-class constituency into an organized culture of opposition, able to set its own objectives and resolve its own dilemmas, requires that working people develop an appreciation of their own collective strength and capability. This is not a matter of replacing "misleaders" with ourselves. It does involve revolutionaries learning how to do certain things which one does not pick up by reading books or participating in internet debates: how to tell the truth to people who will find it painful; how to discover the hidden strengths of the people you relate to; how to disagree when necessary; how to present what is actually won in victories and, as well, what may be won in defeats; how to recognize and respond to "epistemological breaks"* in the routine of working-class life.

I would mention two obstacles to developing this type of a mass, working-class organizing perspective in our sector of the left. First, there is the notion of the irreducible singularity of needs and grievances. This major presupposition of Negri's *Multitude* is widely held, although not commonly argued on a theoretical basis.[10] However, this conception of "multitude" does provide a theoretical basis for the omnipresent opposition to subordinating individual or sectoral priorities to those of any collective. In practice, this undercuts the possibility of implementing a position with sufficient dedication and discipline to determine whether or not it has been, or could have been, successful—or whether the problems were with the position itself or weaknesses in its implementation. This contributes to a never-ending repetition of inadequate and dysfunctional organizing approaches that persist in the absence of an agreed upon context for critical evaluation.

There is a more important problem that resides in a variety of workerist* and syndicalist tendencies that is commonly, though not always, combined with the one just mentioned. This position essentially maintains that the main contribution that radicals can and should make is to keep out of the way of the struggle and avoid providing another layer of oppression or, at best, dead weight on the working class. Of course, we know very well the sad history that gives this position some credibility. Such views were explicit with the C.L.R. James* portion of the Johnson-Forest Tendency,* and I've always felt that certain tendencies in STO took a similar stance. In a different way, a parallel conception runs throughout Negri and Hardt's consistent combination of a good conception of the active and determining role of the working class (proletariat) in the historical process, with various strange, geisty conceptions of implicit consciousness and "swarm intelligence." This typically results in a peculiar form of determinism where the current conditions are understood as a reflection of all that is possible in the given circumstances and are interpreted, "through their good side," as a manifestation of the working class's determining role in the historical saga of capital.

This position downgrades the importance of specific organized approaches to class organization and class consciousness in favor of understanding and recording a decisive materialist dialectic in the structure of capitalist production, a "law" of capitalist development. I'm referring to the way these issues were presented by Martin Glaberman of the Facing Reality* grouping. Thus, a number of issues that I think must be debated and decided by communists as matters of conscious policy—the best mass organizational form, how to develop fully rounded participation in struggles, the relationship of passive majorities to active minorities—are ultimately left to spontaneity, which is believed to be superior to any resolution of them by a "conscious" minority.

Only the assumption that some underlying dynamic will always push these issues ahead in the proper way can justify this approach, and, in my opinion, that is a bad assumption. The immense variety of levels and forms of struggle must contend with the absence of some necessarily unifying underlying dynamic which will group them together, making it as likely that they cancel each other out as that they combine in a more general and fundamental challenge to capital. This is particularly the case when we take into account the factor of ruling-class policy through the more or less conscious exercise of state power. On these points I am something of an Althusserian.*

I want to be clear that the issues of working-class organization cannot be simply reduced to organization of the class and organizations of the communists. Eruptions of popular struggle will always be initiated by minorities before the bulk of their constituency is convinced that the struggle is needed, and certainly before it is generally realized that there is sufficient solidarity to make them productive. There is an entire range of issues concerning the development and organization of such active minorities—I think some of the Italians referred to them as "mass vanguards"*—and their function in the general struggle.

Furthermore, when the initial participants experience some of the intangible benefits of collective resistance, some elements of a counter-hegemonic cultural bloc will begin to develop. These too will have to grow and develop out of small minorities, and will have an organized form that presents both opportunities and obligations. In short, there are a number of layers of working-class organization and consciousness which are in a necessary relationship with each other. These are not a given presupposed structure but a changing framework for political development in which social forces become increasingly self-conscious and individuals become active and creative organizers of the movements from which they emerge.

I have this feeling of being an unconnected oldster preaching to the choir, so I will subside after briefly indicating the changes in approach that I think are dictated by the crisis.[11] We are in a situation where Hegel's famous injunction—*Hic Rhodus, hic saltus*—applies.[12] It's our time to "jump," and the conditions demand that we make a real effort to jump high, far, and often. Where normally the correct approach would be to decide on a point of concentration and commit to a substantial effort to make things work, now I think it is more important to be able to move quickly as events develop. Where normally the correct approach would be to develop some credentials and a "right to speak" through an appropriately protracted and respectful period of familiarization with the forces and conditions, now it is necessary to say what we think and do what we think should be done quicker and more forcefully. Where normally the correct approach is to avoid making ourselves "the issue," now it is necessary to take more risks, including personal ones.

Finally, normally I argue that the best metric for evaluating mass work is the development of cadre, both those who begin as organizers of one type or another, and those who develop out of the organizing process. In these conditions we need something a little more. I don't know exactly how it would be quantified but we must require of ourselves that our activity has a real and growing impact on the balance of forces. If this is not happening under these conditions, something is seriously wrong, and we should not hesitate to change approaches.

Maybe next time for Lenin.

## Mistakes in Our Previous Approaches to Fascism
## November 2015

*This essay was sent to a network of comrades, many of whom were veterans of the 70s and 80s left anti-fascist struggles and beyond.*

Be forewarned, I'm having difficulty formulating what I want to say here.

First, some fragmentary history. Through the mid–1960s and continuing to the present, the left has been weighed down by the approaches to fascism and anti-fascism developed in the Comintern/Cominform framework.[1] Virtually all leftists (including anarchists) see fascism as a tactical form of capitalist rule: a more consistently reactionary and authoritarian capitalist policy option particularly appropriate to moments when the power of capital is under greater-than-usual stress. Based heavily on a flawed understanding of the classical German Nazi archetype, this view collapses fascism into a tendency contained within capitalist reaction. Fascist movements are thought about and acted against in terms of their posited "saving capitalism" function—even when and where they appear to be about something quite different.

With some exceptions, this conception of fascism developed more or less in tandem with a complementary anti-fascist political strategy based on a cross-class popular front* that included—at least in theory—allegedly "progressive," "democratic" elements of the ruling classes and strata. This popular front would supposedly resist the (also alleged) "greater danger" to working-class and popular interests presented by the extreme right wing of the capitalist ruling class and, secondarily, its fascist street force. Left critics of such anti-fascist, anti-ultra-right, anti-monopoly, anti-(anything but capitalism) perspectives, early on myself included, called for an anti-capitalist alternative to it. However, our tentative alternatives also tended to see fascism as just a reactionary mode of capitalist power; and thus the differences with the popular front approach were mainly confined to estimates of the magnitude and immediacy of the fascist (ultra-right, reactionary) danger and the political priority of opposing it. This heritage contributed to a persistent under- (and mis-) estimation of the fascist trends that incubated in this country beginning in the 1970s and undermined any potential political benefits of anti-fascist organizing by keeping it largely confined within liberal reformism.

By the late 70s, Ken Lawrence's examination of William Pierce's National Alliance* and *The Turner Diaries* (1982) and our growing appreciation of the militant agrarian right-wing populism of the Posse Comitatus,* Gordon Kahl,* etc. led STO to clarify its critique of the dominant left conceptions of fascism and anti-fascism.[2] We saw something new in the emergent rightist tendencies in this country. A mixture of reactionary social attitudes and elements of anti-bourgeois, anti-government, anti-imperial, and, to some extent, anti-capitalist sentiments had created a mass constituency for radical neo-fascist movements with the potential to develop a substantial autonomy from any significant sector of capital. An increasingly important strand of right-wing opinion and organization was breaking with traditional reactionary politics that were premised on controlling or capturing the existing structures of capitalist power. Instead, it was promoting and organizing a polarization between a compromising rightist reaction within the system and a radical (neo-fascist) confrontation with the system. This emerging neo-fascism, radical and at times self-consciously revolutionary, challenged the conservative reformists in the broader right-wing milieu. This is made absolutely clear in *The Turner Diaries*, which quickly became a primary document for a movement that extended well beyond Pierce's National Alliance.

Our approach to this neo-fascism encountered a good deal of resistance from the "nothing new here" camp on the left. When they recognized such developments at all, they were only seen as a different tactical manifestation of the systemic white supremacy that had played a long-term functional role in maintaining capitalist power. When increasing numbers of neo-fascists claimed to oppose the "government" and the "system"—and not just the "Jews" and "liberals" who supposedly manipulated both—much of the left dismissed it as posturing and demagoguery; as a tactical facade to hide the strings that were still being pulled by the same string-pullers who had prevailed since post–Civil War Reconstruction. This set the pattern of not taking fascist politics seriously, which I believe is a recipe for disaster.

For some time, I've argued for a different approach to the analysis of fascism, one that doesn't see it as a potential form of capitalist rule but as a reactionary response (potentially a mass one with radical or even revolutionary characteristics) to an increasingly crisis-ridden late capitalism. In this perspective, neo-fascism and various forms of warlordism are understood not as a "worse" form of capitalism, but as the barbarism side of the "socialism or barbarism" options to it. To take the point a step further, at the current time I see the "barbarism" option as an arguably more plausible alternative and threat to global capitalist structures than anything that has emerged on the side of "socialism"—our side. I would like to be wrong about this, but I think this is also the dominant view within global capitalist elites who show little evidence of concern about any potential for emancipatory working-class upsurges.

In practice, the left anti-fascist struggles in the early part of the late-1970s and early-1980s period were limited to episodic responses to a sketchy assortment of publicity seeking, dress-up Klan-Nazis and (a bit later) white racist skinheads in the punk scene who were marginal to much more substantial rightist tendencies that were already apparent. This certainly characterized most of the actions through the 70s in Chicago and, I think, although with less personal knowledge, the same was true elsewhere in the country. The anti-fascist organizing that occurred outside of immediate and specific responses to right-wing provocations neither implemented a strategic plan nor organized a broad defensive response to an actual fascist threat. Instead, the main motivating factor of such work was to promote the politics and expand the cadre of one or another hopeful alphabet vanguards—PLP, SWP, Workers World, CLP, RCP, and, most notably for the points I want to make a bit later, May19/PFOC and WVO.[3]

This particular "no platform" focus on the bizarre and crackpot elements on the right—and they certainly existed—buttressed assumptions that the actual politics and organizational approaches of the political tendencies that were contributing to the emergence of neo-fascism could be caricatured and discounted. The popular view on the left was that the neo-fascist sectors of the right were little more than an opportunistic street force that was managed and manipulated by sectors of the ruling class and the state apparatus. The proclaimed fascists and their potential cadre constituency were characterized as "cowards," who only fought those unwilling or incapable of fighting back—"boneheads," whose ideas were neither seriously held nor worthy of challenge. This is not to say that such charges were never valid; actually, they frequently were … but they were also short-sighted and myopic. And I have to say that they were often equally applicable to the leadership of the anti-fascists. (The depiction of developing fascist radicalism as "stupid" and "cowardly" careerism as well as opportunism also applied to the British anti-fascist organizing of the period—from *Searchlight* to AFA, including the efforts of the British SWP.)[4]

I'm thinking here specifically of WVO's public challenge to the Klan to come and fight in Greensboro* and JBAKC's* equivalent public shouting against the SS Action League and Uptown Patriots in Chicago a few years later. The posturing and rhetoric in the former case contributed heavily to five dead and serious collateral damage to the mass Black movement that was already in retreat. The damage in the latter case was more limited: just some bloody heads and embarrassing pleas for "police protection" from the fascists by supposedly revolutionary anti-fascists, but that was just a bit of good luck.

We frequently encountered leftists who maintained that the opposition of the US state structure to emerging neo-fascist formations—Gordon Kahl's constituency, the Posse Comitatus, the various Christian Identity* nodes and militia formations, the Order/ Brudenschweigen, etc.—was not genuine. This was in the face of repeated armed conflicts with notable casualties, many examples of COINTELPRO-style* police penetration, major legal cases, and RICO jailings.[5] In fact, during that historical period in this country (late 1970s to early 1980s), the cumulative repressive actions directed against radical neo-fascist groups and individuals far exceeded the repression against the left (with the possible exception of the state campaigns against the Puerto Rican independence movement).[6] The repression of right-wing radicalism was very comparable to the wave of COINTELPRO repression that had been directed at the left in the previous decades, and, it seems to me, that from then to the current moment the US capitalist state has continued to be relatively even-handed in its oppression and suppression of opponents that threaten to break with "legitimate" frameworks on either the right or the left. On the international level—although there are a number of other factors in play—the same reality is also fairly clear.

In retrospect, the approach to armed right-wing groups is hard to understand as anything but a liberal appeal for popular support mixed with a sprinkling of adventurist posturing. There was an essential hypocrisy involved in the WVO charges that the Carolina Klan was working with the police (which they were, of course) while they were cooperating with the police themselves to allow a symbolic armed memorial demonstration with no bullets in the guns. The same held for the JBAKC proclamations that the various targeted fascists were actually working for the system while they and many other self-described anti-fascists were busily negotiating with the same system to keep anti-fascist protests on the sidewalk, out of "dangerous" neighborhoods—within the framework of legality. And, of course, there were all too many supposedly on "our side"—like the Southern Poverty Law Center at the extreme margins[7]—that provided explicit, continuing support for the government and the police and did everything possible to remove all potential radical content from anti-fascist organizing.

This leads me to ARA*, which I'd like to treat in a little more detail. It's hard to underestimate how important it was when ARA developed a principled stance against any cooperation with the state under the cover of opposing fascists. This lay necessary groundwork for the conception that we are in a struggle against distinct enemies, fascist and capitalist, which is the only adequate radical framework for anti-fascist organizing in my opinion. Also significant was ARA's attitude towards street militancy. It was willing to actually, not rhetorically, fight fascists, and its militancy went beyond self-promoting street theater and exaggerated, symbolic, public relations "victories." As important as its willingness to fight was the fact that ARA contested fascists for some important public spaces in a conscious and systematic way, understanding that these confrontations with fascists and the state should always be approached as part of a protracted struggle in which they amount to training for forms of extra-legal and quasi-military struggle that will be more important in the future—and not just in anti-fascist work.

I don't deny that at times ARA emphasized physical and quasi-military confrontations with fascists which underestimated the potential risks. In addition, ARA also suffered to some extent from the "fascist bonehead" syndrome, which prevented a full understanding of the autonomous and radical potential of neo-fascist ideology and organizing as well as the extent to which it might become a competitor and alternative organizing focus within "our" constituencies. This undermined ARA's capacity to respond to changes in fascist tactics and organizing approaches—and it certainly didn't help the development of an adequate post-9/11 politics. However, despite such weaknesses, this positive estimate of the ARA experience—especially by contrast with what was done by other folks in other arenas—is essential.

Hopefully this background helps to illuminate what I see as a continuing problem that affects current approaches to "national anarchism"* and "pan-secessionism" in our section of the left. If we begin from Clara Zetkin's prophetic statement that fascism is part of the price we pay for the failures of the revolution[8] (an observation that is probably more meaningful now than she thought it to be almost a century ago), we can see the subjective and objective sides of current dilemmas more clearly.

Looking at the objective side ... what political circumstances—as opposed to hidden manipulations—might motivate anyone to attach anarchism (or for that matter communism) to modifiers like "national" or "pan-secessionist"? The first modifier is an apparent contradiction while the second, at best, is naively utopian. The answer to such questions doesn't lie in some fascist entryist pollution of a gullible left scene. Instead, it can be found in the theoretical and practical weaknesses of left alternatives that rely on faith-based conceptions that capitalism creates gravediggers who will wield their shovels effectively, even when actual evidence of proletarian internationalism is hard to find. These fairly obvious limitations in our politics contribute to the growth of cynicism, pessimism, and passivity in our potential political base that will continue to provide space for "pan-secessionist anarchism" that looks towards red/brown fronts and resilient communities as an alternative to the mass emancipatory working-class struggles that are notable by their absence.

The best way to challenge the branch of neo-fascism that increasingly presents itself as left-wing and anarchist is not through the public exposure of the most questionable of its political stances and the worst of its associates—although there is nothing necessarily wrong with doing this (very carefully). What is much more useful is a serious treatment of the realities of mechanized and automated globalized production processes, of changing class composition, and of fragmented working-class consciousness. This could provide a platform for dealing with an entire range of political dead-ends—not only Third and Fourth Position[9] deviations that affect the left, but also a wide range of reformisms, local utopianisms, primitivisms*, and other in-grown and narcissistic "communities" that also develop out of a pessimism about the prospects for emancipatory class struggle.

I intended to end this with an extended treatment of the way these issues are impacted by various aspects of nationalism. Differentiating and critiquing the political impact of various types of nationalism has never seemed like a particularly difficult topic to me. All nationalism is ultimately hostile to universal emancipation—particularly when it takes on the form of a state (but also, although not to the same extent, when it is embodied in a "party" formation or a movement front). However, there is a clear and qualitative political difference between the nationalisms of oppressed and of oppressing population groups that cannot be ignored or transcended by any approach to revolutionary organizing. However, I've read enough apolitical, moralizing discussion on the topic among anarchists and left communists to make me question whether things are really that simple, so I'll leave this issue for later.

IV. LENIN, LENINISM, AND SOME LEFTOVERS

## Lenin, Leninism, and Some Leftovers
## September 2009, revised May 2022

*This wide-ranging essay was originally an attempt to spark dialog with two anarchist thinkers, Tom Wetzel of the Workers Solidarity Alliance and Larry Gambone, in the hopes of advancing constructive and critical dialog within the North American class struggle anarchist scene. While this narrow intention largely failed, the piece gained some recognition because of its evocative approach to important questions such as the role of organization, the approach to leadership, and the appropriate stance toward the state. Hamerquist prepared a revised version for this volume, though the original is still available online (see Bibliography).*

"Leninist socialism as defined in the period of Stalin contained something wrong somewhere …"

—Comrade Binod, Nepal[1]

This will be a start on some arguments that I have been threatening for a while. I regard myself as a Leninist—frequently to the dismay of others of the ilk—and have always attempted to work to the extent possible within or towards what I view as a Leninist organizational framework … so these are my arguments for the continuing relevance of Lenin. They will probably have no more real impact than my other efforts to jack up the Jacobin[2] spirit among the libertarian left in response to the current flounderings of capital—but a little more discussion might emerge, because what is more fun than debating circumstances long removed and only dimly contextualized and with all alternatives open to caricature. Unfortunately, in the heat of the debate over the political choices of past generations, the most important issues—deciding what to do and beginning to do it in the here and now—can drift further out of focus. I recognize the problem and hope I'm not contributing to it.

173

## *I.*

For revolutionaries, the crucial elements of the period between 1914 and 1918 were the degeneration of the international workers movement into parliamentary reformism and national chauvinism as well as the transformation of proletarian revolutionary organizations and institutions into bulwarks of conservatism and caution. After this came the explosive development of revolutionary potentials in Russia and, to a lesser degree, throughout the world.

During these years Lenin advanced a number of closely related strategic principles. Some reaffirmed radical positions that had been eroded and others were essentially new. First among these principles was the revolutionary obligation to utilize all forms of struggle against one's own imperialism under conditions of imperialist war—including those forms that are "illegal." The goal was to turn the imperialist war into a civil (class) war that supported the aspirations and struggles of peoples oppressed by one's "own" capitalism. Beyond this, Lenin challenged Social Democracy's trajectory towards a junior management role in national capitalisms. We've been living with this reality for decades, but prior to WWI it was central to strategic debates over social democratic and anarcho-syndicalist parliamentary and trade union tactics.

Lenin rejected a "necessary," protracted, intermediate stage for the Russian revolution—and by implication elsewhere in the world—whether justified by the alleged backwardness of economic development, the limitations of working-class consciousness, or any similar reasons. He emphasized the *immediate* anti-capitalist potential—including the possibility of working-class insurrection, a successful challenge to capitalist state power—specifically, although not exclusively, in Russia. Lenin's maximalist strategy began as a small minority faction within the Bolshevik faction that itself was a small minority of the radical sector of the Russian revolutionary process. In the actual context, his stance at the time effectively de-emphasized the guiding, controlling, and managing role of the revolutionary party—a short-lived change that contains important lessons for many subsequent problems in communist theory and practice.

Lenin's strategic perspective included an organizational separation from social democratic and anarchist politics. Other revolutionaries of the period shared substantial agreement with his positions and in some cases developed them earlier and expressed them more carefully and coherently. However, most (with Rosa Luxemburg* as the obvious example) remained indistinct organizational minorities in larger social democratic and (sometimes) anarchist milieus. This limited their capacity to test positions through independent radical organizing initiatives and severely limited their options at moments of revolutionary crisis.

Notwithstanding the huge problems, some of which should have been apparent at the moment and others that are clear in hindsight, the political initiatives associated with Lenin are a revolutionary praxis—warts and all. This Soviet revolutionary period is a crucial episode in the struggle for human liberation and the establishment of communism. It is one of the central human experiences providing hope for a different future. That alone should justify Lenin's continuing importance for any revolutionary—including those with differences extending beyond tactical emphasis to matters of principle.

Lenin fought for his perspective—at significant times in opposition to a Bolshevik majority—through the destruction of the Russian autocratic state, the overthrow of Russian capitalism, and the establishment of what he believed was a transitional "workers' state" as a beachhead for an imminent international proletarian revolution. His politics expedited the development of a revolutionary Bolshevik project—without guaranteeing its permanence or any specific outcomes. By any accounting, this was a monumental historical achievement that still constitutes the clearest attempt to collectively implement what Alain Badiou* calls the "communist hypothesis."[3]

## The Legitimate Critical Review

This revolutionary period in Russia was an immense struggle under extreme conditions and with major limitations on understanding and resources, but, in my opinion, that doesn't adequately explain or justify the eventual outcomes. With dismaying speed, fetishized and mystified organizational forms swallowed an emerging revolutionary practice. Instead of facilitating the emancipation and liberation of the oppressed and exploited, monumental piles of shit in Russia and around the world were the result. These outcomes were not unavoidable collateral damages from a necessary struggle against "class enemies." They were not the inevitable consequence of any "objective conditions." To a significant degree, they were the result of policies and approaches which had available alternatives, and while the mere existence of other options does not prove they would have been more successful in either the long or the short run, could the outcomes have been much worse?

I think it's undeniable that responsibility for the degeneration of the Russian revolution rests on Lenin. Particularly on that Lenin who is not the insurrectionist revolutionary of 1905 and 1917, but the architect of the revolutionary party in 1903 and the theorist of the workers' state and the NEP in 1921–22.[4] This full legacy is complex and ambiguous, but only apologists can't see the elements that undermine the democratic and autonomous popular movements and institutions that must be the substance of the struggle for communism. This Lenin is also relevant to our current problems and potentials—to many important problems where none of us have been inoculated against screwing up—in fact, we have become quite good at it. Accordingly, this darker side of Lenin's legacy does not subtract from his historical significance: it provides additional reasons to take it seriously.

If we are to actually learn from history, we must hold the Bolsheviks and Lenin responsible for how Russia developed and not waste time groping for partial and selective exonerations. However, this should not obscure the fact that the Russian experience is also our collective legacy. If it is scarred by bad answers, most addressed real questions that have not dissolved in the mists of history. We should not approach this collective legacy with shallow and comfortable polarizations, as a moral divide between good and evil or a political divide between proletarian revolutionaries and petty bourgeois dilettantes. A clearer understanding of this legacy will help the left avoid the sterile confrontations between dogmatic and moralistic mindsets that obstruct the discussions and initiatives needed to move ahead in an increasingly cooperative manner.

Most contemporary Marxist-Leninists spend little time on the full range of Leninist politics from the revolutionary period. Instead, they emphasize the leading and guiding role of the centralized vanguard party, conceptualized as the repository of a determinate science of social formations and the ordained leadership of the people's struggles, without which they must inevitably fail. These are the mythic Bolsheviks—"a chain without weak links," in the profoundly mistaken words of Althusser* (1965, 98).

This party-centric approach asserts that only revolutionary movements led by centralized and disciplined parties have significantly challenged capitalist power. I argued from this flawed premise with blissful ignorance for decades, so I certainly understand the hold it exercises on others. A more adequate perception would recognize that the 1917 Bolsheviks came nowhere close to this centralized and disciplined model, while many subsequent revolutionary moments have featured "communist" parties that were centralized and disciplined but no more revolutionary than my television set.

The questionable assertion that communists have made revolutions while anarchists (or Trotskyists in an earlier day) haven't puts an exaggerated blame for all failures and limitations on the equivocation and vacillation of the non–Marxist-Leninist left that failed to challenge for power or to fully support those who did. This removes the incentives to examine the exercise of working-class authority and power prior to, during, and following revolutionary crises, and provides a sectarian barrier to a thorough criticism of the actions of organized revolutionaries in these periods. Real mistakes of commission appear as unavoidable or isolated "accidents." Incompetent policies and attitudes are rationalized and minimized as examples of a revolutionary commitment to the ultimate goal, deflecting attention from many historical examples where the M-L Party has been a major obstacle to revolutionary progress, not just a source of equivocation and vacillation.

However, rejecting this party-centric religion does not require adopting an alternative dogma. Whatever the criticisms of its ultimate goals and the methods selected to reach them, at the time the Soviet experience was accepted by friends and enemies alike as a revolution to overthrow capital. Now, radicals frequently assert that the covert goal of Lenin and the Bolsheviks was to establish a party dictatorship over the working class exercised through a centralized state. This particular view is a feature of a deadening fatalism that is apparent in a wide spectrum of left perspectives. How can we approach politics as if what people and movements do and did, how they understand what they are doing when they are doing it, are not really that significant? But if they can be misled into massive self-sacrificing struggles for transcendent goals that only strengthen what is struggled against—engaging in struggles that end with nothing more than what would have been possible with complete passivity and capitulation to capitalist rule ... what else can we conclude?

This is Hoover's "Masters of Deceit" conception of communism in its anarchist clothing.[5] In fact, while the substitution of vanguard party for revolutionary class, the substitution of the party leadership for a developing critical cadre, the transformation of a revolutionary praxis into a religious view of truth and validity and science, the implementation of the Taylorist factory regime,* indeed the elimination of direct democratic participation in virtually every arena, all happened, they were not part of a covert authoritarian project. The Bolsheviks (and other "successful" communist parties) certainly included fakers and frauds—perhaps even some "capitalist roaders"[6]—but this isn't how the Soviet experience went off path (as it most assuredly did). The actual process was a complex transmogrification of mistaken means initially aimed at legitimate ends. We oversimplify and caricature this process only at the great risk of repeating some of its elements.

Serious discussions of the core issues and questions of Leninism and its successes and failures in Russia are needed to determine if, as Badiou claims, the insurrectionist "communist hypothesis" identified with Lenin is indeed "saturated" (exhausted).[7] I believe that it is not, if it is explicitly separated from the "party-state" formation that emerged in both the Soviet Union and China. However, a more satisfactory answer to such questions requires a more functional political and intellectual framework for the distressingly small cadre of current radicals who are committed to liberatory working-class revolution.

This must be more than a framework for talk. Following Marx, "all mysteries … find their rational solution in human practice and the comprehension of this practice."[8] We have lots of "mysteries," but lack the collective political practice required to evaluate alternative strategic initiatives. In my opinion, the necessary first step in this direction is to bring together social anarchists and those Marxists and Leninists who could live with the lower case "m" and "l"—although they may not have realized it yet. I'm well aware that there are many, perhaps most, in each camp who think this is impossible, unnecessary, or a mistake. I hope that this paper might change some opinions.

But first, back to Lenin. I incorporate aspects of Lenin's positions that I think are relevant and useful and discount and dismiss other aspects without attempting to reconcile contradictions and provide the appearance of systematic coherence. There was a time when I scraped through the *Collected Works* quite diligently, looking for major Lenin positions that appeared "correct" to me—or, at least, ones that were better than Soviet Marxism's permitted texts and the "famous quotations." My emphasis was on *The State and Revolution* (1917), the "Testament" material (1956 [1923]), some stuff from around the 1905 upsurge, and the extensive writings on dual power and insurrection in 1917.[9] The negative comparisons were with *What is To Be Done?* (1902), *"Left-Wing" Communism* (1920), and much of the output from the 10th and 11th Party Congresses.[10] However, I've concluded that such efforts are essentially for historians, not activists. This history is not going to be adequately reinterpreted by the likes of us—at least not before the development of the struggle makes the effort superfluous.

### *"Vanguard Party"*

One implication of my position is that it is essentially pointless to try to determine what parts of Lenin are more authentically "Leninist." However, this is not a reason to ignore the recurring themes in his writing and activity that have current ramifications. The one that is directly relevant to this piece concerns the nature and role of the "vanguard party," and I would like to spend some time on it.

There is no doubt that Lenin was committed to the conception and the development of a unified, disciplined, and centralized revolutionary party—a cadre party able to act as the political/military leadership of the working class. Much more problematic and far less clear in Lenin's writings and political practice (if not for the "Leninists" who succeeded him … ) is the conception of the party as a core institution that should aim to unify, discipline, and centralize the entire working class and/or the "revolutionary people" around itself.

All of these terms, "unified," "disciplined," "centralized," etc., are ambiguous. Lenin interpreted and applied them all differently at different points—sometimes dramatically so, as with the famous critique of the "spontaneous movement" in *What is To Be Done?*[11] followed by the subsequent, not so famous, critique of the critique a few years later in "The Reorganization of the Party" (1905). Lenin wanted a revolutionary organization that

was "professional," even in 1905 when he called for a membership composition of "one Social-Democratic intellectual to several
hundred Social-Democratic workers." He wanted an organization that could think critically, even when he called for "one-tenth
theory and nine-tenths practice." He wanted an organization that
could act decisively and exercise effective discipline, even when
he said "criticism ... must be quite free ... not only at Party meetings, but also at public meetings" (1906). Althusser's* historically
laughable statement about Lenin building the Bolshevik party as
the essential subjective element of the Russian revolutionary process, "a chain without weak links," presents the common core of
the dominant Marxist-Leninist conception of the vanguard role of
the party:

> Lenin was correct to see in it [the political circumstances
> of Russia in 1917—d.h.] the *objective conditions* of a
> Russian revolution, and to forge its *subjective conditions*,
> the means of a decisive assault on the weak link in the
> imperialist chain, in a Communist Party that was a chain
> without weak links. (1965, 98; emphasis in original)

Althusser's theoretical argument for the centrality of the party
rests on his understanding of the famous *What is to Be Done?*
critique of spontaneity (see 1965, 171fn57). Most of the current
Marxist-Leninist constellation still hold that rigid and ahistorical
view, actually more characteristic of Kautsky and Plekhanov* than
Lenin.[12] This is despite the fact that this critique is exactly what
Lenin modified in the 1905 documents mentioned above, while
most of Luxemburg's contemporaneous criticisms of *What is to
Be Done?*,[13] which she viewed as Kautskyist, have been vindicated
by historical developments.

Many anarchists assert that the *What is to Be Done?* critique
of mass spontaneity, at least as it has come to be interpreted, effectively denies the capacity of the working class to emancipate itself
and robs the conception of communism of its central dynamic: the
expansion of working-class autonomy and human freedom. They

argue that this underlies a number of the policy mistakes that followed the Russian October. I think they are certainly right on the first point and probably at least partially right on the second. The common M-L conception of the revolutionary party elevates centralized party command over popular creativity and initiative, and there is no doubt that this should be explicitly confronted and reversed to maximize revolutionary potentials. That was true in 1917. It is more clearly true now.

The problems with the militarized structure of command and discipline that was consolidated in the Russian party and the Communist International within a few months of Lenin's death are obvious, and there is no point in compiling another "what's wrong" list for Chapter Six of Stalin's *Foundations of Leninism* (1953). We've heard enough of "iron discipline" and know quite well that it is hardly true that once the "line is determined, organization determines everything." However, the trajectory that these issues followed out of the Russian revolution does raise some interesting questions. Is there a clear path from Lenin's approach to revolutionary organization to the Third International's orthodoxy?[14] If there isn't, is there a central weakness within Lenin's perspective that facilitated this development? Finally, why doesn't the general recognition of the problems of "actually existing socialism"* lead to a more critical approach to communist organization among thinking Leninists?

The historical questions are complicated. At the outset, there is Lenin's Kautskian *What is to be Done?* argument for the necessity to introduce revolutionary consciousness into the working class from the "outside."[15] Almost twenty years later, we have the terrible statements in *"Left-Wing" Communism* (1922) that ridicule any proposed distinction or contradiction between the dictatorship of the proletariat and the dictatorship of a party in the name of the proletariat.[16] On the other hand, we have Lenin's explicit recognition, paralleling Luxemburg's observations in "The Mass Strike" (1906) and Gramsci's* in the *L'Ordine Nuovo* period (1968),[17] that the masses of people were more revolutionary than the social democrats and the majority of Bolsheviks in the upsurges of 1905 and 1917. Then there are the well-known examples of major strategic differences within the Bolsheviks being tolerated and even openly debated beyond the party under the most extreme circumstances. For example, the "strikebreaking" of Kamenev and Zinoviev.

Lenin frequently referred to the backwardness of the party cadre and leadership, their inability to "think" and propensity to "administrative solutions" that resolved ideological issues through bureaucratic authority. This might be grounds to criticize Lenin for an exaggerated sense of his own capacities, but it does indicate that he did not think the vanguard party was infallible—as many alleged followers do.

Then there are Lenin's late writings where he is so concerned with the increasingly bureaucratic character of Soviet power, that he proposes a reorganization that would empower the non-party "Workers and Peasants Inspectorate" to oversee the functioning of the elements of the state and government and … the party. This also is hardly compatible with an exaggerated sense of what the communist party is and what it can do. In fact, it seems more like a foreshadowing of the positive aspect of the Chinese Cultural Revolution,* capsulized in the slogan "Bombard the Party Headquarters."*

There are conflicting strands in Lenin's politics. In one, the distinctively Leninist elements are in opposition to the future Bolshevik degeneration. In the other, his positions are significant contributions to that same process. On one side is Lenin's general, nuanced approach to the issues of debate and criticism that are codified under the heading of democratic centralism. On the other side is his propensity to conflate the concepts of centralization and unification in ways that led to mechanical and instrumental management techniques rather than the expansion of popular participation in the revolutionary process. I'm raising these issues not only because they have substantial intrinsic historic interest, but also because the questions involved and the range of inadequate answers to them still plague us.

In 1977, long after Lenin and Stalin had left the stage, L. Althusser published a series of articles for the 22nd Congress of the French Communist Party. In a belated and unsuccessful attempt to confront the problems of Soviet Marxism and the failures of its own strategic perspective, the French Party took advantage of Moscow's increasingly flaccid authority and moved towards the Eurocommunist stance of the Spanish and Italian parties.[18] Althusser, however, was a spokesperson for a minority tendency in the French party. He had been on record as sympathetic to Maoism, had endorsed the ambivalent 70/30 attitude the Chinese Communists took towards Stalin, and seemed to agree with the Chinese hostility to the post-1956 Soviet critique of Stalinism.[19] Althusser was also opposed to the parliamentary reformism and "socialist humanism" of Eurocommunism, again following Chinese positions which were addressed to "Comrade Togliatti," the Italian Comintern veteran who was an early advocate of Eurocommunism.[20]

Althusser's articles and the proposals they advanced were thinly veiled criticisms from the left of the proposed changes in the party's attitude towards democracy and state power, including its renewed emphasis on cross-class unity and the "peaceful parliamentary transition to socialism." However, in 1977 these positions no longer fit a pro-Chinese stance, and Althusser's alternative program was limited to proposals to promote fuller debate and discussion of strategic issues within the French Party. The prospects for his initiatives were dim since, as Althusser noted, despite the 22nd Congress's heavy emphasis on increased openness and democracy in society, it neither presented nor entertained initiatives to expand them within the party.

Althusser's interventions immediately raised the issues of democratic centralism as it had come to be understood in Communist parties a half century after the Russian Revolution. With few exceptions, the emphasis in this conception was on centralism. The second term, democracy, is seldom more than an afterthought with dangerous potentials for weakening the needed discipline and resolve. To the extent it exists, such "democracy" is always guided and managed—usually with a very heavy hand. Political challenges to basic strategic approaches or major theoretical concepts are seldom "in order." Open discussions of differences are generally limited to questions of "political line" and are only permitted during highly structured pre–Congress/Convention periods. Genuine differences are hard to formulate, and minority arguments can only be presented to the membership with great difficulty and only during pre–Convention periods. No "horizontal" political discussion or contact is permitted within the party; everything is channeled up through the structure and—sometimes—back down to the rank and file. Finally, there is no right, and very little possibility, to raise differences within the party outside of its framework, however relevant and important the issues might be.

Implementation of this regime created ignorant and acritical communists around the world, doggedly convinced of their collective capacity to provide infallible leadership for the working class despite individually not knowing much of anything—including what was happening in the Communist movement or within the leadership of their own party. Of course, another result was huge turnover and mass defections, all of which are lumped together as "deviations" and "factionalism"—charges that carried serious weight in party circles. Not only did such charges invoke visceral fears of losing contact with the revolution, as perverse as that may seem now, they also were colored by the fates of left and right "factionalists" in situations where Communists had some power.

With a typical lack of references, Althusser argued that "Lenin was against factions" and asserted that "the Party today expects *something else* [other than factions], and it is right" (1977; emphasis in original). His reform was to suggest that party discussions on strategy should not be limited to specific periods before Congresses and that the rank and file should be aware of the differences that existed within their leadership—the existing situation in the Italian and Spanish parties. This is as far as Althusser was willing to go, and, predictably, his limited proposals went down the tube anyway. This was a sad and feeble protest.

In point of fact, Althusser's proposed "reforms" for the French Communist Party fell far short of actual Bolshevik practice up to the "temporary" ban on factions at the 10th Congress of the CPSU in 1921. The attack on factions at the 10th Congress was aimed primarily at the so-called "Workers' Opposition" of Kollontai and Shliapnikov, a substantial party grouping that was critical of the state-capitalist features of the NEP and opposed to increasing bureaucratization and the general substitution of party authority for working-class power that were also outcomes of the 10th Congress. The ban on factions was presented as a temporary measure required by extraordinary circumstances, and it is significant that Lenin argued against sanctions on the Workers' Opposition that would have excluded them from future leadership roles in the party. Not that this made much difference a few years down the road.

Significantly, Lenin's argument against factions was not actually on the predictable grounds of maintaining unity and discipline, but rather because factional divisions obstructed a full discussion of outstanding issues in the entire party. This is directly opposed to the usual arguments where anti-factional "unity" is ensured by hierarchical buffers that prevent the rank and file from understanding the issues, and enforced by barriers against horizontal contacts within the party and bans on open political discussions of any important issue outside of the party framework.

In short, I would argue that there is no historical reason to doubt that Lenin's general position on party discipline at the 10th Congress was pretty much the same as the position that he had argued more than a decade before:

> The principle of democratic centralism and autonomy for local Party organisations implies universal and full *freedom to criticise* so long as this does not disturb the *unity of a definite action*. (Lenin 1906; emphasis in original)

Whether Lenin's practice was generally in line with this position is open to argument, and there is no doubt that the formulation is susceptible to different interpretations. However, I know of no contrary statement from Lenin, and it does describe how he worked at some crucial junctures even if there were some opportunistic modifications to fit the circumstances. I'm not looking to justify or condemn his position on such issues. My point is that this position conflicts in principle with the current understanding of democratic centralism that is accepted and reinforced by Althusser and many others who define themselves as Marxist-Leninist. It's significant that currently both critics and worshippers credit Lenin with the same position on democracy within the party as the one clearly held by Stalin and, to some extent, Trotsky—although it is a position that is clearly at odds with Lenin's explicit arguments in favor of clear, sharp, and open political debate.

## Centralization and Unity

Whatever one's attitude towards the Bolsheviks, the issues of organizational discipline and political unity are still relevant concerns for revolutionaries. Here I would make a short side trip to consider Larry Gambone's approach to these issues in an organization of anarchist revolutionaries, most notable a recent blog post on the "Porcupine Blog" (Gambone 2009). I'm not sure whether I fully agree with his position either in general or with respect to Lenin's theoretical attitudes toward class and state, but I was struck with what he sees as the central weakness of Lenin's line of argument. Gambone asserts that Lenin conflates the concepts of centralization and unity, and I think this is a good way to characterize some problems with Lenin's positions on the role of the party in relation to the practical issues that were confronted after the seizure of power.

Gambone rightly sees organizational centralization as a problematic surrogate for political unification. By itself, the most extreme centralization in a party-type organization does not guarantee political unity—any more than it does in a military organization. There can be no real unity around positions that are not understood. Political unity in a disciplined organization is inconceivable without a critical and a legitimately contested approach to all major strategic and theoretical issues.

This contrasts with the Stalinist conception of the party that is based on a military model of leadership and discipline reinforced by a leadership monopoly of a pseudo-scientific "theory" that gives it unique access to "objective truth." When this process of bureaucratized centralization expands beyond the party and governs more and more aspects of society, it constricts the possibilities for autonomous development, replacing potentials for actual unity with an imprinted uniformity. Thankfully, this model almost always has its cracks and imperfections, but to the extent that it is consistently applied and enforced, it is a blueprint for religious cults, not revolutionary organizations.

The beginning of self-government in the Russian revolutionary process required cultivation. It could not survive the command centralization of Soviet society. Of course, centralization never occurs in a political vacuum, and post-revolutionary Russia confronted real problems that cannot be reduced to an abstract lust for power by the Bolsheviks. As the likelihood of successful working-class insurgencies in Europe faded, the strategic problems of holding together the poor peasant/working-class popular base for Soviet power grew more pressing. The main specters haunting the Soviets were not the Kolchaks or Denikins, the Allied Intervention, or any other attempt of the defeated ruling class to retake state power: it was the "Revolutionary Paris/Counter-Revolutionary France" dichotomy.[21] The first-generation Bolsheviks were always preoccupied with the memory and fate of the Paris Commune.

The Soviet response to the weakening of the strategic class alliance was to accelerate production, based on limited and narrow economic notions of the forces of production, to meet the sometimes conflicting demands and needs of the working-class minority (a small one) and the peasant majority (a large one). Lenin's approach can be clearly seen in his remarks to the 11th CPSU Congress: less and less priority was put on transforming the relations of production and reproduction through the expansion of democratic and participatory institutions, and when moves in this direction potentially conflicted with economic growth, as they almost always did, the initiatives were routinely crushed.

It was true that economic growth was needed to satisfy the practical expectations that people had of the revolution and to maintain the class alliance between workers and peasants. However, when the growth was not easily achieved, an increasingly centralized party authority opted for capitalist conceptions of industrial efficiency: Taylorism and one-man management.[22] The centralization of the party assumed an increasingly technocratic character, implementing its leadership and "guiding role" through its monopoly of positions of bureaucratic authority. This essentially ended any discussions about alternative approaches. Where attempts to expand popular control emerged, they first were seen as disruptive and—rather quickly—as counter-revolutionary.

All sorts of bad things derived from this supposed efficiency through centralization: the notion of workers' organizations as "transmission belts" for industrial policy, the formation of a professional military, one-man management of the firm, the eradication of organized left opposition in the country. It is true that until he died, Lenin opposed one centralizing element: the heavy pressure to limit or eliminate the right of secession for nations historically oppressed by Russia. However, that struggle was also eventually a losing one—doomed in substantial part by the priority on party-"guided" and managed development that was blinded by the peculiar bias that the Chinese call the "theory of the productive forces."[23]

## II.

I think that many contemporary Leninist conceptions of revolutionary organization are fundamentally misconceived, but my alternative to them—one that I am perversely determined to also call Leninist—regards the role of the party and of its cadre of communists as equally important, although with a different content. Since we are concerned with discussions of substance, not the labeling of categories, it may be confusing—even self-defeating—to assert a questionable claim to "Leninism." I hope my attachment to the term comes across as more than stubbornness, since I mean it to go to the continuing relevance of Lenin's approach to the "art" of insurrection, which I intend to consider in a later section. I'll continue to be an uncomfortable Leninist until a more appropriate label is developed.

I've written a good deal on the topic of revolutionary organization. This has emphasized the development of disciplined and organized revolutionary cadre able to think critically and act collectively and decisively. Rather than repeating the arguments that I have used or indicating the changes in my views over some four decades, I'd like to make some observations on more practical and immediate issues of organization and perspective as I see them presented—or avoided—by class struggle anarchism and some contemporary left Marxists.

I should be clear from the outset that I've never been that familiar with anarchist tendencies and arguments and may have lost touch with some emerging trends in Leninism and neo-Marxism, and I will try to clarify my views without making extensive critiques of arguments which I may not adequately understand. I will be referencing Tom Wetzel of the Worker Solidarity Alliance[24] and I have just cited Larry Gambone. They both express substantial positions on questions I think are important. However, I have not read many of their writings and my understanding of their positions may be inaccurate or incomplete.

I'm interested in Wetzel's writings on working-class organization and culture; his specific criticisms of Bolshevik attitudes towards working-class autonomy; and the base-building, dual power/dual organization perspective which he advances. Wetzel appears to embrace a class analysis of capitalism that hasn't persuaded me, but I do recognize the problems that it addresses for understanding post-revolutionary Russia and China.

This section will deal with a few topics, somewhat jumbled together and in no necessary order: the issue of "representation," social anarchist conceptions of dual organization and social insertion, Badiou's conception of the "event,"* and possibly some speculation about that Kasama* masthead slogan: "without state power, all else is illusion."[25]

I think that most of us (but not all) can agree that many strategic problems concern how to conceptualize and implement Marx's injunction (which was also Bakunin's) that the emancipation of the working class can only be accomplished by that class itself. We can certainly agree with Wetzel that these problems have to be approached in light of the variations and unevenness in the understandings and activities of the international working class, and the differences in objective socio-economic circumstances which segment it. It is also helpful to consider these problems in light of the range of policies and institutions, both repressive and incorporative, that constitute the exercise of capitalist state power.

*The Communist Manifesto* (Marx and Engels 1848) spells out a couple of general principles for the relationship of communists to the mass struggles of working people. Communists should "represent" the interests of the whole in the movements of parts, and they should "represent" the interests of the future in movements of the present. Responses to these notions vary. Lifestyle anarchists, even before they objected to any group claiming to have the intellectual roadmap to the "future" or to "know" the interests of the "whole," would be skeptical of this entire notion since they tend to see efforts of a smaller group to project and implement appropriate strategies and objectives for a larger group or for any of its individual members as authoritarian. This leaves them with some problems in the face of capitalist power, which has no inhibitions about crushing isolated, small-scale initiatives towards self-rule, but they still do present a potent source of resistance to virtually any left political strategy for a so-called advanced capitalist society.

Some other radical autonomists have a slightly different critique of representation, less concerned with its restrictions on individual liberty and more concerned with the issue of "substitutionism."* They see the changing class composition of the working class as the motor and primary determinant of historical change, more or less independent of the conscious intent of its participants. Implicitly, and frequently explicitly, the importance of ideology and self-conscious organization in a process of the class becoming "for itself"[26] is replaced by an assumption of an underlying historic dynamic. This position can develop from a "workerist"* outlook of the Johnson-Forest* or Italian variety, or from some version of the "irreducible singularities" conception in Negri's* notion of the "Multitude." It often argues that virtually every organized intervention by communists has and will result in a net subtraction from the working-class struggle, and the best course for communists is to stand aside or self-consciously limit their role to helping out and "describing"—following some variant of Staughton Lynd's notion of "accompaniment."[27]

Wetzel makes it fairly clear that he does not share these positions (for example, in "Anarchism, Class Struggle and Political Organization" [2009]), although I think some of his comrades may slip in that direction. He, along with most class struggle social anarchists, appreciates the unevenness in consciousness and development in the working class and the consequent role for an organized revolutionary minority to motivate and consolidate projects that advance and expand the general struggle. This necessarily entails a "representation" of the interests and potentials of social groups that are not organized and politically unified by a revolutionary organization that hopefully is. However, it does not necessarily imply any delegation of authority from the one to the other.

I intend to raise some questions, and potentially differences, with this perspective, but I agree with the general thrust of the approach. However, before getting further into those subjects, I want to briefly consider current attitudes in sections of the Marxist-Leninist left that don't see the emancipation of the working class (and humanity) as the role and responsibility of that class. Relying on the positions Lenin advances in *"Left-Wing" Communism*, most of the MLM [Marxist-Leninist-Maoist] fragments disregard the problems inherent in the representation of the working class by a minority segment of that class. Consider these positions of Mike Ely on the *Kasama** site, which tends to be more thoughtful:

> Socialist Revolution does not require that conscious self-identification by sociological class be a defining feature.
>
> What led the oppressed in some cases were radical political forces (the communists generally) who saw themselves as *representatives* of the working class (and its objective interests)—and who won the allegiance of important sections of that class (often minorities, but significant sections none the less). (Ely 2009; emphasis in original)

The logical implication of these comments is that the revolutionary overthrow of the state power of the capitalist class can, and indeed must, be accomplished by a movement that in no sense is the working class organized "in and for itself." The emergence of a working class capable of achieving universal liberation in the process of its own self-emancipation is presented as a dysfunctional and utopian conception derived from a class-reductionist perspective. To the extent it remains as an eventual goal, it is an objective to be achieved with the assistance of the authoritarian tools provided by a prior capture of the state.

I should indicate an area of agreement with a feature of this position that isn't fully expressed in the selections I have cited. It raises some important questions for revolutionary strategy in what Gramsci called the "war of maneuver"*; issues of qualitative leaps, revolutionary breaks, and the response to "events"* in the Badiou sense. It recognizes that the reduction of popular movements of resistance and refusal to a simple class polarization is no more likely than the reduction of the entire capitalist social order to domination by the economic element "in the last instance."[28] I will return to this point from the other side in criticisms of some incrementalist and evolutionary features in class struggle/social anarchist perspectives.

Remaining with Gramscian categories, Ely discounts the conception of the "directive [*dirigenti*] class" which accords a unique role in the revolutionary process to the working class.[29] This is unfortunate, since Gramsci's term has the merit of emphasizing the distinctions between "leadership" and "domination" (command) in this role. The errors and confusions on this topic are very relevant to the trajectory of "actually existing socialism"—to the problems that underlie Binod's "something wrong somewhere" that I cited at the beginning of this paper.

Any capacity for these politics to respond to the rapid, but temporary and reversible, shifts in political potentials in epistemological break* situations, is overshadowed by the massive problems of communists positioning "themselves as representatives ... of the working class (and its ... objective interests)" prior to establishing a social practice that can provide a genuine democratic legitimacy for such a representation. The problems become even more intractable when the vanguard party sees itself as "representative," not only of an underdeveloped working class, but of an entire "revolutionary people," composed of a number of classes and strata and a bewildering array of internal contradictions, and then proposes to utilize the instrumentalities of state power to implement its own, quite subjective conception of the objective interests of (other) people.

I'm not arguing that revolutions or major steps towards them can't be accomplished by vanguards with only minority segments of the working classes in active and conscious support. They can— but only with real limitations that cannot be talked away. The seizure of the state by vanguards that claim to be acting in the objective interests of social classes does not answer the question about whether they actually are implementing such interests and whether they will continue to do so after they possess the instrumentalities of state power. These underlying issues will only be displaced to the conception of "Socialism," where they will predictably confound any assertion that some workerless "workers' state" or non-participatory "New Democratic" people's state actually is *their state* for either the workers or the people.

This displacement of the problem is clear in the history of all those "Socialist Revolutions" captained by a self-proclaimed proxy for the working class (or for a coalition of progressive classes). The real test if a seizure of power has initiated a trajectory towards human liberation is whether working-class and popular self-organization and self-rule is expanding. By that test these regimes fail and so, to a substantial degree, did the movements, fronts, and coalitions that led to them. They don't provide significant concrete steps towards replacing the administration of people with the administration of things.* None of them have led to increasing democracy, to authentic and expanding popular participation, or to any discernible "withering away"* of the power and functions of the bureaucratic state.

While many modern Maoist positions appear to be oblivious to these issues, there are some substantial arguments that elements of the Chinese revolutionary experience may provide some answers to these problems, and not just illustrations of them. The thrust of these arguments is that Mao's approach to contradictions among the people, combined with the radical and anti-bureaucratic thrust of the Cultural Revolution, might have provided a workable alternative to the failed trajectory of the Soviet Union—if it had gained hegemony in the Chinese Communist Party and successfully reversed some seriously mistaken policies in that party.

These arguments present Mao's approach to contradictions among the people as a model that would limit rule by command, mandate the expansion of open critical debate, and criticize the subordination of these priorities to "efficiency," most notably including efficiency in the expansion of material production. Significant elements within the Chinese Cultural Revolution did call for establishment of a Commune State with all elected officials subject to immediate recall. This was a direct confrontation with the emerging bureaucratic nomenclature that originated a call for a mass movement to "bombard the [party] headquarters."

According to this perspective, these features of Maoism are a variant of democratic centralism that sees the dangers of the bureaucratization of the post-revolutionary state, which Lenin did also late in life, but makes a much more significant attempt to reverse the process through continuing popular class struggle. In this view, the mistaken line that various parties have adopted, not the party-centric model itself, is the problem. Going further with the argument: since a clear alternative developed in China and was almost victorious, the hegemony of that mistaken line is not inevitable. Although the Cultural Revolution was ultimately unsuccessful, it could conceivably have succeeded and replaced the perspectives that had captured the Chinese party with categorical alternatives.

I would like to agree with this view, but I can't. This history isn't my field, but I was active during the crucial moments and paid some attention to what was happening. I remember the impact of Mao's "On the Correct Handling of Contradictions Among the People" (1957) and the Hundred Flowers Campaign that was presented in the same document.[30] The argument that disagreement wasn't necessarily treason to the revolution and betrayal of the party and could—and should—be handled through open democratic discussion was refreshing. It all appeared to be a much more balanced and comprehensive response to the issues that had finally emerged for Communists (who were well behind the awareness curve as usual) with the secret denunciation of Stalin's "cult of the personality" at the 20th Congress of the CPSU.[31] It was also a welcome break from *Peking Review*'s implausible "Great Leap Forward" economic stories about backyard steel production and

Mao's ability to grow record-size melons in his window box.

Some believe that this approach to non-antagonistic contradictions implies an actual alternative conception of revolutionary organization that was eventually defeated. I don't agree.

We should be way past the point where we accept best readings of these historic documents and expect that there were or will be good faith applications of them in practice. So let me offer a more skeptical, "worst" reading of Mao on " … Contradictions Among the People." Here is a key passage:

> But this freedom is freedom with leadership and democracy is democracy under centralized guidance, it is not anarchy. (Mao 1957)

Further into the argument we reach Section VIII, containing the "hundred flowers bloom … hundred schools contend" passage. This still sounds good, but relatively quickly we encounter a set of the rules for dividing the "flowers" from the "poisonous weeds." Consider rules nos. 2 and 5 that Mao indicates are the most important: number 2 stresses that "weeds" include ideas and criticisms that will not be "*beneficial to* socialism." Who decides what is beneficial and what is not? Number 5 provides a clue to the answer: Flowers "should help to strengthen, and not shake off or weaken, the leadership of the Communist Party."

This clarifies the content of the "democracy under centralized guidance" and provides a better framework for understanding the limits of positions about reasoned discussion, patient persuasion, open contention of different ideas, and the necessity to avoid arbitrary command and coercive tactics. Unfortunately, we have a near century of collective experience that demonstrates that such "worst" interpretations are the ones most likely to have actually happened.

In this instance, the historical backdrop is particularly relevant. Mao presented his speech, "Contradictions Among the People," to a major Chinese political meeting in February of 1957—after Khrushchev's secret speech* to the Soviet 20th Congress; after the

Hungarian and Suez events; and well after tensions had mounted with the Soviet Union over industrial aid and economic policy, over the pending Soviet reversal of the excommunication of Yugoslavia, over the Sino-Indian border conflict, over the Sino-Russian border, over the Quemoy Matsu incidents, and over the increasing centrality of the "Three Peacefuls" in Soviet ideology and Russian state policy.[32]

When these factors are introduced—and there also are others related to the voluntarist and highly mystified approach to economic growth of the "Great Leap Forward"—a subtext of real issues is readily apparent for virtually every element of Mao's discussion. However, these actual issues that should have been commonly understood and democratically discussed—certainly in the party and, I think, also generally in the society—remained mystified and in some cases deliberately falsified. In actual practice, the "leadership" and "centralized guidance" role that Mao endorsed for the party in this speech provided an effective barrier that denied the masses of people—and probably the bulk of party cadres as well—any opportunity for informed and timely participation in a debate over the real alternatives that would determine the future of "their" society.

This long after the fact, we should have little doubt that the left elements in the Cultural Revolution had a more accurate understanding of the situation in China than Mao, assuming that Mao genuinely believed all that he was saying. However, it is also true that this experience demonstrates that no basic reform of the Chinese party/state was possible without calling the party-centric model into question, and this questioning would include a critique of the last three words in Mao's conception of "democracy under centralized guidance."

*Transitions*

The results of these workerless "workers' states," governing "for" the working class while ruling on the backs of actual working people, have been increasingly bureaucratized, repressive, and exploitative societies. Such societies may be "socialist" in some superficial, public relations branding sense, but, notwithstanding a good deal of quickly forgotten propagandistic apologetics, there is no evidence that these displacements of the representation dilemma to a post-revolutionary society have illuminated any path in the direction of communism.

There is no shortage of stubborn self-deception on these issues in every segment of the left (although some promote it more aggressively), but it is hard to deny that the types of authoritarian and exploitative social formations that have emerged out of major revolutionary struggles, rather than being transitional steps to communism, have proven to be seed beds for evolutionary and counter-revolutionary reversions to the most barbaric capitalist archetypes. This process, combined with the futile attempts to rationalize and justify it, have resulted in disastrous impacts on revolutionary morale that muddy all popular liberatory revolutionary vision.

I opened this piece with a remark from a leading Maoist in Nepal, identified as Comrade Binod. Of course, there is a lot in the interview that stays with the traditional party-centric formulas, although these predictable left-Maoist positions seem a bit at odds with the plaintive "something wrong, somewhere" comment that casts its shadow over growing questions about the model of revolution that had been accepted. Comrade Binod makes it clear that his concerns revolve around popular participation, individual freedom, and the legitimacy of the exercise of power under circumstances where the strategic task of a popular insurrection is on the order of the day.

Let me return to that Kasama quote, "without state power, all else is illusion." The actual illusion is that any capture of a state by any self-proclaimed leadership is necessarily a step towards communism—whether or not its "leadership" is of the working class or of a broader and vaguer "revolutionary people" that includes the working class. Any actual step towards communist society must include some discernible movement towards the administration of things, not people, and the substitution of "re-education" for the physical elimination of "class enemies" is not such. Nor is it a significant revolutionary advance to replace the capitalist state with a different external authority that continues to administer people as if they were things—or potentially wayward children.

What is needed is genuinely democratic participation in all major social decisions, not fabricated near-unanimities that hide the real dominance of technocratic notions of efficiency. There must be real steps towards expanding the individual freedom and autonomy necessary to make these changes real and substantive, not merely decorative. This is all radically incompatible with personality cults and the near-deification of leaders or leaderships, but only such changes will produce a different kind of state, a "Commune State" that will conceivably "wither away." This is not an argument against the possible need to exercise power against the former ruling class, but it indicates some narrow limits on methods that can be employed without deforming ultimate objectives.

The modern attempts to reconcile *The Manifesto* roles for communists with the notion that the working class must emancipate itself have led to this dilemma: on the one side, as Alonzo Alcazar said recently, "we are almost afraid to say 'we'";[33] and on the other side, the self-emancipation of the working class is put on the back burner until the "Socialist Revolution" is won by an internally disciplined party leading a disparate and only partially self-conscious constituency that lacks any capacity to discipline "its" vanguard. Radicals must determine what to do and how to do it somewhere between these equally inadequate alternatives, recognizing that we will not stumble into insights that resolve all dilemmas. The issues will have to be constantly re-investigated and the proposed solutions reinvigorated in the light of changing conditions and developing potentials. This need for the constant re-examination of premises based on a working feedback loop between the development and the implementation of policies requires an organized, disciplined, and structured approach to revolutionary political work.

## Democracy?

I'm citing some excerpts from Wetzel's 2009 article, "Anarchism, Class Struggle and Political Organization." The selections indicate elements of his conception of anarchist political organization and strategy and contrast them with those of a "vanguard party":

> From the point of view of "organized anarchism with a class struggle perspective," two kinds of organization are needed: (1) forms of mass organization through which ordinary people can grow and develop their collective strength, and (2) political organizations of the anarchist or libertarian socialist minority. ...

> Bakunin had said that the role of anarchist activists was a "leadership of ideas."

> But disseminating ideas isn't the only form of influence. Working with others of diverse views in mass organizations and struggles, exhibiting a genuine commitment ... makes it more likely one's ideas will be taken seriously ... .

> The idea of a "vanguard party" is that a political organization is to try ... to achieve a hegemonic position within mass movements [and] ... use this position of dominant influence to eventually achieve power for its party. ... This means congealing the party's power through various methods of hierarchical control. This is formal leadership power and not just influence. ...

> The aim of libertarian socialism is that the masses them-
> selves should achieve power, through mass direct democ-
> racy, not that a leadership group should do so through a
> party gaining control of a state. Reflecting this, the aim of
> the libertarian Left activists should be to encourage self-
> management of movements/organizations.

Presumably Wetzel has other writings on the subject since, for
example, these say nothing about the various questions of internal
unity and organizational discipline. I should probably note that
while most advocates of the vanguard party would regard Wetzel's
description as a caricature, I find it to be a reasonably accurate presentation of the way most such groups function once they reach a
certain threshold of size and influence.

However, despite this area of agreement, there are some gaps
and some questions that may indicate significant differences. I'd
like to consider some class struggle social anarchist positions on
organization and strategy. These will include issues of democracy and participation within mass struggle; questions around the
legality and legitimacy of capitalist power with respect to potentially military dimensions of the struggle; the concept of "social
insertion"; and some approaches to workplace organizing. I will
end this by returning to the question of insurrection.

Here is the major problem that I see in these selections and in
my understanding of the general approach. It posits an organization of revolutionary anarchists that relates to mass struggles in a
collective and organized way, it recognizes that this organization
should advance distinctively anarchist ideas, and it provides a list
of things that "vanguard parties" supposedly think and do which
revolutionary anarchist organizations should not think and do.
But there's still not enough to answer some very basic questions
facing any revolutionary strategy: What are the concrete potentials? What should be done? What are appropriate metrics for
evaluating our work?

I've raised the importance of recognizing that we have a collective radical history, and that it is important to have a good handle on the facts of this history before making major judgments on its implications and motivations. I want to spell this out in a little more detail since I think it has particular relevance to these anarchist critiques of Leninism and to some issues of current approaches to work.

I have no overriding compulsion to defend major Leninist political interventions—past or present, general or specific. The essential need for participatory democracy in the course of struggle was degraded by the nested structures of Third International organizational centralism: an inner ring where the party leadership is the general staff and the cadre are the disciplined soldiers; an outer ring where the party is the general staff and the working classes are the grunts—or perhaps the collateral damage. However, I do think we can only learn from criticizing these past experiences if two conditions are met: First, that the nature and significance of the issues addressed should be evaluated independently of the actions taken to address them. Second, that the actions taken should be evaluated separately from the justifications offered for these actions. These conditions help provide an adequate factual groundwork before provisional judgments become hardened— which is particularly important when these judgments take on a moralistic aspect.

The anarchist alternative to vanguardism presents greater democratic participation as the generic answer to most of the problems of revolutionary strategy. This tends to exclude any possibility that the immediate issues of democracy and participation— and their limitations or restrictions—weren't the only questions, or even necessarily the pivotal ones, in various episodes of struggle. This has two consequences: it reduces the responsibility on current revolutionaries for formulating their own positions about the underlying issues within various historical situations, and it promotes the tendency to make premature and exaggerated moral judgments about matters that haven't been adequately considered on a political level.

There can be a cost for being too quick to conclude a political analysis and draw moral conclusions. The accounting may come in the increased likelihood that in some marginally different circumstances parallel mistakes of commission will be made. It may also come as collateral damage from failures to collectively confront real issues in an organized way. Such errors of omission can result in important lost opportunities and even major setbacks.

When current struggles are the focus, the discussions tend to be more realistic. Consider the recent anarchist exchanges over the English Oil Workers' job actions[34] that had elements that were both undeniably popular and undeniably reactionary and anti-internationalist. It was much easier to see the problems than the solutions in a situation where it was necessary that something be done ... and it's hard to see any way in which "more democracy" would have been particularly helpful.

There are going to be complex issues of democracy, participation, and militancy whenever mass democratic struggles intersect with revolutionary groups that are attempting to intervene in them. Class struggle anarchism tends to gloss over the tensions, contradictions, and conflicts that are a necessary part of this intersection, notwithstanding any understanding of their general possibility as implied by Wetzel's notion of "unevenness."

Let me approach the issue from another aspect. Another well-known Marxist proposition is that the "ideas of the ruling class are the ruling ideas"[35] (understanding "ideas" in the strongest sense, including a range of cultural norms, many of which are not clearly "thought"). These ruling ideas are backed by the momentum of institutionalized historical inertia and reinforced by the exercise of both repressive and incorporative aspects of capitalist state power. "Normally," in most areas of the globe, even when they are resisting, working people and the working class are thinking, believing, and acting within some variant of capitalist ideology and capitalist culture. And in "normal" times, no accurate index of popular opinion will show that the masses of people are with the revolutionaries, because, in fact, they are not. This is an aspect of reality that actually does matter—notwithstanding various spontaneists, who see the working class always doing exactly what is possible in the given circumstances, no more and no less. It is a material fact that limits the applicability of "democracy."

The ruling-class ideas are not simply mirrored in the subordinated classes. The "high culture" of the actual rulers does not apply clichéd homilies like "Be all that you can be" or "With hard work, you can accomplish anything" to their own privileged lives. The ruling class does not question its own potential for class solidarity because "people won't stick together," although it certainly promotes such notions among the overwhelming majorities that are oppressed and exploited. The primary manifestation of the dominance of the ruling ideas on popular attitudes is the mass buy-in to the "There Is No Alternative"* mantra: the acceptance of the inevitability and essential rightness of the major features of the status quo and the ultimate folly and futility of collective resistance to it. For the majority of people, this attitude predominates even while they are engaged in struggles and resistance that stretch the framework of capitalist legitimacy. While these ruling ideas are never the only ideas within the oppressed and dominated working classes, they determine the important segments of working-class consciousness that Gramsci characterizes as "common sense."[36]

Looking at the same issues in a different framework, episodes of mass and class struggle that imply a struggle against the capitalist system always include elements of a struggle for "better terms" within capitalism, for reforms. Clearly, there will be moments in such struggles when participatory majorities tacitly or explicitly acknowledge their subordination in exchange for selective concessions. Such struggles that de-emphasize internationalism or defer possibilities to expand the opposition to white supremacy are the norm in this country.

Revolutionaries have no interest in any reinforcement of this subordinated working-class consciousness, whether or not it is "democratically" determined. When revolutionaries cave in to such popular opinions, which certainly may be incorporated in "democratic" decisions, the results can be just as damaging as any authoritarian manipulation. I don't see how Wetzel "democratically" deals with situations where revolutionaries should confront and challenge strongly held positions within the class and among the people.

For revolutionaries and revolutionary organizations, including anarchist ones, certain principles should be axiomatic—across all types of borders; an injury to one is an injury to all;[37] under all circumstances, it is good and therefore "right to rebel."[38] The validity of these principles is established through revolutionary political practice over the long haul, not by decisions of the moment, no matter how participatory and democratic the process may be. Periodic democratic reaffirmations of our principles are certainly welcome, but with or without such validation, they will remain as our operating assumptions. Unless there are basic changes in the strategy and the purposes and objectives of the struggle, revolutionaries will attempt to win broader support for them whatever the polling indicates. Of course, there are some extremely stupid and counterproductive ways of doing this that should be avoided.

Where I agree with the anarchist perspective is that no "thinking head and acting body"* notions and no mystified embodiment of the prospects for revolution in some individual "genius" is a substitute for actual changes in the collective understanding of what is—and of what is possible. This understanding can only develop and become a real social force through the experience of active resistance to the power of capital and the construction of a popular cultural alternative to capitalist "civilization." Notions of the general "objective" interests of some broader social group may be helpful to this process, and sometimes it is needed when it might not be so helpful, but such normative ideas are no substitute for decisions that the actual participants in the struggle recognize as their own.

Revolutionaries will normally encounter the issues of democracy and participation in complex situations where the issues of who should decide and who should participate are not clear-cut. In most cases, we will be a minority working within a larger minority—frequently not that much larger—under conditions where the domination of capital is at least potentially under challenge, where some resistance to its command has developed, and where there is a need to internalize and generalize the collective experience of struggle to effectively expand it and make the break with the "ruling ideas" as durable as possible.

Any expectation that greater democratic participation will provide the best answers to all such questions obscures the possibility that it can substitute lowest common denominator approaches for less comfortable and less popular initiatives that might prove to be more productive. It is not unlikely that a formally democratic and participatory approach will result in decisions that will not move the struggle forward, at least not in the view of the organized militants. At such moments in a struggle, a confrontation with a democratically developed "common sense" is likely to be important.

The problem is not only that operational participatory majorities will frequently diverge from "majorities" in a broader, quantitative, sociological view. Even internally, there is no guarantee that formal democratic procedures will promote the expansion and intensification of a continuing struggle. In fact, there will be many times when such "democracy" will cripple it. Such contradictions will frequently be reflected in tensions between the rank and file—including its effective leadership in "normal" conditions—and the organizing projects of revolutionary groups. It will be reflected more productively in tensions between emergent mass vanguards* and the elements tied to the existing class compromises.

This is not an argument against rank-and-file democracy and in favor of leadership and guidance of the struggle by organized groups of revolutionaries. More often than not, M-L formations are the first to capitulate to lowest common denominator politics. As Luxemburg forecast for socialist parties in general, they are typically an organized drag on revolutionary potentials and the setters and enforcers of bureaucratic limits at times when masses of people are breaking with them.[39] They are seldom the Jacobin insurrectionists—on balance, unfortunately, I would say.

This doesn't mean that revolutionaries must always urge the fight forward. Many of us have experienced strikes or comparable actions which have broken out of the institutionalized scripted routines and have seen a flowering of new leadership with new experiences of militant success and different conceptions of what success actually means. This upsurge of participation in a struggle, along with the more inclusive and substantive democratic discussion among the participants, can lead towards more basic confrontations with capitalist economic and political power. These waves of enthusiasm can also promote tactics that are not sustainable and objectives that are not attainable. This is not always a bad thing, but neither is it always good. It can result in significant and predictable setbacks and even lead to that "Revolutionary Suicide" that some Black Panthers perversely presented as a goal, or maybe it was a prediction.[40]

As a willing participant in the 60s, I have many examples of such situations, and they still flare up regularly at moments, like the height of the anti-globalization struggle. The result can be militant majorities of the moment that do not properly calculate the gaps and unevenness between what they are willing to do, and what they and others will support over time. Frequently, the root cause is that the experience of ruling-class repression is also "uneven" in distribution, and, more significantly, it is unevenly understood. Popular struggles can create militant operational majorities that do not appreciate that they have an enemy with the demonstrated willingness to kill hundreds of thousands to maintain power. They don't understand that they have an enemy that is also able to fine-tune repression, making its impact maliciously selective and compellingly divisive.

There will be points where it is important to retrench, consolidating advances and acknowledging losses, even while additional victories still seem attainable to many participants in the struggle. It will be unpopular, but it may be right to question or challenge a militant majority under such conditions. Of course, this should be done with the greatest of care, because nothing is more important than the willingness to fight collectively for important objectives, although they may appear to be "unrealistic." The very worst position for revolutionary groups is to be behind the struggle when the action starts, counseling caution and timidity, patience and the long view.

Organized revolutionary groups have made mistakes in all areas and in every conceivable direction. However, no listing of past or potential mistakes takes away the need for an organized activist project, a project that is more than a stance and a vision; one that raises the need to take risks, including the risk of being quite wrong, to help transform the political context and balance of forces. Without such a project, we will be either just waiting for the "event"*—pretty much guaranteeing that it will impact us more than we impact it—or bogged down in a deadening march through the institutions* that ties us tighter and tighter to the modes of operation that are realistic within them and binding ourselves to people who will almost certainly fall on the wrong side in an upsurge.

Beyond the issue of whether revolutionaries must organize themselves separately as a base from which to participate in class and popular mass struggles, there is the issue of the political content of that work. I agree with Gambone that the revolutionary group should be disciplined and that it should be politically unified along coherent ideological lines. However, the questions still remain: What does it do ... and how?

The vagueness of Wetzel's approach raises another problem. A potentially revolutionary working-class movement is a mortal threat to the ruling class, and any revolutionary grouping that attempts to implement a perspective towards this end will be recognized as a threat as soon as it begins to have some impact. The space for "legal" struggle has been much more constricted in this country in the fairly recent past; it is essentially absent right now in many other capitalist countries. If our movement mounts a less-feeble challenge to power, a continuation of open "legal" advocacy of anti-capitalist revolution is not a likely possibility. How does

Wetzel propose to deal with the power of the capitalist state and the potential for an expansion of repression? Will these issues never materialize because the US left is destined to remain a tolerated nuisance on the margins, providing a fig leaf of tolerance and openness to support the hegemonic power? I don't think so. In my experience, these issues have developed almost overnight in the past. It could happen again.

The questions of "legality" lead directly to the problems/potentials of military forms of struggle, and these also must be treated in a clear fashion. We know that these are immediate issues in much of the world, so how can they be off the table in the center of capitalist power? Is the assumption that the problems are so overwhelming that we should operate on the premise that legality will be the norm and not an improbability? This is a risky assumption for obvious reasons. One reason that may be less obvious is the growing presence of other revolutionary tendencies, from neo-fascist to national anarchist,* that explicitly do not accept it, and are increasingly attracted to modern theories of asymmetric, "Fourth Generation Warfare."[41]

Wetzel doesn't pursue these issues in what I've read, and I don't intend to pursue them here. I have to assume that he might think it is a discussion for another time and place—and another method and format—as I do also.

However, we are left with the situation where Wetzel appears to rely on a cooperative capitalist state standing aside until it is too late for a successful defense, allowing us to develop an effective counterpower that contends only with our bumbling and with working-class inertia. There is no indication of any responsibility for revolutionaries to prepare for the forceful destruction of the state apparatus of capitalism, when and where political circumstances make it possible. Not to mention the opposite responsibility to prevent premature or otherwise problematic military initiatives.

Instead, Wetzel offers a gradual and prolonged process of creating a dual power alternative through incremental steps which will "wither away" the capitalist counterpower.[42] This does not take adequate account of the very "unevenness" of struggle that Wetzel raises. It doesn't consider how today's advances can obstruct tomorrow's struggles—how concessions in one area can facilitate repression in another. It doesn't take account of other political players with other agendas who are not going to be content to sit back and watch. In short, I think it is a perspective with serious utopian downsides that will have a great difficulty transcending the "unevenness" of the struggle.

## "Social Insertion"

I want to make some comments on "social insertion," an aspect of some class struggle social anarchist perspectives that Wetzel endorses. I understand that this conception was initially projected to broaden the political approach for Latin American anarchist groups with a clandestine, armed-struggle background and focus. These groups encountered major problems relating to mass, working-class constituencies and mass struggles under changing political conditions. The notion must have some connection to the southern cone guerilla movements and their "continental strategy" that was influenced by the anarchist Abraham Guillen, a comrade of Durruti, and someone whose writings on armed struggle and revolutionary strategy I've always liked.[43]

Before I understood the origins of the concept, I had interpreted it as a welcome corrective to tendencies among US anarchists to confine political work within incestuous "scenes" and milieus, branded by generational and class privilege. But even with a more accurate understanding of the concept, I see some problems with Wetzel's brief description of it. I'd make two points. First, Wetzel appears to assume that organizations of revolutionaries are destined to be dominated by a declassed stratum, able to treat its living circumstances and class role as lifestyle options. While that may be an accurate description of present reality in this country, hopefully it is a reality that can be surpassed, and hopefully revolutionaries with working-class origins and working-class futures will play an increasingly central role more akin to the situation amongst the Chicago anarcho-syndicalists, the historic IWW, and, to a lesser extent, to some aspects of Communist Party and Trotskyist experience. Certainly, this change in social composition should be part of the short-range objectives of any revolutionary movement, and, at least under conditions of basic legality, there is no justification for not prioritizing it. In fact, in my opinion, the extent to which this objective is met and working-class "organic intellectuals" develop is an important test of the strategic perspectives that are being implemented.

Second, and perhaps more important, revolutionary groups must understand the potential impact of mass upsurges on their structures and methods and have the flexibility to respond to them. With modern possibilities for social movement and with instantaneous global communication, there may be moments when newly activated forces from the social base flood the political organizations with new ideas and new people who don't need to be inserted because they already come from the workplace and the community.

*Workplace Organizing*

When I look at the practical application of class struggle anarchist perspectives in this country, I'm not struck by the differences with Marxist-Leninist vanguardism as much as by similarities with M-L conservatism and incrementalism. Clear differences in political stance don't appear to result in significantly different approaches to work. If I was a naive visitor from Mars, I might think that—looking towards broader unity—this might have a potential good side. We know better than that. So, I'm more concerned with the bad side: with the common promotion of frameworks for struggle that fight for today's gains without seeing their potential to be tomorrow's problems, frameworks that too often incorporate the struggle within capital, thereby helping it adapt to changing circumstances.

I only want to make a few brief points limited to some issues in workplace organizing: the attitude towards contract unionism and "union reform" and the attitude towards the shop steward/committeeman post. This will take me quickly into areas where my lack of detailed knowledge of actual anarchist practice might result in exaggerations and other mistakes. As I have said, my reading has been limited and narrow, particularly with respect to approaches outside of North America. I would welcome corrections on any of this.

The tactical attitude towards unions, and particularly towards the workplace and the process of production, is an important question for the left—one with a range of options, not all of which are exclusive. One common approach is to emphasize work in organized workplaces that mobilizes a sufficient rank-and-file base to eventually capture and "reform" dysfunctional or collaborationist unions and revitalize "class struggle" unionism. Another, slightly less favored, is to emphasize work in unorganized situations (going "deeper into the class" as some less objectionable M-L groups say), intending to eventually organize and certify a union, or to decertify a "bad" union in favor of a "good" one. Then there are possibilities with "independent" and with dual unions, or alternatively, a "base committee" approach.

(I have had some experiences with all of the above, none particularly successful, but have always favored yet another option: organize a direct-action, mass grouping of workers at the point of production that can begin to understand the relevance of class issues beyond their particular shop floor—whatever the nature of the union or whether or not there is one. This approach has its problems as well, but they are a matter for a different discussion.)

It appears to me that class struggle social anarchism trends in this country tend to opt for more traditional approaches within the union reform genre. I don't think this is the case with Wetzel, based on his extended exchange with Carl Davidson that is appended to the article I've been citing.[44] However, there appears to be a bit of contract unionism, "boring from within," and NLRB fetishism in IWW circles.[45] Again, I may be factually wrong here, but, if I am not, this is questionable in this country, where trade unions and union contracts have formal juridical status and limits that constrict trade union organizing within a framework that explicitly recognizes and actively enforces the legitimacy of capitalist property rights and management prerogatives. The focus on contract unionism is usually a diversion from the issues of power in the workplace toward a quasi-parliamentary struggle for influence within the union—a form of struggle that the overwhelming majority of workers avoid like the plague. It is a diversion from the immediate arena of management command and worker resistance where the understanding of the potential power of autonomous organization can best be developed.

For those M-L groups whose ideal situation is to capture an elected paid union leadership position, or at least to become part of the organizing or educational staff, these factors do not present any problems. Their working objective is the accumulation of positions of influence and authority within reform movements. Wetzel is completely correct in criticizing this conceptualization of a revolutionary "leading role" that amounts to placing communists and their allies in leadership positions in reform movements and organizations. The situation is, or at least it should be, much more complicated for revolutionaries who are attempting to build centers of autonomous activity that challenge all forms of delegated authority.

Short of becoming a paid official, which is almost always a disaster, the closest approach to the actual class struggle normally available within the union reform perspective only gives radicals sufficient access and influence to open up negotiations with the union structure and its paid lawyers and organizers, acting as proxies for management. Even the best of such union-oriented work is forced to focus on the type of worker, the union militant, who is frequently a careerist and is recognized as such by peers—a "politician" who may talk a good militant and radical line when they are among the "outs" in the union, but only until they become the "ins." Such folks do not normally emerge as part of a militant organic leadership of significant struggles and, in fact, frequently turn out to be an additional layer of obstacles.

But what about the shop steward/shop committeeman? Is that a different position that can help radicals coalesce a revolutionary political base? I don't think so. Groups I have worked with in the past looked at the British shop stewards movement[46] as an organizing model, but found it inadequate, at least for this country. In the first place, there were significant differences in circumstances. The British union system at the time did not have legally binding specific term contracts that outlawed job actions, and the British shop stewards movement was not bound from the outset by those "no-strike" strictures as any parallel formation in this country would be. In Britain, the shop stewards grouping was able to organize job actions independently of the union structure, cutting across industrial divisions and union jurisdictions, even including the potential to initiate political strikes or a national general strike. There were clearly limits, but at least the British shop stewards generally represented workers to unions and management. In this country, shop stewards must enforce the contract and generally represent unions and management to workers.

Despite the fact that almost every left perspective shares the goal, the question of whether revolutionaries active in workplaces should aim to become shop stewards or similar officials is no slam dunk—not if the goal is revolutionary organizing work at the workplace. Shop steward credentials are not that hard to come by for radicals in most organized workplaces, unless they are completely socially dysfunctional. However, despite their cachet in radical subcultures, in the workplace the essence of the steward's role is to enforce labor discipline on other workers. That is the quid pro quo of the grievance system. Any steward who does not go along will not be an effective representative of the workers. Any steward who does go along will have problems "representing the interests of the future in the movements of the present."

The shop floor is the base point where workers can exercise their potential power over the work process. The steward function is a delegation of that power to an institution with a prior commitment not to employ it. It is infinitely better to have workers who still retain some trade unionist illusions learn for themselves from the contradictions impacting this role, rather than having revolutionaries acting as good reformists in the pursuit of some skewed notion of efficiency. I don't want to extend any of these arguments too far since, as I have said, I'm no longer that close to the actual discussions of people doing this work. I do think it is a topic area that should be pursued.

### Conclusion

I've recently read a report by an Irish social anarchist about a tour he took around the US and his impressions of the anarchist movement. He treated "insurrectionist anarchism" as essentially the anarchist primitivism* of the Eugene variant. Many working-class oriented social anarchists appear willing to cede the politics of insurrection to various "post-left" elements, including the "crazies" among the lifestyle anarchists, and treat it as an element of generational extremism, a posture that will collapse in the face of any real repression, if not the mere possibility of repression, such as followed after 9/11.

I think that the issue of insurrection—the basic reason to take Lenin seriously—is an essential element of a revolutionary perspective right now. Most class struggle social anarchists would probably disagree, but I think this conclusion is a clear implication from Wetzel's concept of "unevenness." Given the ebbs and flows of the revolutionary process in various geographies and institutional frameworks, and the different impacts of alternative policies of suppression and incorporation, it's unlikely that any political perspective can advance incrementally towards a revolutionary transformation. There will need to be moments where an exercise of collective will—a leap into the realm of the possible with no guarantees—will break the normal routines. As the class struggle develops globally in distinct territories with different stages of development and different rates of change forming a complex mosaic, the issue of whether to take power when it appears possible, but perhaps also problematic, will inevitably emerge. The revolutionary response will either be more or less prepared—or unprepared, and therefore certainly inadequate.

The development of mass revolutionary potential is the result of sharp breaks and new normals that can produce a stratum of insurrectionists who may not even have been reformists yesterday. Alain Badiou, whom I must get around to reading (instead of reading about), has this conception of "event"—a sharp epochal change that transforms potentials for revolutionaries, if they recognize what is happening and are not trapped in old paradigms until the time is passed. The new revolutionaries made possible by the event are not discovered through a process of patiently arguing and convincing, they create and discover themselves through unexpected leaps in perception and self-conception that happen in actions, fights, and struggles.[47]

In this context, we should be aware of some specific liabilities that are tied to our ultimate goals as communists. We look to promote a universalistic liberatory future. But the very "unevenness" of the political circumstances creates obstacles to our perspective that are advantages to certain of our radical rivals. Rivals who also look to take advantage of an "event," but in ways that threaten to unleash a centrifugal spiral into barbarism.

# V. ANTI-REPRESSION

### Three Tendencies on Repression
### Fragments of an Unfinished Piece
*no date*

First tendency after a casual disregard of repression is to consider it as an overriding ruling-class inclination, but as a blunt instrument applied casually and haphazardly;

Second tendency is to be overwhelmed by the potential sophistication and universality of the repressive apparatus and the limitations of our capacities to respond;

Third tendency is to understand we have a conscious opponent, but one subject to a range of contradictions and resulting political limits—although not absolute ones.

## Repression
## Fall 2001

*This document originally appeared in the second issue of the* Anti-Racist Action Research Bulletin *as an unsigned editorial. The reader should also note that between the first issue where Hamerquist's essay "Third Position" appeared and the second issue containing this essay, the 9/11 attacks had taken place and the landscape of mass state repression had changed dramatically.*

Even in very small towns, ARA* is finding an increasingly sophisticated police response to its confrontations with fascists. This response is clearly organized and coordinated at the regional and federal levels, and this is probably only the tip of an iceberg that includes a good deal of international cooperation. Beyond our anti-fascist and anti-racist work, we are also part of a general radical insurgency both in spirit and in many cases in body. There is no doubt that the state is organizing countermeasures to this insurgency. This necessitates a clearer understanding of state repression on our part.

Everyone in our section of the movement is generally aware of state repression, but a general awareness isn't going to cut it. The bizarre arrest of Jaggi Singh and the sting operation leading up to the arrests of the Germinal Five in Quebec should not be seen as isolated incidents, but as part of a policy.[1] The federal grand juries operating in the Northwest and in Michigan and the increasingly coordinated response to every situation where a black bloc develops also point to an emerging repressive policy.

There is no doubt that the state is taking us seriously. We should also take ourselves seriously. Playing the innocent victim is not serious. Treating repressive policies as if they were reflexive reactions of idiots and thugs is not serious. Much of the content of movement talk about "criminalizing dissent," about mass and pre-emptive arrests, about police brutality and "non-lethal weaponry" substitutes a liberal public relations stance, and an ineffectual one at that, for an analysis. We won't get anywhere or gain anything by reacting to incidents of repression with appeals to civil libertarian rights to protest. The state isn't committed to these "rules of the game," and the movement isn't either—or at least it shouldn't be.

It is quite unlikely that "criminalizing dissent" or any other clumsy and generalized strong state posture will be the major element of repressive policy. To the contrary, when the movement reaches the level that we have reached, the most important features of repression will come from the doctrines of counterinsurgency and low-intensity warfare. These doctrines emphasize mapping, encapsulating, and eventually determining the direction of the movement. We should be examining our encounters with state repression from this perspective. The reactionary, rhetorical law and order crap that is a staple of ruling-class propaganda should be dismissed with the contempt it deserves.

We intend to deal with the issues of repression in the near future. This will include counterinsurgency policies, some of the limitations on the use of these policies, and some ways of countering them. We also want to look at some specific examples, both current and historical, to see if anything helpful can be learned. Any contributions in this area are welcome.

## On Some Historical Examples of Repression
## April 2011

*This piece was sent as an email to comrades in order to share some candid reflections about experiences Hamerquist and other had with state repression.*

Repression can be a broad or a narrow topic. I aim to go in the latter direction and focus on a couple of specific areas of state repression that impact the revolutionary left. Perhaps a different title, "things we should have figured out, but we're slow," would be appropriate. However, there is a danger that this approach might lose some broader aspects of the issue in a mass of details and anecdotes, so I will begin with some general propositions.

The basic structure of capital, both the reality and the book,[1] rests on the appearance of an "exchange of equal values" disguising a reality that is an "appropriation without exchange." The capitalist ruling class has a general interest in cloaking this reality in social forms and ideologies that can enlist dominated majorities as participants and even administrators in their own subordination.

Foucault's "carceral logic" explains this behavior as "something like an inner compulsion indistinguishable from our will, immanent to and inseparable from our subjectivity itself" (Hardt and Negri 2003, 329). This social discipline underlies Engels's observation that the "best form of rule for capital" is a parliamentary democracy where real power relations can be hidden behind a competition between different interests, in which everyone appears to get what they deserve and are "worth."[2] These processes are clearly a part of the repressive aspect of capitalism and a major element in its general elasticity, but they should not be confused with the overt exercise of command over a subject population that will be the emphasis here. However, they are an important ruling-class advantage that will not be given away, and they do provide some limitations on overt repression. Their persistence in our corner of the world is why notions of a ruling-class drive to maximize repression—or to institute fascism—should be viewed with substantial skepticism.

There are real questions whether the global capitalist system is changing in ways that maximize repression and reduce the functional value of formal democracy for the ruling class. These are consequences of the narrowing limits on the capacity of capitalist governmental structures to "deliver political goods" (Robb 2009), and the growing weight of state and non-state repressive capacities on "hollowed out"* governmental formations. (Lewis and Leys 2010). In these changing political circumstances, repressive policies can evolve and transform rapidly and unpredictably. It's easy to forget this point when the left focuses too narrowly on time-specific policies, incidents, and experiences.

That said, let's get narrow. I'm assuming familiarity with the *New State Repression* (Lawrence 1985) thesis that locates systematic political repression as an element of a low-intensity conflict/counterinsurgency ruling-class strategy, and not as the outcome of some inherent capitalist tendency towards the erosion of bourgeois democratic legality and "rights."

In the early 80s, the Sojourner Truth Organization* brought together a number of groups that were under substantial police pressure to coordinate a political response to repression. Given the participants, this was a doomed effort and I can only wonder what we were thinking. Predictably, little survived past the first meeting. Despite a formal agreement on the main argument of *New State Repression*, there was no genuine commitment to its criticisms of the claims of "innocence," "frame-up," "provocation," and the assertions of *"rights"* that dominated left responses to repression. All of these groups, except STO, ultimately embraced this "united front" posture for their own political defense. This was despite the fact that their repression was clearly related to their distinctive political stances that explicitly challenged capitalist power and, if anything, over-emphasized illegal work and armed struggle.

This produced an ineffectual response to their repression, based on implausible notions that "everyone's 'rights' are under attack," which disrupted serious discussion of their actual experienced repression and the development of a plausible and coherent radical political response to it. Unfortunately, it seems to me that this is still the dominant approach in the US left, although I'd welcome evidence that I'm wrong.

After this still-born organizational initiative, a small group of us continued practical work in the area. This was based on involvement with many of the major political defense cases and with the "anti–Red Squad" class action suits in New York, Chicago, and Los Angeles.[3] This experience included work with the National Lawyers Guild, *Counterspy*, and the *Covert Action Information Bulletin* on the continuing analysis of the information gained from the initial capture of the COINTELPRO* documents and from the Church and Pike Committees.[4] We were also involved in significant local investigations into the Chicago Red Squad and the Mississippi State Sovereignty Commission.[5] Most important, we had extensive direct political relations with most of the groups and individuals in the Black, Mexican, Puerto Rican, and Native movements that were experiencing systematic surveillance and penetration from the state, which provided the basis for their legal and extra-legal repression and disruption. We aimed to document the lessons learned about the nature and trajectory of police and extra-police repression of political tendencies that were viewed as dangerous by ruling-class fractions, and to organize the information in a useful form. We hoped to develop informer/provocateur profiles and case studies of significant experiences of political repression.

We also intended to check our hypothesis that the Kitson/Everleigh counterinsurgency strategy[6] that had emerged in response to the upsurge of national liberation and socialist struggles following WWII was actually becoming the dominant policy motivation underlying political repression in this country. It's important to see how the policies associated with this counterinsurgency model developed and became more central, without losing track of some features of political repression that don't fit the model.

The changes in the state treatment of communist activity and the CPUSA help in understanding this trajectory. Initially, the US state (FBI) had approached communism as a social pathology, an asset of a foreign enemy that lacked any potential to develop a political base but was a danger as a "fifth column." The proposed cure for this "sickness" was a combination of surgery and quarantine for the infected population and the inoculation of the "healthy" population through exposure of the doctrine. Following WWII, these policies were embodied in a wave of repression that criminalized communist organization (Communist Control Act) and communist ideology (Smith Act) and that jailed the entire CPUSA leadership.

However, as international class and anti-imperialist struggle movements produced a much broader popular base for anti-imperialist and anti-capitalist politics, this traditional policing approach became increasingly counterproductive. The policy change towards national liberation by the Carter Administration in the late 70s marked a clear erosion of the traditional repression models and its gradual replacement with counterinsurgency doctrine.

It's important to recall the circumstances of the late 60s and the 70s in this country. The political climate was increasingly hostile to forcible government action in general and to police and policing in specific. A flood of damaging information on state repression that normally would be closely held became broadly available. Some of this was leaked and some was captured. Some key players in the repressive structures went through ideological conversions. This included cops of all sorts—not only the occasional ideological convert, but a cohort of participants in repressive initiatives. Information came from flipped agents and informants who felt misused by the system when they found themselves in political and legal hot water, sometimes facing jail time and more often career impasses. Some of these were reacting from being maneuvered into public exposure or other disruptive life changes—and this is not to forget the role of the cash nexus with those "recanters" who objected to the cuts in their piece rate payments as the information they provided lost value.

These circumstances provided us with background information on the operation of dozens of informer/provocateurs. Some of these were major operations with far-ranging impacts, like Doug Durham in AIM; William O'Neill in the Chicago Panthers; the Childs brothers, aka "Solo," in the CPUSA; and John Dial in the Mexican/Southern Cone support structure.[7] Other examples, more local and "typical," were gathered from a wide variety of movement sources.

(Towards the end of the project, this work included material about the state use of informers and provocateurs against neo-fascist groupings. One of the more frustrating elements of radical left myopia is the mindset that can't accept the possibility that a capitalist state would utilize counterinsurgency methods to repress a radical challenge from its right. Hopefully, this view has become less pervasive.)

We developed the information through careful readings of numerous government and court documents as well as through direct and indirect interviews. There were sufficient common features in these case studies to develop something of an informer profile. It is rather straightforward stuff and the basic organizational defense countermeasures are hardly rocket science.

Despite TV depictions, political informants are almost never undercover cops. In general, they are not the most stable types and aren't working out of principled ideological motivations. In the cases where they believed in pro-capitalist politics, it was very difficult for them to plausibly debate and advocate revolutionary positions they did not hold. In a number of such cases, they ended up as converts to the left (or so they said). Such informants were most effective in situations where they did not have to think and argue about politics but could regurgitate a line in slogan form or in macho stance. Unfortunately, then as now, the US left was quite generous in providing such opportunities.

A simple lesson is that any political grouping that is (or might be) working outside of the framework of capitalist legality should pay specific attention to who is working with them. Make sure to pursue questions of family and employment background (without getting anal), questions of unusual access to resources, and questions of any excessive avoidance or embracing of physical and legal risk. Perhaps most important, don't tolerate any form of anti-social behavior because an individual is doing "valuable" political work, is strategically positioned, has technical capabilities, or is otherwise "important." When security questions are raised about individuals, deal with them promptly and frontally without relying on organizational techniques, particular hierarchical structures, and "need to know" restrictions. These don't normally work at all, often drawing more police attention and maximizing damage from police penetration while creating their own problems of unaccountable leadership which can render the police penetration superfluous.

Finally, avoid the terrible self-delusion that this stuff doesn't really matter very much, and that it will be good enough to make sure that any agents who may be in the ranks do effective political work. This posture frequently draws support from a specific aspect of Bolshevik history in the following form: "Although their leadership was penetrated by the Tsarist Okhrana for decades, the Bolsheviks managed a successful revolution." That's a rationalization that Lenin perpetuated ... also an illusion that can get people killed.

So, on to a few observations of more general relevance. We found that the state is particularly concerned with maintaining and extending its "human intelligence" capabilities (informers and provocateurs). Downplaying its reliance on human intelligence—on actual penetration by agents—and exaggerating the significance of spying hardware and technical methodologies, provides the state a number of practical and ideological advantages, some obvious and some not so much. The image of an Orwellian state with overwhelming capacities to impose sanctions and to limit the possibilities for effective radical action does have real ideological weight and propaganda value.

However, without dismissing the importance of population mapping and modeling, remote surveillance methodologies, digital forensics, etc. these methods are normally quite costly and cumbersome for the state. Most important, at moments of elevated struggle they are too passive and reactive to have an impact on rapidly changing conditions. Consequently, in many cases we found that technological surveillance was instituted as a result of human intelligence and used to cover the fact that the group was not only spied on but penetrated. At times this meant losing crucial items of evidence in legal proceedings from the inability or unwillingness to disclose the basis on which they had been obtained.

Another variation on this theme used a cooperative media to promote *Reader's Digest* versions of events in major political arrests. These "explained" policing successes with "hand of God" stories and fortuitous "accidents" at crucial moments: the nosey neighbor, the vigilant janitor, the stupid traffic violation. These were also managed so as to maximize the cover for any informants who were still in place. We should look very hard at everything of that nature.

It should be assumed that it is not likely to be a casual and haphazard act when the state exposes an informant. At times, it's a preemptive action to harvest some benefits before the asset is lost for one or another reason. In more important cases it might have a dual purpose of exposing an unproductive informant to help credential and position more productive and versatile ones. There are numerous documented instances where individuals were accused of being informants, some falsely and some not, with evidence that was developed by actual informants and provocateurs with access to state resources. This happened in my experience with COINTELPRO,* which targeted the CPUSA and the Black Panthers. There are similar examples in various international movements—not to mention in state action against neo-fascist groupings in this country such as the "Order,"* the Posse Comitatus,* and the post-Pierce National Alliance.*

Let me go off topic to consider some important ways that concrete repression doesn't fit neatly within the counterinsurgency paradigm that I favor. Given the reality that actual class rule involves complicated political overdeterminations, including both incorporative concessions and fragmenting repressions, it is certainly possible that some ruling-class fractions will be less interested in the best way to repress an actual or potential radical opposition than in seizing an opportunity to improve its political leverage or economic advantage in some other areas. For example, it is pure cover story to consider "homeland security" to be an optimally efficient response to "terrorism." In fact, its arbitrary and comic book aspects promote mass cynicism about any need for a larger repressive role for a larger state. The "repression" involved here is another manifestation of crony capitalism, not an attempt to neutralize a real threat.

The repressive apparatus is increasingly reluctant to put its human assets in radical groupings at risk for extraneous political purposes that have very minor repressive impacts. This became a factor, for example, in the abandonment of the HUAC/exposure mode of state repression with Congressman McDonald's crash and burn demise—although it was not the only, or the most important, consideration in that process.[8]

We should also recognize a distorting intervention of "politics" in repression from our side of the process. This can involve cases where the radical group courts repression, both its own and that of broader circles, as part of a political strategy that emphasizes symbolic organizing around figures of heroic opposition. This is doubly serendipitous for the state. It's relieved of the necessity to expose its human assets to make a public case, and actually gains possibilities to expand such assets and capabilities at little cost or risk. This happens, for example, when state repression is met with the variant of radical stupidity that creates new "traitors" and "penitenti"* by placing unreasonable demands on weak and wavering cadres. These are then retroactively snitchjacketed and become the explanation for past security failures. This works out conveniently both for the state, which can protect its real operational assets, and for the incompetent leadership of radical groups, which can mask their own failures with moral condemnations of turned cadre.

I'm working up to some major points and perhaps it is best to get to them directly:

1. The state repression that we should worry about the most is not focused on "illegalizing dissent," and it is not aimed at putting the radical leadership in jail and decapitating the movement.

2. The primary function of state repression is not intelligence gathering, it is an intervention into a radical opposition aimed at influencing and, if possible, determining its politics.

3. There is no necessary correlation between the choice of a target for state repression and the political effectiveness or strategic importance of the targeted organization or its leadership.

The notion that the state is actually aiming to jail "everyone who disagrees"—or all "peace lovers"—is nonsense. To the contrary, there is a good bit of evidence of the reluctance to criminalize dissent and the willingness to minimize its costs. There are many cases where the state deliberately chooses not to treat radical opposition as criminal, even when it is clearly "criminal" and when both the information and the power to take such action exists.

There is reason to believe that certain instances of repression are selected and implemented primarily to credential incompetent and corrupt political leaderships. In some cases, pre-emptive arrests play a major role in the formation of leadership of mass insurgencies. I'm not only thinking of Egypt and the Google Guy, but also certain leaders and "spokespeople" for anti-globalization protests who are conveniently rounded up before they are confronted with major issues of tactics and strategies, and then released for the appropriate press conferences and celebrity trials that are more likely to increase name recognition than result in hard time.[9]

Rather than extend this further, I will end with an example that may be familiar to some of you, but probably not most: the "Solo" operation that penetrated the leadership of the CPUSA and, ultimately, the international communist movement. I will hit some high points; for greater detail, google "Solo Morris Childs CPUSA."

"Solo" began when the FBI recruited two Chicago brothers who had left the CP in a factional dispute in the late 1940s. One of them, Morris, had been a fairly major figure, the editor of the party newspaper for a time. In the early 50s, the FBI convinced the brothers and their wives to rejoin the CP as informants and set up Morris Child with a completely subsidized jewelry business front that provided cover for frequent trips abroad.

Over roughly a quarter century, the Solo operation provided a direct window for the FBI into the political and financial relationship between the US and Soviet parties. At crucial points—e.g., the 20th Congress critique of Stalin and the "81 Party" Congress split between the Soviets and the Chinese—it provided an effective tool to intervene in a number of political conjunctures, domestically and internationally.[10]

The Solo operation provided conclusive proof that for decades the Soviet Union had directly financed the US party. This charge was always a major contention of the official campaign against the party, but this proof for it was not made public at the cost of major political embarrassments for J. Edgar himself.[11] Clearly, the very narrow circles of high-level politicos who were aware of the existence of the operation—all of whom were committed to the public fight against communism—thought the military-strategic-political value of the penetration outweighed the propaganda value of exposing the relationship. The penetration created numerous possibilities to encapsulate radical potentials domestically and globally, while institutionalizing incompetent "revolutionary" leadership by funneling them resources in ways that made political account-ability a joke. I think that there is evidence that similar motivations underlie some current repressive initiatives.

The circumstances which grounded the Solo operation are also instructive. After Hoover's death, and with the exposure of COINTELPRO by the Media, PA operation, the FBI became increasingly preoccupied with justifying its campaigns against Martin Luther King, Jr., which had created widespread suspicions that it was complicit in his assassination.

The well-known book by David Garrow (1981), *The FBI and Martin Luther King, Jr.*, raised a new FBI justification for treating King as a closet communist. It argued that credible information supporting this conclusion had been gathered from a high-level FBI penetration of the CPUSA which they had named Solo. At the time, we assumed that the FBI had planted the information in Garrow's book, and we made attempts to look into it further—including (don't laugh) contacting the leadership of the CPUSA. I'm not sure of the actual sequence of events, but according to the subsequent FBI-sponsored book on the Solo operation (Barron 1997), the furor over the Garrow book, combined with some other problems in maintaining the cover for the operation, led to its termination. Morris Childs disappeared, but his official biogra-phy has a photograph of him getting the Medal of Freedom from Reagan to go along with the Order of Lenin he had gotten earlier from Brezhnev.

We approached the CPUSA and recommended a damage assessment of the Solo operation (don't laugh).[12]

# VI. ANALYSIS

## On Transnational Capitalism
**March 2022**

(Contemporary) capitalism is a transnational economic/financial system with an emerging transnational ruling class that increasingly recognizes it is facing growing risks of secular crises* that have existential significance. These risks are complicated by uncertainty resulting from "black swan" impacts[1] and by political/cultural state apparatuses that increasingly lack the capacity to deal with contradictions between segments of capital and between capital and its restive oppressed and exploited populations. The basic economic premise of this transnational capitalist system— the unfettered flow of capital to areas of maximum returns—constantly undermines and hollows the brittle and corrupt state and regulatory institutions that are its major hopes for maintaining and renewing a stable legitimacy. Though this social formation is extremely unstable, there is no real possibility that its basic financial architecture will collapse back into a nation-state-based imperial structure.

This framework encompasses the "hollow state" notions taken from Colin Leys and John Robb;[2] the significance of "financialization" following the 2008–9 crisis that was aided by the work of Yves Smith and Michael Hudson;[3] and the "flailing and churning" characterization of contemporary capitalism, which belongs to Dave Ranney (2014).

## Email to K on the Iraq War
### ca. 2005

*This was written as part of a discussion regarding the causes of the US invasion and occupation of Iraq and how the left should relate to it. A number of points in this email reference previous correspondence; these should be clear from the context.*

I want to respond tentatively because I'm unsure of my own positions and don't want to stick out my neck too far. Also because, as with all serious questions, the "answers" don't exist some place but will be determined in struggle. The trick will be to approach the struggle prepared to think and act creatively. Who can illuminate this path better than a worn-out commie, living far out in the woods and unprepared to take much responsibility for constructing "acts to the end"*?

You are certainly right that classic inter-imperialist rivalries motivated by economic considerations are still a factor. Obviously, part of the ruling-class reaction against the neocons[1] in this country is based on notions of prioritizing the interests of US capital. The global strategy document just released by the CIA's "think tank," the National Intelligence Council, appears to be arguing in part from such premises when it projects that a polarization with China will be the decisive reality for the next few decades.

My argument is that these contradictions are rapidly becoming less important and that the growing influence of the neocons demonstrates this fact. Not only are they being superseded, where they continue to be a factor the content has changed. It makes a real difference if the inter-imperialist contradictions focus on "divvying up the booty" or the "different strategies of rule." To the extent that you regard them as essentially similar in function, I think you are mistaken.

238

Let me indicate two ways in which the apparent inter-imperialist rivalries can be a mystifying shell for a content of contradictions around priorities and strategies of rule.

First, the neocons' perspective involves taking risks and making sacrifices in terms of the structures and institutions of capitalist rule in the center. The Iraqi "extension of democracy"[2] proceeded through a transparent manipulation of facts against the clearly evident majority opinion of virtually every conceivable constituency. This sort of thing exposes the reality that parliamentary structures in the center don't determine policy and weakens those important hegemonic mechanisms. A further risk that the neocons willingly assume is that the fruits of structural adjustment and market domination might be brought home, undermining the social wage and reducing national privileges for the center working classes—and, as a consequence, undermining the flexibility to incorporate dissent and part of the material basis for relative domestic tranquility. There are differences among segments of the ruling class and thus among imperialist states about the wisdom of this. It is the same difference that exists within national ruling classes and was evident in this country in the Kerry campaign.[3] It is not a traditional inter-imperialist conflict.

Second, in my opinion all of the neocon variants mean to scrap major aspects of existing state relations to ensure that capitalist power can be actively employed in the major areas of crisis ("system perturbations"!) that they see developing in the "Non-Integrating Gap."[4] Thus, both Niall Ferguson and Thomas Barnett[5] propose new international structures of rule, disregarding the UN and existing multinational arrangements in ways that potentially downgrade or even eliminate the role of states that are currently major players. There are major conflict potentials here, for example, in France and Russia seeing a diminished role in the future—perhaps even becoming more an object than a subject of the use of capitalist power.

Let me look at the issue in another way—raised by your invocation of Halliburton.[6] Of course, all capitalists want to maximize returns and competitive advantages. This should be a beginning assumption of any analysis, however, not its major conclusion. Ruling-class policy must consider policy in areas where there are conflicts between blocs of capital, where the gain of one may well be the loss of another. It must act in areas where there is no simple and clear relationship between short-term and long-term "profits"—where there are major problems in determining the likely consequences of policy alternatives, because these may be affected by conscious and organized actors, by political resistance, which is not susceptible to the available metrics.

Two questions, then: what might lead a bloc of capital, such as "big oil," to see its economic interest in this particular Iraq policy; and what is the evidence that they actually exerted political pressure in this direction?

There is actual evidence that the oil industry in Britain and the US counseled against this policy in general and against the long-term military occupation of Iraq in particular. They argued that the potential disruption in the area was risky and that they had worked successfully with the existing political structures, institutions, and elites in the Middle East for the better part of a century (remember that the same interests were lukewarm to the intervention in Afghanistan as well because of the potential damage to oil transport arrangements from the Caucasus). I know of no evidence that any segment of the oil cartel publicly argued in favor of regime change in Iraq. If this happened, it would certainly have been out of character.

Beware of truisms like the *Monthly Review* editorial which trumpets that Iraq is all about oil reserves and supply routes etc., a position that says exactly nothing more than capitalism is about the interests of capital. How those interests are understood and differences within the ruling class about how they are implemented are the issue.

This situation is not like those referenced in the famous Gen. Smedley Butler quote, "I [the US Marines] went into Guatemala for United Fruit" ... etc.[7] The operative parallel to the current situation is not United Fruit in Guatemala, but Dow Chemical in Vietnam. Dow went bankrupt. This is why I think it is childish economic determinism to draw a line of causality from "oil imperialism" to Halliburton to Cheney to the war. The more likely causality goes in the opposite direction. Halliburton has the "Iraq contract" because their competitors would be more likely to pack up and leave after a dose of kidnappings, "IEDs," and suicide bombings. Halliburton is an effect, not the cause, of the policy.

It is easier to argue that "oil imperialism" dictated the very different policy of Bush, Sr., Baker, Powell, and Scowcroft in the first Iraq war. Remember that Cheney was Secretary of Defense before he was CEO of Halliburton. Indeed, he was Secretary of Defense during the first Gulf War. It is probably believed that he was an opponent of the policy at that time and wanted to March on Baghdad and "FINISH THE JOB." Not true. In a speech in Seattle in 1992, Cheney said:

> How many additional casualties is Saddam worth? … I think we got it right, both when we expelled him from Kuwait, but also when the president made the decision that we'd achieved our objectives and we were not going to go get bogged down in the problems of trying to take over and govern Iraq. (Connelly 2004).

The stated objectives in the first Gulf War focused on oil. Iraq invaded Kuwait, claiming that it was stealing oil from Iraq's southern fields through slant drilling techniques. The US argued that intervention was required to prevent an Iraqi invasion of Saudi Arabia, the world's major oil reserve and oil producer as well as the major lever to prevent any recurrence of the OPEC problems that had emerged in the early 70s.[8]

Clearly, Cheney's position has changed 180 degrees. Can anyone seriously believe that this happened because he got a Halliburton job? In order to get some contracts for his erstwhile employer? Not likely. None of these worthies are preoccupied by worries about income, theirs or their companies'. In fact, as

Cheney regularly and honestly says, his position changed because his estimate of the nature of the global threat to capitalism, including the oil industry, changed. He bought into the neocons' analysis and, wisely or not, from the perspective of capital, he is acting and arguing accordingly.

Let me stop here, although there is much more to consider on the economic field, such as the significance of the trade and currency imbalances, the disputes over agricultural and business subsidies, the political significance of transnational corporate consolidation, the fact that "foreign" capital constitutes 25% of the US equities market, etc.

## Barack, Badiou, and Bilal al Hasan
## January 2010

*This essay originally appeared on the anti-fascist blog Three Way Fight (Hamerquist 2010).*

Author's introduction:
A few years ago I argued that significant changes in capitalist power and policy should require changes in the way the left approached global politics and working-class revolution.[1] At the time, my focus was on globalization, the neo-conservative phenomenon, and the war in Iraq.

This piece attempts to expand the discussion to include the impact of a global economic crisis and a different political face for the ruling class in the US. I hope to open up two questions: the first concerns the origins, objectives, and implications of ruling-class strategic policy—particularly with respect to the flexibility to reconsider and change it. The other, and more important, question concerns the development of a more useful conceptual framework for the left. On the second point I rely substantially on Negri* and Hardt's critical treatment of the political framework associated with the Leninist theory of Imperialism—particularly as it was developed in their work *Empire* (2000). In case it is not completely clear from the context, this does not entail acceptance of major aspects of Negri's approach to class analysis and revolutionary strategy. Some of these issues are considered in more detail in continuing discussions on the *Three Way Fight* website.[2]

*d.h., 2022*

Obama has made his speech on Afghanistan, and we should think about what it entails and implies.[3]

The majority of the US left looks at these issues in the context of classical conceptions of imperialism, emphasizing the interests of US capital in maintaining and extending its dominant position: in the first place, against popular anti-imperialist movements; but with increasing frequency, also against purported imperialist rivals.

Two examples:

This war is not about "defending the American people"—but establishing a stable US domination over a highly strategic arc reaching from Iran ... to Pakistan. ... It is a war for consolidating US domination in large parts of the world. (Ely, *Kasama\**, 12/2/2009)

All this, apart from the religious aspect ... is about oil. But not just oil, but all other resources, and not just resources, but the control of those resources and the fear of a rising multi-polarity being led by the Chinese with accompaniment by a renewed belligerence of Russia and the rising economic power of Brazil and India among others (the BRIC nations). (Miles, *Znet*, 12/4/2009)[4]

I realize these short excerpts don't adequately express either Ely or Miles's full positions. However, taking them as they stand, whatever their other merits, neither helps explain why Obama is implementing this particular policy and not another—potentially quite different—one.

"Protecting the US"—establishing an "arc of domination" in Southwest Asia—acting against a "rising multi-polarity" within the global capitalist system—these may or may not point to some of the motivations that underlie US policy in general, but the goal of "US domination" could arguably be implemented through policies which were quite different. Non-military interventions could be pursued rather than costly and unpromising wars. A concentration on mounting problems closer to the "homeland" could be prioritized to ensure there actually was a more "stable" base from which to expand "US domination."

The other day I ran across this in a column by Tom Friedman, perhaps the best-known publicist for global capitalism:

Frankly, if I had my wish we would be on our way out of Afghanistan not in, we would be letting Pakistan figure out which Taliban they want to conspire with and which one they want to fight, we would be letting Israelis and Palestinians figure out on their own how to make peace, we would be taking $100 billion out of the Pentagon budget to make us independent of imported oil. (Friedman 2010)

There is no question whether Friedman would prefer a stable US domination over this section of the world—this "strategic arc." Of course he would. There is no question that Friedman is worried about the weakening of US economic power relative to its capitalist competition and to the challenges it faces—he's written a number of irritating books on the subject. But there is also no question that he supports a substantially different approach from the current Obama policy. This possibility for substantially different ruling-class policies from sectors and spokespeople of the class that share substantial agreements on assumptions and objectives, should motivate us to look beyond our own generic "explanations." This is particularly true when, as is the case here, these explanations are firmly rooted in the political categories of a past where we didn't do all that well.

So what "facts" support these postulated US imperialist objectives in Afghanistan? Do the gas pipelines, the narcotics trade, the copper mining proposals, and similar factors create a clear interest for US capital that is appropriately pursued by this grotesquely asymmetric use of military force? Which US ruling-class fractions have organized to promote these interests? Where is the trail of influence from these alleged interests to the adopted policy?

If the goal in Afghanistan actually is that of "consolidating US domination," one obvious objective would be establishing a friendly and stable pro-capitalist regime. Exactly how does a more consolidated domination emerge out of increasingly destabilized territories and regimes? An institutionalized and protracted external domination is certainly implied by the Obama policy, but this will make Afghanistan and the region less friendly and a whole lot less stable, not more so.

It is hard to see how a "stable consolidated US domination" might develop out of these policies under the best conditions. If it is also assumed that US policy is confronting a "rising multi-polarity" based in rival centers of capitalist power that are looking to gain some relative advantage, failure is virtually guaranteed. This leaves us with a postulated goal—stable, consolidated domination—that would be completely at odds with the means—military conquest and occupation by limited forces. My firm belief is that the ruling class does not subject itself to stress tests that it has no reason to believe it can pass. We must find better explanations for what is happening than these.

Let's look a little closer at the "rising multi-polarity" version of inter-imperialist conflict that is presented by Miles. There is no doubt that there are inter-imperialist conflicts and contradictions in the region, but what is their relationship to this Afghanistan policy? Does any potential inter-imperialist conflict over Afghan resources or its strategic location (US/NATO vs. BRIC is the one Miles proposes) outweigh the historic conflicts in the region— between Russia and China, between China and India, between India and Pakistan? Does it outweigh all three countries' counterparty status, or the dependence of the BRIC states on inter-imperialist coordination to maintain stability in the international financial and commodity markets? Does it outweigh their common interests in managing internal populist unrest—perhaps with Chinese Uyghurs and Russian Chechens—or threats to Russia's interests in the formerly Soviet "stans"? Does it outweigh the common interests of these rivals in combatting "terrorism," such as that flowing from Naxalite peasant insurgency,[5] from newly marginalized Chinese workers, or from neo-fascist tendencies in the ruling Hindu elites and among the Russian National Bolsheviks?[6] I'd say no, inter-imperialist contradictions don't outweigh these factors, and if there were any possibilities that they might, we wouldn't be in Afghanistan in the way that we are—nor in Iraq, for that matter.

In short, most left explanations of the underpinnings and objectives of Obama's Afghanistan policy don't provide an adequate explanation of the concrete policy, of the adaptations it might undergo in the future, nor of the policy alternatives to it—such as Friedman's—that may or may not be viable. Actually, they are worse than inadequate because, sometimes explicitly and sometimes by default, they contribute to the widespread left common sense that holds that it is not particularly important to look for coherent explanations of specific ruling-class policies. Perhaps because, as Kolko has said, there are no such explanations since ruling-class policies are just an incoherent result of the interplay of the most immediate and crass motives of economic and political self and sectoral interest.[7]

Other analyses come to similar results without utilizing Kolko's variant of chaos theory. They see US capitalism being pushed towards desperation, making it prone to fundamentally illogical, even irrational, positions—to "mistakes." Such positions were more popular and more explicit during the previous administration—particularly with respect to Iraq policy. The Bush regime was easy to picture as ignorant and venal, mistake-prone and even incompetent from a ruling-class perspective. It was easy but, I think, essentially wrong. This mindset contributes to a dumb left optimism in which analyses of ruling-class motives and perspectives are regarded as unproductive and unnecessary. In the process, all the important distinctions between a radical and a liberal opposition to ruling-class policies get muddy. For a case in point, look at the pervasive overestimation of the different policies that a supposedly more clear-headed incoming Obama administration would pursue. Many on the left went this route and are still scrambling to catch up.

In fact, except for some unimportant, largely cosmetic trappings, Obama is much the same as Bush. In Afghanistan, Obama hopes to apply some lessons and experiences learned from Iraq and in doing so is incurring very real domestic costs and taking significant risks just as Bush did, most notably in Iraq. Despite much public rhetoric to the contrary (particularly from the remnants of the Bush camp now that it is removed from policy-making), the policy directions chosen by both administrations place the hegemony and domestic stability of the US, the "sole superpower," at risk, but nevertheless are still rational attempts to defend and extend capitalist power when the frame of reference is global, not national, and political, economic, and social stability in the US is not the primary point of reference. (I think that Panitch and Gindin and, particularly, David Harvey, have a parallel position on some of these points, particularly in terms of economic processes—however their political conclusions may be quite different from mine.)[8]

How might global capitalist interests be operative in Obama's Afghanistan policies? A full answer includes the structural elements of the current economic crisis and is beyond the scope of this argument. However, there are clear hints of a partial answer in the language that Obama used to present his policy at West Point— especially when it is augmented by the language used a few days later in Oslo when he accepted his bizarre award of a "Peace Prize."

Obama said that the policy towards Afghanistan was part of a strategic response to a real danger from "disorderly regions, failed states, diffuse enemies." In the Nobel speech he stressed in Bush-like phrases, "I face the world as it is [and] evil does exist in the world."[9]

I wrote down the former phrase at the time I heard it, but I've seen no reference to it in the commentary on that speech. Hopefully, at least some of the Fourth Generation War websites will eventually pick it up.[10] I'm sure that the invocation of evil in the Oslo presentation was not missed, but without the earlier passage as a context, it becomes a rhetorical flourish with only an ambiguous practical significance.

However, taken together, these phrases point towards a rationale for Afghanistan policy that makes some sense for a global ruling class facing a secular crisis*, if not for a national US ruling class focused on internal stability and on maintaining its relative power position in a classically imperialist structure. Consequently, unlike Tom Engelhardt, I do not find Obama's pursuit of a very expensive Afghan policy instead of a "reasonable jobs program at home" to be a "strange wonder of the world" (Engelhardt 2009).

This Obama statement opens some important questions: What is the danger in Afghanistan? Who is responding to the danger and in what ways? Focusing on these questions, not the logical errors, factual irrelevancies, and the bloated patriotic rhetoric which filled both the West Point and Oslo speeches, will open some possibilities to position what is happening within the context of global capital and international class struggle.

I'd suggest three working hypotheses, recognizing that their validity is provisional. Their similarity with certain elements of the Negri/Hardt approach should be noted:

1. At the end of the last century, the global capitalist system rapidly extended the penetration of what used to be called the "second" and "third" worlds. It now faces a growing difficulty profitably utilizing the labor that it has "freed" and endowed with new needs and demands. This increasingly marginalized labor force is also increasingly mobile. This is one underpinning for a general populist threat to global capital that contains both liberatory and reactionary elements. The problems and conflicts, the social turmoil that this process entails, cannot be quarantined even under the best of circumstances, and it now affects the entire system, including the capitalist core areas.

   A variety of political projects with a diverse array of antagonisms and accommodations to the global capitalist system are attempting to organize this growing base of fundamental discontent. Global capital sees the populist threat as the major current challenge to its continued dominance and is focused on developing a response to its jihadist components. This is a real priority that is acknowledged and implemented by virtually all national segments of capital. It is not a pretext or a facade to provide space and resources to pursue other goals, although it will certainly be used for such purposes if and when the opportunity develops.

2. The collapse of the global financialization system and the serious cyclical crisis that is related to it have exposed structural limitations on capitalist accumulation. The growing problems with maintaining profitability and cultural hegemony within the core areas of the capitalist system are compounded by the emergence of the issues of the gap in the core. This has increased the awareness among capitalist elites of the need for major structural adjustments, but this awareness is constrained in the core by the increasingly limited flexibility for material and incorporative concessions to the working classes. The same limitations restrict the tools, particularly the non-military tools, available to deal with political challenges in gap regions—such as Afghanistan.

These factors combine to undercut the ruling-class confidence that capitalist development has enough momentum to surmount the complex of emerging threats and instabilities. Certainly, any confidence that these challenges can be dealt with simultaneously is weakened. In place of the eroding confidence that capitalism can automatically incorporate all potential futures is a growing recognition that history may not have ended and that securing the future prospects for capitalism requires at least a major restructuring of its disciplinary apparatus and a risky reordering of political and economic priorities.

3. There are major issues with the current organization and application of capitalist power. To efficiently advance the interests of capital, global political and economic considerations should determine the rational use of power, but this power is politically organized within an increasingly dysfunctional nation-state framework. This is a problem at the top when military capabilities become inflexible and unwieldy—not properly oriented to asymmetric non-state threats where specific

and rapidly changing political factors must outweigh technical military considerations. At least potentially, it is also a problem from below when the structures of privilege and subordinated participation through formal parliamentarism that have provided some stable national bases for capitalist power don't work in the ways that they have historically.

I intend to say a few things about how I see these three points in play in Afghanistan policy. First, although it may already be apparent, I should make it explicit that these points assume the essential validity of Negri's point in *Empire*: "The United States does not, and indeed, no nation-state can today, form the center of an imperialist project." (Hardt and Negri 2003, xiv)

It may be less obvious, but my argument will diverge significantly from another Negri position: "The guarantee that Empire offers to globalized capital does not involve a micropolitical and/or microadministrative management of populations. The apparatus of command has no access to the local spaces and the determinate temporal sequences of life" (Hardt and Negri 2003, 344). I think that this is a mistaken and dangerous view. In my opinion, such a "management of populations" is exactly what is being developed and with some success.

Remember a few short decades ago when Carter and Brzeziński schemed to bring down the Soviet Union by giving it "its own Vietnam" in Afghanistan.[11] Are any rival national centers of capitalist power oriented towards entangling the US in Afghanistan this way? I think not—and also with respect to Iraq. This certainly cannot be explained by a fear of US military and economic power, which has demonstrated increasingly clear limits. I find the best explanation to be that, notwithstanding the talk of conflicts with China and "a rising multi-polarity," the global ruling elites increasingly subordinate inter-imperialist rivalries to a growing appreciation of common enemies and common risks. This emergent sense of an overriding common interest is reflected in the virtually universal support of every state for what is called the "war on terror."

It is reflected in the generalized cooperation to regain some equilibrium in global financial systems and commodity markets.

In distinction to Negri, who places minimal weight on all elements of consciousness and organization—including those that might impact ruling-class policies—I think there is an emerging global capitalist project lurking beneath the Obama pronouncements, and it is important that we understand it. I want to speculate about this process in two areas: one with implications for the gap (warzone), and particularly the "non-integrating" seams in the gap; the other with implications for the old core (homeland). (I'm assuming some familiarity with these gap/core categories from Thomas Barnett that I have been using; however, their meaning should be obvious from the context.)[12]

Afghanistan is both a specific problem and a manifestation of more general ones in an important regional zone of disorder. For global capital, Afghanistan is an opportunity to experiment with new ways to discipline increasingly unruly populations while maintaining and even extending capitalist control over global flows of capital and labor. It is an opportunity, as well, to develop better techniques to disorient and demobilize emerging challenges to capital's global disciplinary regime. At its core, I believe that the Obama "surge" is such a test of new methods and new tools. It is a concrete project in which most sections of global capital share definite common interests. Of course, it is not a project that represents an overt and thorough-going ruling-class consensus. There are remaining conflicts and contradictions on important issues, and these are sometimes quite evident in policy differences—particularly on questions of tactics. But, I think, the underlying common interest is pretty clear to capital and should be to anti-capital as well.

(Before getting further into these questions of ruling-class policy, I would like to inject a parenthetical note of caution: It is hard to raise such issues without implying that ruling-class policy is more consciously calculated and coordinated than the available evidence shows. What I say here will be subject to such a reading. So from the outset I want to be clear that I don't mean to deny that there is, and will always be, a range of contradictory factors, elements of controversy and indeterminacy, not to mention incompetence, that go into the formation of ruling-class policy. I hope what I say doesn't lead to the substitution of assumed conspiracies for a concrete investigation of actual processes. This can lead to a host of political problems that frequently end in passivity and defeatism.

However, in this instance I'm more worried about the opposite problem: the underestimation of the extent and impact of the organization and planning that goes into maintaining capitalist power. The fact is that any approach we take to radical political organizing will have to make some operating assumptions on this issue before the investigations that could establish their validity are complete and when the most pertinent results are not widely available. In our situation, I think that it is prudent to adopt the protective principle of ecological science and work from the assumption of the worst case. Considering the massive resources the capitalist state devotes to its own defense, and assuming that this produces some usable product, this is probably not only the prudent course, but the wise one as well. As Mao might have learned before leaving the scene, it's very important to avoid any tendency to underestimate the enemy—and that means strategically, not just tactically.)[13]

To me, it seems that the Afghanistan surge is not oriented to a victory over the Taliban, the eradication of al-Qaeda, or any type of nation building. I think that "winning" in Afghanistan is not about establishing a relatively stable pro-capitalist nation-state that is a more docile part of a US sphere of influence (a completely utopian objective under any scenario). Instead, consider Afghanistan as Obama described it: a "failed state" in a "disorderly region" containing "diffuse enemies." Afghanistan is the archetypical disorderly region, and it is not insignificant that it has many features placing it on the dark side of the establishment's Manichaean discourses on Evil. If the force structure focused on Afghanistan is clearly unable to achieve a traditional military victory that should indicate to us, not that it is some kind of a mistake, but that it is probably meant to achieve different goals.

A more likely goal of this policy is that it is a test, oriented towards developing and controlling balkanized enclaves through direct relations with empowered reactionary elements of civil society, bypassing centralized governmental structures, including compradorial ones. This will be an attempt to relate directly to all sides of all existing social divisions, hoping to gain effective control over the resources of the underground and illegal economy and to fragment any potential nationalist or internationalist resistance that has an anti-capitalist aspect to it. In pursuing such objectives, the tacit assumption is that the "disorderly region" will remain disorderly and that these methods of domination are being worked out for the long haul and have more than a provisional and local significance.

Notably, the surge discounts the significance of the imperialist-initiated "national" borders—with Pakistan, with the ex-Soviet "stans," with Iran—while building up centrifugal pressures towards micro-states and ethnic fiefdoms with their accompanying internal borders—both geographic and social. But even while implementing this segmenting project, the surge can and will utilize organizational forms and policies that are as transnational as those of the jihadists, while providing an effective deniability of the blood trail back to the actual originators of the policy.

This approach can be detected in what was said and what was not said in the speeches. Note the careful reference to direct contact with local officials and leaders, bypassing the Kabul central authority with its ethnic limitations that make further "military training" beside the point. Note the careful reference to the surge of "civilian" experts on agricultural (read: drug) policy and other sensitive issues. Note the careful lack of reference to the surge of "civilian" and military contractors which is equal or greater numerically and certainly in the breadth of function to that of the formal military forces. Note the lack of mention of any public accountability, benchmarks, or timetables for these contractors, either military or "civilian," or for the operation of the military's Joint Special Operations Command (JSOC, McChrystal's last gig)[14] which functions covertly throughout the region without even the feeble political oversight that nominally constrains the CIA. Finally, note well the absence of any mention of who and what is involved in the expanding operations in Pakistan.

What is emerging out of this are secret intelligence gatherings and arms distribution systems and other military capabilities, most of which are privatized and—although this is far from their defining feature—exceptionally profitable. Elements of the US ruling elite (with clear international connections) have actively pursued this goal since the mid–twentieth century. The pursuit intensified following the collapse of the Soviet Union and the emergence of new forms of Muslim insurgency. DYNCORP, L-3, FLUOR, XE Services, etc.,[15] all of whom are acknowledged players in Afghanistan, are such assets for capital, able to circumvent the limitations on state militaries and provide deniability to actual policy makers—sufficiently flexible and robust to respond quickly to shifting needs while bypassing the bureaucratic parliamentary filters.

This looks something like a rerun on a global scale of the Pinkertonized class warfare of the nineteenth century in this country.[16] But it is more than that. There is a particularly modern character to these formations: they are operating within the context of a global capitalism, not within a national state, and they are confronted with structural limits on capitalism that were not a factor in the period of the Molly Maguires or the Moyer, Pettibone, and Haywood trial.[17]

As emerging oppositions have become less susceptible to a gradual, evolutionary political incorporation within the framework of capitalist expansion, they also have become more difficult to eliminate by traditional military or police methods because their social preconditions are constantly regenerated by essential dynamics of capital accumulation. Consequently, I think that we must assume that the privatized, multinationally-staffed contractors that are already doing the targeting for the drones and the hit squads in Pakistan and elsewhere will have developed networks of covert operatives and agents of influence that will enlarge their potential uses and increase their importance in the near future. If these paramilitaries can develop sufficient information to accurately target jihadist leaders, they can also be positioned to more fundamentally affect the tactics of the resistance through systematic penetration and an increasingly tight encapsulation. One likely result will be more anomalies in the mold of al-Qaeda in Mesopotamia—more of those "terrorists" most likely to demoralize a revolutionary population and expedite an expanded counterinsurgency.

These new tools do not and will not operate autonomously. Their oversight may be strategic rather than operational, but there is not much doubt who will ultimately provide the money and determine the jobs. It will not be any section of the state apparatus that is remotely accountable, you can bet on that … But it will be elements and appendages of the global ruling class, you can bet on that as well.

As capital develops these capacities with respect to jihadists, there will be ramifications shortly down the road for other situations and other resistances—think Haiti. These will impact anticapitalist movements with radically different agendas and perspectives than most Islamic radicals. The capacities that are being developed in this privatized force structure will push beyond repression and suppression of external (to this country) populisms to policies that influence and distort the character and objectives of all oppositions, internally as well as externally, class-based as well as populist.

To recap, capital currently faces a real danger from populism in the gap, and the gap is increasingly less defined and limited by geography because of the mobility of populations and the increasing access to information and new forms of communication. Moreover, the current crisis confounds all of the forms of capitalist triumphalism, including that of the Barnetts and the Friedmans

(Thomas, not Milton), because there is no longer any compelling evidence that the gap is shrinking in any real sense. This means that the challenges to global capital from this populism will become larger and more urgent, rather than dwindling into only marginal significance.

Afghanistan is one of the regions of the world where, for the historical moment, global capital has some flexibility to respond to these dangers experimentally, with minimal worries about issues of moral standing or legitimacy in the exercise of power. However, such operations can hardly hope to achieve a social equilibrium in Afghanistan in any meaningful time frame and they are even less likely to initiate favorable trends on a broader scale. The likelihood is that the more effective these new methods prove to be, the more they will make themselves needed—and the more expensive, economically and politically, they will become.

This points to the linkage between the issues in the gap and some emerging questions of capitalist hegemony in the core. The economic and cultural cushions that have supported hegemony in the core are wearing thin as the actual and prospective actions in the gap are becoming more costly, and now with significant elements of the costs in blood. That is the problem for capital, and it is a large one. As more resources have to be directed at fundamental instabilities in the gap and their actual and potential spillovers into the core, the problems of maintaining an adequate hegemonic flexibility at home grow larger.

The global dominance of capital has rested on its hegemony in stable nation-states in the core. For a variety of historical reasons, these are regions where the ruling class is, and probably must be, concerned with maintaining legitimacy in the exercise of power and avoiding the collateral damages from an excessive reliance on repression. In these base areas it has been possible to both maintain and disguise essential capitalist rule through a network of incorporative privileges—but these are increasingly hard to sustain, politically or economically, and it is impossible to expand them significantly except in the most localized conditions.

The requirements and conditions for capitalist stability change as a range of tensions emerge between its globalized pursuit of surplus value and its nation-based system of rule, and, increasingly, they will be set by larger issues of global power and profit. To avoid a general spiral down towards the pit, capitalist priorities cannot be limited within national borders or allowed to be overly influenced by nationalist sentiment. But this is no easy course. Certainly, in this country it is almost hopelessly hard for the ruling class to politically explain the rescue of multinational and foreign financial institutions while sacrificing Detroit, the borrowing of billions to finance wars that make no sense while a pathetic health care "reform" must be deficit neutral. If it happens, as it well may, it will be hard to explain bailing out Spain, Greece, and Austria rather than California. But there is no framework of global capitalist legitimacy as a base from which to adjudicate the resulting conflicts.

An increase in authoritarianism and repression can only be an inadequate and partial, probably temporary, solution, because any general resort to reliance on repressive methods will accumulate its own risk factors. The maintenance of political equilibrium in the core nations depends on an essential passivity which contains grievances and undercuts capacities and potentials for mass collective resistance. Many aspects of capitalist discipline and control are obscured by this accepted subordination—more accurately, a repressive self-discipline that limits natural resistances to oppression and authority. This culture is a major part of capitalist strength and resiliency, and it is not an advantage that will easily be surrendered. Consequently, I think that major increases in repression and, particularly, overtly imposing elements of a repressive authoritarian "world government" in the US or elsewhere presents unacceptable risks—at least for now.

This leaves capital struggling to develop more effective methods to discipline new populations and regions, while facing growing problems maintaining social cohesion and a non-police-centered discipline in its traditional centers, where material conditions are also deteriorating. One possible general response of capital to this dilemma, the one that I believe will eventually predominate, is what has been called global social democracy. (Following Walden Bello [2008], although he appears to have recently backed away from his conception.)

Since the vision of shared prosperity has become a pretty threadbare joke, and significant improvements in material conditions are not a general possibility, such a new form of social democracy must provide its own new alternative to the Fordist* wage/consumption underpinning for class collaboration. And it is not hard to see what will be central to any such alternative. It will be fear: "Fear is the ultimate guarantee of the new segmentations" (Hardt and Negri 2003, 339).

The primary fear will be of an enemy that might emerge from the populist reaction to capital. An enemy consisting of "fanatics who hate us and our freedom," to paraphrase from the house of George. An enemy that is mainly in the gap, but that is expected to materialize in the core as well. An enemy pictured as anti-modern, anti-liberatory, and neo-fascist—a picture that has plausibility because it points to significant reactionary elements of existing mass populist movements.

On the one hand, this fear will be generated from capital's recognition and popularization of actual dangers from the right to its continued hegemony. It will be magnified and embroidered as segments of the ruling class appreciate the usefulness of a new set of "enemies" to replace the popular narrative of the "communist danger." (It's beyond the scope of this argument, but I think that another largely fabricated contribution to this popular "fear" will emerge through the manipulation and marketing of the ecological crisis to confine alternative responses within essentially Malthusian assumptions, defining the essential ecological problem as too many "other people.")

We had a major historical experience in WWII with a repressive right-wing structure of authoritarian rule in this country. This was not just a manifestation of imperialism at war. It was also a global response from capital to a perceived threat from a trans-capitalist fascism and a potential threat from communism.[18] This provided a framework that incorporated the willing participation of the overwhelming bulk of the left and progressive forces under the rubric of a popular front* against fascism, greased by a return to a militarized full employment. Despite its repressive content, the process presented itself and is still commonly viewed as a continuation of the social democratic momentum of the New Deal.

Currently, big sections of the near-left—at least in this country and probably throughout most of the other "developed" areas—are more than open to a refurbished variant of the same structure. The other side of this possibility and, in a sense, the proof of its real potential, lies in the lack of a militant anti-war movement after a decade of exquisitely rotten wars; in the lack of class-conscious, anti-capitalist militancy, solidarity, and internationalism at a time of capitalist crisis that is increasing exploitation, marginalization, and oppression around the world.

What I have argued above is sketchy and tentative, but I am relatively confident of some points. We are living in the aftermath of an extended revolutionary process that had its debatable successes. But these were rapidly transformed into limits that are now obstacles to a more basic struggle against capital. To think seriously about revolutionary politics, we must challenge some left presuppositions and develop new catgories of strategic analysis that fit the qualitatively changed circumstances of the present period. However, while we cannot adequately deal with new political questions without a clearer understanding of the struggles of the past century, an understanding that avoids both nostalgia and meaningless recriminations, we are going to have to act, moving ahead with whatever intellectual, moral, and material resources are available to us, well before we have this adequately grounded understanding of our collective past.

I'd like to finish this piece with a more explicit treatment of attempts to refurbish one of the old categories—that of anti-imperialist national liberation. Given the emergence of important mass populist movements in the gap in response to a generalized crisis of living conditions there, it is logical that there would be a renewed interest in the revolutionary potentials of mass struggles of oppressed peoples against external political and economic domination.

A recent discussion on a more limited topic on the Unity and Struggle website includes a comment by mlove that raised a point that I think is a good starting place: "We need to revisit the Third Worldist imagination—not the politics of the national bourgeoisie (radical or otherwise), but the masses who resisted and provided a potential alternative to capitalist Bandung modernization—the 'third revolution'"[19] (Unity and Struggle 2009).

I certainly agree that this "third revolution" should be revisited in light of the current conditions. But it should be clear from the outset that yesterday's potentials are not easily resurrected. It is an illusion to think that the movements for national liberation can be rebuilt and produce different and better outcomes, if only some obvious mistakes are not made a second time. The weight of the past, including its failures, combines with transformed present circumstances to qualitatively change what can and should be done in the future—closing some possibilities and opening others. I'm sure that mlove would agree that the revisiting of the "third revolution" should start from a critical reconsideration of whether it still might provide a "potential alternative to capitalist Bandung modernization"—or if it ever did.

Here again I want to begin with a passage from Negri, although with the usual ambivalence because he offers so much else with which to disagree: "From India to Algeria and Cuba to Vietnam, *the state is the poisoned gift of national liberation.*" (Hardt and Negri 2003, 136; emphasis in the original)

In my opinion, cross-class coalitions in oppressed nations, challenging imperialist power and demanding national independence and socialism, were the most important element of the international struggle against capital for much of the last century. But I agree with Negri that they will not play that role going ahead. We aren't confronting Lenin's Imperialism, which for the benefit of the censors he called capitalism's highest stage while actually thinking it was its end point—just a step short of international working-class revolution. This conception of imperialism is no longer strategically relevant. The set of possibilities that constituted its antithesis (i.e., anti-imperialist national liberation) is politically exhausted and will not be revived by the new populisms which appropriate some of its characteristics—not even when these go well beyond rhetorical posturing and include a rejection of some elements of global capital, as they do from time to time.

The historic national liberation struggle was indelibly marked and increasingly limited by the specific context in which it developed—a context which has been decisively modified. This changed context has two important and closely related elements.

First, classically, imperialist domination was a relationship between a developed capitalism and an exploitable "outside," as Luxemburg conceptualized it. Imperialism was an external force over the "Third World," and the class alignments and attitudes in both metropolis and periphery reflected this. The most powerful imperialist states essentially pillaged and destroyed non-capitalist societies by appropriating their surpluses and dumping their economic and social problems on them.

The economic side of this process and its essentially transitional character are forecasted in the well-known passages on the tendency of capital towards the creation of a world market in the *Grundrisse* (Marx 1939, 408–10). Now this transition is essentially complete and these ex-colonial societies for the most part have been thoroughly incorporated into global capitalist production and thoroughly penetrated by capitalist institutions and ideologies. They have developed into capitalist societies and, while they are typically a different form of capitalism than in the core, they are still part of capitalism and are no longer an outside to its global system. Here it should also be noted that this capitalist global system has now also subsumed the "Second World" and is scavenging the carcasses of "actually existing socialism"* and obliterating any trace of that "different path" to political and economic development.

The social classes of these postcolonial regions have interfaced with globalized ruling and ruled class structures. Little remains to anchor a progressive multi-class front against a clearly defined imperialist oppressor nation. Instead, a progressive momentum requires coalitions of working classes and marginalized strata in the gap that have a more concrete anti-capitalist and internationalist orientation: an orientation that aims for solidarity with all similar forms of resistance and that particularly opposes the forms in which domestic and foreign capital are combined into unified ruling structures and policies—in "their" states and quasi-states.

Second, during the classic period of anti-imperialist struggle in the mid-twentieth century, it was widely accepted that "socialism," as embodied by the so-called socialist bloc, was a real alternative path to modernization and economic development. It was believed that socialism, despite its problems, was a viable base from which to challenge both capitalist markets and capitalist culture. The more progressive and radical anti-imperialist movements all specified that their political objectives included national independence *and* socialism.

When this "actually existing socialism" proved illusory for the global working-class struggle, it likewise disappointed the movements for national liberation. Any possible progressive trajectory for a cross-class anti-imperialist movement looking towards gaining state power in an independent nation and joining a socialist camp was rapidly eroded. No socialist camp meant no sustainable alternative to the capitalist world market, which translated to little genuine sovereignty and power from formal "national independence" and even less of a genuinely liberatory content from the "victories" of national liberation movements.

It is strange now to have to recall this amalgam of ideological perversions that grew out of the ... democratic hopes of socialist representation ... And while we say our farewells we cannot but remember how many ideological

by-products, more or less fascist, the great historical experiences of socialism were condemned to drag in their wake,
some merely useless sparks and others devastating infer-
nos. (Hardt and Negri 2004, 255)

This dual historical failure of both "socialism" and "anti-
imperialism" left more than political vacuums. They left a disil-
lusionment and cynicism that provide a social base for the anti-
capitalism of the right as well as for secessionist orientations that
seek special solutions and unique benefits for some in a rotten
combination with a general dehumanization of living conditions
for many.

In his late 2008 presentation, "Is the Word 'Communism'
Forever Doomed?," Alain Badiou* has presented a framework
that I think is helpful in settling accounts with our collective past.
I'm a newcomer to Badiou and certainly don't have an adequate
understanding of his recent positions, much less his earlier ones.
However, what I think I understand I like a great deal and it will be
the basis of the rest of what I write here.

"Our problems are much more the problems of Marx than the
problems of Lenin ..." (Badiou 2008). The "problems of Lenin,"
according to Badiou, fit within an extended phase of the revolutionary process, "from 1917, the Russian Revolution, to 1976, the
end of the Cultural Revolution in China." This is a phase that has
ended with a generally acknowledged string of failures to achieve
the fundamental stated objective—a rapid transition from local
seizures of state power to an inclusive, stateless, communist society. As I have said above, I think that the massive upsurge of the
national liberation struggle, the reason why it contained much
greater revolutionary potential than the earlier nationalisms of the
nineteenth century, is inextricably linked with this phase of the
communist project and similarly tied to its failures.

We are left with the problem placed by Bilal al Hasan in a more
limited context: "The question here is what comes after the end of
a revolution and its failure?" (Haddad 2009)[20]

Badiou argues for a conceptual return to the standpoints of the nineteenth century, but not on the premise that a simple class polarization can be resurrected through some act of political will. He is concerned with an issue of philosophical stance—with posing the idea of communism in terms of the "conditions of its identity"—a nineteenth-century problem—and not as a question of "the victory of the communist hypothesis" (Badiou 2008)—the problem of Lenin and the party/state and of the revolutionary movement for most of the past century.

This line of argument is relevant to the revisiting of Third World revolution. Badiou indicates the elements of the communist hypothesis in the nineteenth century as combining "the idea of communism as a popular mass movement with the notion of savior of all." The original conception of communism was that of a multiform struggle that would embody and culminate in universal emancipation through the "process of the Decline of the State" (Badiou 2008).

In my opinion, the core element in this conception is the inseparable linkage of the notion of "savior of all," stressing the universality of the project, with the destruction of the state—a state that is sometimes defined expansively by Badiou as "all that limits the possibility of collective creation" (Badiou, 2008). The vanguard parties and revolutionary blocs characteristic of the twentieth century had a different orientation. In Badiou's terms they were party/state formations which might seize and hold power locally but could not transform social relations because their essential character incorporated features of a state. Thus, they inevitably became the antagonist of the mass "Communist movement." But only through such a movement, which is necessarily "beyond the state," can communism be achieved.

It is quite clear that even the best of the national liberation fronts were essentially party/state formations. They functioned even more as shadow governments than did the vanguard parties. The discipline they enforced was more overtly military and not subject to even the more or less hypothetical democratic forms of vanguard parties or to the objective limits that are inherent in a defined class base.

These movements were nationalist (including some more hopeful pan-nationalist and "continental" formations that were of limited temporal and geographic duration). At their best, they treated liberation as more a matter of autonomy and expanded rights of self-determination than of internationalism and solidarity. This is demonstrated indirectly by how unique the Guevara experience was. This view was supported in an ultimately damaging way by the Maoist version of Marxism when it elevated the conception of self-reliance, "Juche" as Kim Il-Sung presented it, over that of internationalism.

These issues are coming to the front currently around questions of the character of the populist resistance to global capital, particularly, but not exclusively, in the gap. To what extent do these developments project a fascist, rather than a liberatory, alternative to global capital? To what extent are they contained or containable within neo-colonial limits? These are important issues that I've written about in some of the discussions previously cited. I'm not going into them substantively here except to note the importance of recognizing that no general recognition of contradictory potentials can or should substitute for concrete evaluations of specific cases. And our goal in such concrete evaluations should always be more than clarifying problems and limitations, it must also include a real attempt to discover and build on the best possibilities.

That said, we should also be categorically clear that universal liberation is not to be achieved through movements structured to limit creative participation, whether or not this is presented as an element of their "self-determination" and cultural autonomy. This is particularly relevant concerning the oppression of women and attitudes towards the use of force and violence. I will leave these points as they stand for now, but feel obliged to confess that I've been around long enough to have made major mistakes on all conceivable sides of such questions.

## Financialization and Hegemony
## October 2011

*This piece was originally posted to the* Khukuri Theory* *blog in response to an essay by Anselm Jappe, a German Marxist philosopher and contributor to the German journal* Krisis. *Hamerquist revised and slightly edited the essay for its inclusion in this volume.*[1]

" … that which in them divides itself from the old"
　—Alain Badiou, *Théorie de la contradiction* (1975)[2]

A recent article by Anselm Jappe states:

> [Karl Marx] foresaw the eventuality that some day the capitalist machine would stop running on its own, through the exhaustion of its dynamic. Why? Capitalist commodity production contains, from its very inception an internal contradiction, a veritable time bomb built into its very structure. (Jappe 2011)

We have waited a long time for this "veritable time bomb." It's not as if propositions such as "the capitalist machine would stop running on its own" have been validated by historical experience. Whether Jappe provides a good rendering of Marx is open to a discussion that I will avoid for now, but regardless of what Marx said or meant—and both questions are debatable—it is hardly sufficient for our current circumstances.

　This same conclusion extends to a more familiar passage in *The Communist Manifesto*:

> All fixed, fast frozen relations, with their train of ancient and venerable prejudices and opinions, are swept away, all new-formed ones become antiquated before they can ossify. All that is solid melts into air, all that is holy is pro-

faned, and man is at last compelled to face with sober senses his real condition of life and his relations with his kind. (Marx and Engels 1848)

Little in our collective experience demonstrates a capitalist compulsion on the working class to soberly confront "real conditions" and "relations," and a good deal of our experience supports very different conclusions. Without such a revolutionary anti-capitalist subject, without a revolutionary program and the organized will to respond to the mass potentials created in a capitalist crisis, communism will "remain an ideal that will be always yet to come" (Bosteels 2011, 280).

Assume that we are experiencing a disruption of a previous equilibrium. There are hopeful signs in this situation, but every upsurge of mass resistance tends to fetishize various short-of-revolution possibilities that are more likely to fit into a new, non-emancipatory equilibrium than to provide a foundation for a revolutionary advance. Without a functioning revolutionary subject any new equilibrium will be essentially capitalist.

The elasticity of capitalist power is demonstrated in the limits on the anti-capitalist possibilities that emerge at moments of heightened contradiction and crisis. This elevates illusory popular objectives into political substitutes for revolutionary communism that can dominate radical politics for generations.

So how should we respond? I like this formulation from the younger Badiou* as a starting point: "It is never 'the masses', nor the 'movement' that as a whole carry the principle of engenderment of the new, but that which in them divides itself from the old" (Badiou 1975, cit. Bosteels 2011, 136).

The new potentials that develop in the explosively expanded struggles of periods of capitalist crisis aren't necessarily cumulative or irreversible. The Badiou formulation raises the contradictory character of this process and the importance of countering the strategic unevenness through organized political interventions. Before capitalism can be overthrown, some very uncomfortable elements of the internal dialectic between the communist component of a mass movement and the mass popular constituency of that movement will have to be confronted to prevent popular insurgencies from overdosing on their own victories—real and illusory. Badiou notes that far too often, "once the mass festivals of democracy are over, things make place for the modernist restoration of order among workers and bosses" (Badiou 1976, cit. Bosteels 2011, 279).

Contrary to Jappe, capitalism will not topple "through … exhaustion." It will not "stop running on its own." It must be overthrown by a politically conscious, mass counter-force, and the primary issue for us concerns how such a force might develop. I'm more a Leninist than a Marxist on such questions and think that these issues underscore the importance of Lenin's position on the "art" of revolution. Although Lenin would certainly have disagreed, I think that rather than an extension and elaboration, this is a break with Marx—certainly it is a break with the Marx of Jappe, which implies capital might collapse from the working out of a simple internal contradiction.

## Financialization

There is another weakness in the Jappe article. He shows little interest in connecting the general questions of revolutionary process with this particular capitalist crisis, dismissing the possibility that "financialization" might explain key features of this crisis without proposing any alternative way to understand it. Unlike Jappe, I see the development of financialization as a significant disturbance to the capitalist equilibrium of our recent past that is central to this current crisis.

Jappe argues that the expanded system of financialization may have deferred and redirected a more basic crisis in capitalist accumulation but that it is not an important causal factor in its own right. Instead it amounts to an attempt to disguise the underlying reality of capitalist power by creating a false opposition between a "good" and a "bad" form of capitalism. In a certain sense this is not particularly controversial among anti-capitalist revolutionaries. It's true enough that the global financial system and its crisis should not—really cannot—be approached separately from the global circumstances for capitalism. But who on the anti-capitalist left thinks differently on this question? The distinctions between a "bad" capitalist financial system and a "good" productive capitalism are features of populist tendencies and institutional reformists—with some neo-fascists among the former, and some social democrats among the latter. Not many of those folks regard themselves as revolutionary anti-capitalists and fewer still merit such a description.

When this "bad capitalism" view is adopted by a genuinely radical tendency, the cause is less likely to be a mistaken understanding of the "capitalist machine" than a reasonable lack of confidence that Jappe's "veritable time bomb" will ever actually detonate. And as I have said above, there are grounds for such pessimism that Jappe would be well advised to consider.

When financialization is seen as an independent variable with only a contingent relationship to some idealized capitalism—or when it is reduced to that same idealized "simple" capitalism—our ability to understand its actual impact will be severely reduced. And in the same process, so will our ability to clarify and implement the political interventions that can counter the tendencies for the emerging mass resistance to collapse back into itself; greasing the emergence of some new, non-liberatory stage that might or might not be something that looks like an equilibrium.

I'd like to develop a counter-argument to Jappe's with respect to financialization and the unique role the capitalist state assumes in the current crisis, but some preliminary points are needed. What I intend to argue begins from material that is fairly new to me—although possibly not so much to others—and I'd welcome questions and challenges. In part, this material is based on the Bosteels book *Badiou and Politics* (2011), which I've cited a few times in the earlier argument, but the primary point of reference is the argument presented in Giovanni Arrighi's book, *The Long Twentieth Century* (1994).

I did find some debatable themes in what I have read from Arrighi. One that is relevant to an understanding of this crisis is his recurring fixation on finding a new capitalist hegemon emerging between the "signal" and the "terminal" crisis of the current "'organic core' of the capitalist world-economy" (Arrighi 1994, 332). At an earlier date, a greater Japan was Arrighi's candidate for hegemon. More recently, shortly before Arrighi's death and with Japan in a prolonged stagnation that was stretching into its third decade, he appears to assign the role to China. Laying aside whether or not these estimates were properly based in socio-economic fact, this strand of Arrighi's approach is biased towards the possibility of a new long wave of capitalist accumulation, a "new equilibrium," with all of the non-revolutionary implications that this would involve.

In my opinion, this lingering reluctance to see a break in the pattern of essentially repetitive cycles of capital accumulation, although on larger scales and with shorter durations, is a major weakness, even taking into account Arrighi's recognition that there are some qualitative changes from one cycle to the next that do imply broader and deeper questions about future possibilities. However, there is another strand of Arrighi's presentation that I like much more. Consider this passage from the concluding chapter of the book:

> The uncontainability of violence in the contemporary world is closely associated with the withering away of the modern system of territorial states as the primary locus of world power. ... Combined with the internalization of world-scale processes of production and exchange within the organizational domains of transnational corporations and with the resurgence of suprastatal world financial markets, these unprecedented restrictions and expectations have translated into strong pressures to relocate the authority of nation-states both upward and downward. (Arrighi 1994, 331)

*Hollow\* states*

Arrighi died in early 2009 and all versions and updates of *The Long Twentieth Century* were finished well before the events of 2008/2009. Nevertheless, this passage is relevant to the period initiated by the current crisis. The "withering away of the modern system of territorial states" raises the "hollow state" issue that I've been kicking around recently. The "suprastatal world financial markets," which Arrighi sees as major active factors precipitating the "withering" process, are just another way of presenting the disruptive impacts of an active and growing—and increasingly problematic—global financial system.

I wouldn't characterize the results as Arrighi does in this citation, as "strong pressures to relocate the authority of national-states both upward and downward." Rather than relocating the authority up and down, it seems to me that the new sources of authority trends are relocating at a diagonal from the previous institutional frameworks. More important, the processes of breakdown in hegemony and command occur at a distance in both space and time from the counter-processes that might activate new and relocated sites of command and acquiescence—the new "networks of coercion" (Arrighi 1994, xi) that will be essential to any new cycle of capitalist accumulation. But perhaps this is more a disagreement with language than substance.

Consider another aspect of his argument:

> In the scheme of things proposed here, the close historical tie between capitalism and the modern interstate system is just as much one of contradiction as it is one of unity. We must take into account the fact that ... "capitalism and national states grew up together, and presumably depended on each other in some way, yet capitalists and centers of capital accumulation often offered concerted resistance to the extension of state power." In our account, the division of the world into competing political jurisdictions does not necessarily benefit the capitalist accumulation of capital. (Arrighi 1994, 32; quoting Tilly 1984, 140)

According to Arrighi, the emergence of the worldwide capitalist system has involved distinct historic cycles of accumulation linked to the emergence of dominant hegemonic political structures, primarily nation-states, that "can credibly claim to be the motor force of a general expansion of the *collective* power of rulers *vis-à-vis* subjects" (Arrighi 1994, 30; emphasis in original). These hegemonic political structures play a distinct role in both expediting and defending specific capitalist accumulation processes. However, Arrighi perceptively notes that they also are the center of "territorialist" complexes of state formations and civil societies that embody "modes of rule … or logics of power" (Arrighi 1994, 33) that are distinct from those of capitalist modes of production.

These differences are currently exacerbated to the point of rupture by the increasing influence of the suprastate elements of capital accumulation: transnational corporations; global productive processes and labor flows; and, above all, global financial markets dealing with magnitudes far in excess of any measure of the values of actual production—and more and more commonly far in excess of the economic resources commanded by and encompassed within any state formation. All of this becomes less and less compatible with the viability and the success of any of these "competing political jurisdictions."

Let me turn around the Arrighi citation and ask, isn't it also true and perhaps more relevant that the current mode of "accumulation of capital" does not fully "benefit" any "political jurisdiction"? If the growing organization of production within transnational economic structures, combined with the importance of the global pursuit of fictitious capital, translates "into strong pressures to relocate the authority of nation-states both upward and downward," it also qualitatively disrupts the traditional state forms, bringing the viability of the bourgeois category of nation-state into question. This produces problems in either relocating the various state functions "upward," to the transnational level, or "downward," to more local forms or to those emerging quasi-state functional capacities in what previously was considered the private sphere. Thus the emergence of the phenomena of "hollow states" that can't provide the essential "networks of coercion" and the viable common ruling-class project on which development of new sites of capitalist accumulation depend.

Whereas Arrighi emphasizes the division of the world into competing territorial political jurisdictions that don't adequately facilitate capital accumulation, the other side of the contradiction is equally important. The current accumulation of (largely fictitious) capital does not necessarily benefit any unique array of "political jurisdictions." Instead, it undermines most without much discrimination. This extends from the inability of local and regional governments to control adequate revenue streams to allow them to deliver political goods to their constituents; and to the inability of supranational capitalist governmental structures to impose discipline on their national or regional components—or on particular segments of capital. The tendency towards various types of financial crisis in this late stage of capitalist development presents the "territorialist" state complexes with major dilemmas. Specifically, it is increasingly difficult to implement a capitalist resolution of a financial crisis through the existing territorial nation-state institutional structures without disrupting those structures and eroding essential elements of their internal hegemonic character. This is a reality that we can see in the news of the day—and I mean this quite literally.

**Ferguson**
**March 2015**

*The original version of this essay was sent to an email list of comrades in response to an article posted on the communist blog* Insurgent Notes. *The piece comments on the impact of events in Ferguson, MO—the suburb of St. Louis where Mike Brown was murdered by the police in 2014, sparking several weeks of militant protests across the United States. Hamerquist edited and slightly revised this text for this volume.*

A passage from a long article on *Insurgent Notes* lists some factors that impacted the recent struggles in Ferguson:

> The events surrounding Michael Brown's murder are the product of a complex set of historical developments in the St. Louis area. Those developments include: the central place of Missouri in the struggle over slavery; patterns of racial discrimination across the better part of the twentieth century; deindustrialization and the emergence of the *financial and real estate sectors* as centers of economic activity over the last forty years; policing practices; and the development of a "new whiteness" in the post–Civil Rights era. (Garvey 2014; emphasis added)

Our interest in this topic begins with the mass disrespect for capitalist order that spread across this country from Ferguson. Without questioning the relevance of these historical factors, they have been operative over a substantial time span in many communities, not only in St. Louis or Ferguson, without producing comparable upheavals. I doubt these historical continuities will provide much help in understanding what might be distinctive and new in these struggles.

I think that the most relevant factor raised here is this: "deindustrialization and the emergence of the financial and real estate sectors as centers of economic activity over the last forty years." It directs our attention to relatively recent political/economic changes that are significant determinants of current "policing practices." From this starting point, we can develop more adequate categories to understand emerging contradictions between ruling class and state formations, and the limitations of our traditional approaches to class and class struggle—a rethinking that I think is needed.

I had never heard of Ferguson, Missouri until the past few months. However, I do recall Emerson Electric, a large multinational electrical equipment manufacturer whose headquarters happens to be located there. In the 70s, Ferguson included an electrical equipment plant employing thousands that was a major target for factory organizing by the STO analog in St. Louis.[1] This factory and virtually all Emerson manufacturing facilities are long gone from Ferguson and for the most part from the US, gone in search of lower wages around the world. But Emerson's corporate headquarters are still in Ferguson, a short distance down the road from the QuikStop at the epicenter of the recent struggle.

Over the decades, while Emerson transitioned from a large regional manufacturer into a major global conglomerate, Ferguson transitioned from an overwhelmingly white, factory-centric industrial village to a largely Black community with a growing population of young potential proletarians with dim prospects for the relatively stable wage slavery that Emerson used to provide.

These changes produced a Ferguson in which the "Third World" was increasingly manifest in the "First World" (as Negri* puts it), a change characterized by "the close proximity of extremely unequal populations, which creates ... a situation of permanent social danger ... and requires the powerful apparatuses of the society of control to ensure separation and guarantee the new management ... of social space" (Hardt and Negri 2003, 336–37). Parallels with recent "riots" around the world have more political relevance to Ferguson and its aftermath than its historical roots in white privilege and white supremacy—not that these roots don't also factor into the situation.

In the mid-1970s, the primary interest for capital in Ferguson was "labor peace" and a docile and sustainable work force for Emerson Electric (also Granite City Steel, the General Motors and Ford operations, the old McDonnell Douglas). Today we can see many "Fergusons" in the United States, places where industrial operations have moved on and out. What remains requires fewer and more narrowly trained workers than the "Fordist"* functions that were previously important concerns of the local. Regional capitalist state apparatuses no longer have the same centrality.

The political focus of capitalism's Fergusons has shifted from development of a popular "legitimacy" based on a viable social infrastructure and an expanding base of consumption, towards increasingly single-minded promotions of the FIRE sector of capital.[2] In places like Ferguson, these changed priorities privatize broader areas of social life to develop new revenue streams for capital. They are focused on siphoning off rents from the underground economies that develop from the material and social wreckage of deindustrialization and marginalization.

The changed circumstances require structures and policies capable of maintaining a centralized command over compact populations who are increasingly excluded from the wage slavery side of capitalism. None of this is conducive to an equitable allocation of resources or to political stability, and it requires a basis for political legitimacy that cannot be Fordist or social democratic.

This is a broader story than just Ferguson. The increasing reliance on asset inflation and more extensive and intensive forms of rent extraction has undermined the classic market capitalist approach to social equilibrium throughout the country, along with Keynes's* sanguine forecasted "euthanasia of the rentier": "I see, therefore, the rentier aspect of capitalism as a transitional phase which will disappear when it has done its work" (Keynes 1936, 376). From the perspective of capital, this sea-change in emphasis has benefits, but also costs. There are the obvious benefits from reducing the average social wage as well as from the atomization and fragmentation of a modern working class that had been schooled by a collective experience of social production. But these benefits are offset by exposing the fictions of the free exchange of equals between capital and labor, and the necessity of more—and more overt—reliance on the police power of the state.

This jeopardizes a passive TINA* consent to the necessary order of things in exchange for profit and revenue increases that might be short-lived, and potentially at cross purposes with long-term systemic requirements. These contradictions produce social impacts that are both the outcomes and the motors of the "hollowing"* of state apparatuses. The impacts are evident throughout US capitalist society, but they have some specific features in its Fergusons.

There are thousands of local and regional governments and agencies like Ferguson, Missouri. They face decaying infrastructures, diminishing tax bases, and reduced transfer payments from Washington that necessitate an increasing reliance on revenue from licenses, permits, fines, and fees to pay for ballooning expenses from expanding bureaucracies, capital "improvements," and "business-friendly" inducements. In Ferguson as elsewhere, these "rents" are extracted and enforced by policing and incarceration practices that maximize the atomizing and impoverishing impacts on poor communities—particularly the elements of those communities that are increasingly dependent on informal segments of the economy.

The process becomes more onerous over time, as the individualized impacts merge into a broadened awareness of collective grievance and common oppression that legitimates popular resistance. This results in more frequent and larger outbreaks of collective struggle, although the clashes may remain episodic.

At previous moments in our history, the accumulation of points of collective resistance has led to material concessions—or at least a plausible promise for them. Differences with the past are made clear when the privatization and "austerity" that define capital's current stance is contrasted with the concessions, both material and incorporative, that characterized the so-called "Great Society" response to the urban riots of the 60s.[3]

In the first place, the pressure towards increasing repression to "guarantee the new management" (Hardt and Negri 2003) in our Fergusons is based on the growing impact of public debt. As infrastructure decays and tax revenues stagnate, fiscally challenged local and regional state apparatuses rely increasingly on increased debt to maintain or improve their relative competitiveness. In the process, they become involved with leveraged and manipulated financial markets and provide sectors of global capital with a financial interest in the rent-extractive potentials of fee-based revenue streams from the Fergusons writ large across the country.

These sectors of finance capital easily dominate and manipulate local political elites and are insulated from localized protest and reform pressures. Even in the best cases, the local and regional capitalist state apparatuses routinely succumb to pressures to focus narrowly on short-term and sectoral capitalist interests. J. P. Morgan's role in the bankruptcy of several Alabama localities demonstrates some of the possibilities for overt corruption.[4]

Combine this reality with the growing expenses and political risks involved in major structural reforms or in taking a precautionary approach to the cumulative social costs of capitalist production, and the likelihood of local state apparatuses basing their actions on a concern for capitalism's general viability becomes slim. They have little capacity to see the general capitalist class interest in the social reproduction of labor and the maintenance of adequate demand. Even if this interest could be recognized, they have little ability to implement appropriate measures.

In an abstract sense, a more conciliatory and incorporative approach to the conflicts and contradictions that flow from deindustrialization and marginalization (possibly including a massive Keynesian reformist push towards "good jobs" and some significant measures of wealth redistribution) might outweigh the incapacity and corruption of local political elites. But any such policy transformation would need access to resources without being hamstrung by the need to find some compensating revenue to "pay" for them. Nothing like this is politically or economically possible for regional and local state apparatuses with no control over their own currencies and little real fiscal flexibility. In the remote possibility they might be inclined to make an attempt, they lack any real ability to successfully "tax the rich."

Some of these macroeconomic tools might be theoretically available to capitalism at the nation-state (or transnational) level; however, a revitalized Fordism is not much more practical for the United States or for a capitalist structure such as the Eurozone. Notwithstanding the fact that the "pay as you go" requirements[5] have been—and will be—quickly abandoned for matters of "war" and "security" and for rescues of various TBTF financial entities,[6] the chances are remote for any contemporary "New New Deal" scheme anywhere in the capitalist metropolis. Consider this statement by a member of the left bloc in Syriza*: "If you are going to apply such a programme, as Syriza has proclaimed, which is not radical—Syriza's programme is just moderate Keynesianism—you need to think seriously of how you are going to get out of the confines of the Eurozone" (Lapasivitas 2015).

Nixon thought that we were all becoming Keynesians in 1971,[7] but classical Keynesianism is certainly not the path being taken today at the nation-state and transnational levels in the "West." In fact, from the point of view of global capital such a position would hardly be rational. In the current situation, the broad-based concessions required for such a rescue from above are counter to both the perceived and the real interests of the sectors of global capital that are dominant at present. The short-term risks to the profitability of existing investment—particularly its speculative and leveraged/financialized component—outweigh any ruling-class worries about the bleak outlook for capitalist stability in the metropolis. Hopes for such major capitalist concessions only provide fever dreams for a politically exhausted social democracy.

Changes in the structural and ideological circumstances at the nation-state level support a ruling-class strategy—neo-liberal austerity and privatization of the commons—that excludes potentials for Fordism. This strategy includes an array of intensified repression that is imposed and enforced directly by police and military power, and indirectly via a vast array of disciplinary structures and processes that are increasingly opaque/insensitive to (and removed from) the subjects that are disciplined.

Established power currently needs a new basis for capitalist hegemony not dependent on a Keynesian plausible promise of an expanded and broadened material stake in the system. Its alternative presents a reconstituted social basis for hegemony, a consensus resting on fear of the "permanent social danger" (Hardt and Negri 2003) from the growing populations, both external and internal, that are excluded from the possibilities of the current conjuncture. In this way, the capitalist "West" produces a general need for its latently rebellious Fergusons to substantiate the visions of thugs and barbarians challenging "civilization"—not only at the gates but from within the very heartland. But only if the challenges can be reliably domesticated.

At the risk of introducing more elements of indeterminacy, I want to dispel any ideas that I'm arguing that the state is weakening or "withering"* and becoming a less central issue for radical strategy than it was previously. If anything, I think that the role of the state is becoming more important and more complicated, particularly in the arenas that make Badiou's imperative to remain "at a distance from the state"* such a crucial principle (Badiou 2010, 192).

It's important to dispel the left common sense view that the capitalist state is a "tool," a ruling-class instrumentality with a "monopoly on legitimate violence,"[8] applicable as needed to advance the interests of the capitalist class or some fragment of it. In that perspective, the capitalist ruling class and the capitalist state become interchangeable descriptive categories and alternative state policies are reduced to alternative approaches of major ruling-class fractions with formally "representative" and "democratic" parliamentary structures reduced to window dressing.

This position has some similarity to the notion of the "hollowing" of the state that I support. Both assume an expansion of state and non-state repression and recognize the importance of a strategic anti-parliamentarism—of maintaining a politics "at a distance from the state." However, there are significant differences. Left "common sense" sees an emerging capitalist consensus towards a more repressive "leviathan" state—on an inexorable trajectory towards fascism.

The conception of the "hollowing" of the state has significantly different political implications. This recent statement from Black Agenda Report's Glen Ford illustrates some of these:

> The conclusion is obvious: the Obama administration is determined to escalate and expand the national counter-insurgency police mission begun in the late Sixties in response to the Black Liberation Movement, a policy that has led to the establishment of a Black Mass Incarceration State. (Ford 2015)

I don't question the historical facts behind the argument, however this formulation has problems. Without minimizing its impacts, it's important to recognize the complexity and contradiction in Black oppression in this country. If such a repressive ruling-class mission has been hegemonic during the past period, what explains why racial repression is only elevated to genocide fifty years after the crucial challenge to capitalist authority had developed and been largely countered? I doubt that Ford thinks this delay in the "mission" resulted from a previous independence of the state. The core of his argument is not really "obvious." Particularly if contemporaneous changes in imperial attitudes towards the broader national liberation movements in the world are considered, the incorporative side of US capitalism's response to the Black Liberation insurgency of the late 60s and early 70s are as apparent as are its efforts to suppress and crush the challenge.

These incorporative features were explicit in the so-called "Great Society" agenda and in the emergence of a neo-colonial Black middle class with its Black mayors and police chiefs, etc. These factors had impacts on this society that are at least as important as the increasingly militarized policing and more extensive and intensive applications of counterinsurgency doctrines in situations like Ferguson.

The political changes in this country cannot be adequately understood as the US ruling class wielding an increasingly racist state power against an increasingly multinational working class; abandoning pretenses of democracy and popular participation to reveal the racially organized class dictatorship that was there all along. That's too simple and not supported by sufficient facts. Most important, it directs our attention away from new elements in the situation that demand reworking our political approach.

To provide some context for this point, let me make a brief excursion to Michael Heinrich's conception of the capitalist state based on chapter 11 of Marx's *Capital* (Heinrich 2012). Heinrich argues that the overriding and distinctive function of the capitalist state is the promotion and defense of a mode of production in which all classes have a limited equality, circumscribed by the boundaries of a specifically capitalist rule set. Any capture of the state by any bloc of capital will undermine its capacity to discipline the diverse elements and interests of the capitalist class into an effective administration of the policies that will serve capital's changing needs. If the capitalist state functions as an armed executive, enforcing the immediate political and economic interests of the strongest elements of the capitalist class, it will be at the expense of the flexibility and adaptability of the capitalist system.

For Heinrich, the capitalist state needs a real autonomy from specific competitive capitalist interests, in order to develop a general capitalist class interest that can be presented as a general interest of the entire society. To avoid undermining the mystifications of power and class that give this system of minority domination its resilience, the state needs some independence from every ruling-class sector—or at least the plausible appearance of such relative independence.

Capitalist nation-states have a long and complicated relationship to the development of their national capitalisms. Historically, the US federal state has assumed major responsibilities for infrastructure development and for many aspects of the reproduction and training of the labor force. While these state functions clearly benefit capitalism over time, the most "political" of the elements of the capitalist class routinely oppose them irrespective of whether they are clearly in their middle- and long-term class interests. Their priority is to guard against any possibility that any public project, pro-capital or not, becomes a significant subtraction from short-term profit. Sometimes they are successful—sometimes not so much.

Sharper contradictions develop when class and mass struggle pressure the state to expand both the level of social consumption and a facade of popular participation and democratic legitimacy. Faced with situations that call for incorporative reforms in the general capitalist interest, state policies and apparatuses often conflict with major organized ruling-class fractions that oppose any actions that might increase their costs or reduce their revenues. In the real world, this means significant opposition from capital to any substantive reforms—again, an opposition that is not always successful.

Up to this point I've been assuming a generic capitalist state based loosely on US conditions. However, if the state is not a simple ruling-class tool it is also not just a disembodied function. State power is constituted and operates through a set of historically developed bureaucratic institutions—concrete structures, each of them with their own limiting characteristics and internal inertia, and with their unique levels of effectiveness and dysfunction.

While the general functional role of the state is to advance the general and long-term interests of capitalism, these interests are not transparent goals. "A state is not a well-oiled machine, but an ensemble of relations traversed by struggle and subject to competing political pressures" (Seymour 2014). At every level of the state structure, the actual policies emerge from a context of class and social struggle. However, there are no guarantees that they are the appropriate objectives for any group, or that they are being implemented in the most effective manner. Clearly, this "ensemble of relations" can become dysfunctional if it lacks sufficient flexibility and autonomy to contain the competition between and within the defining social classes. Although the interests of capitalism as a system require a state apparatus that can subordinate short-term and sectoral capitalist interests to the general stability of the system, it is seldom self-evident which policies will be most effective to achieve these ends.

This opens the field to capitalist competition, and no bloc of capital will deliberately risk its profits and comparative advantages—its survival—for a vaguely understood general class interest. All attempts to deal with the conditions for the social reproduction of "free" labor or for the efficient realization of surplus value will be in tension with some short-term interests of certain sectors of capital. These distinctive, partial interests are likely to be more clearly understood and forcefully advanced than the alternative policies they respond to.

A careful state pursuit of a genuinely "class conscious" capitalist course is made even less likely when, as is normally the case, long-term objectives are also both contentious and ambiguous and there is a range of differences in opinion over how to achieve them.

As state structures become less sensitive to the long-term health of capitalism, the system has few alternatives to the organization of dominance and subordination that is mislabeled as "representative government." The so-called "self-equilibrating market"[9] is certainly not an option. It is bound by capitalist assumptions and logic that can't deal with the larger social costs of capitalist production: the restricted development of productive forces, anthropogenic climate change, the general ecological degeneration, etc.

The limits of capitalism are essentially determined by this unstable domination of an overwhelming majority by a tiny minority. No temporarily ascendant ruling-class bloc will evade these limits through capturing and manipulating the state apparatus. When any sector of the apparatus becomes merely the enforcement arm for the immediate interests of a specific capitalist class fraction, this will damage the longer-term prospects for that apparatus—increasing frictions within the ruling class and weakening capital's capacity to leverage popular struggles against the effects of its rule into a new basis of command over those who are ruled.

There are practical political implications to the increasing brittleness of state apparatuses. One that is particularly germane at local and regional levels akin to Ferguson, is the entrapment of popular initiatives in identity-based self-governing schemes, assortments of illusory reforms, and hollow promises of autonomy. These approaches eventually wind up revitalizing a localized element of capitalist domination. In some ways this parallels the dilemmas of union reform strategies that achieve "victories" where workers end up administering their own subordination. "Victories" in this arena will leave us with a few more Black police chiefs, Black mayors, possibly even Black presidents, overseeing an accelerating trend towards failed states and dysfunctional state apparatuses.

This clarifies the basic differences between viewing the capitalist state as increasingly "hollow" and viewing it as having been captured by specific sectors of capital and subordinated to the pursuit of their narrow interests. The unspoken corollary of the capture thesis follows the ill-fated "third period" German Communist policy: "After the Nazis, Us." It hopefully assumes that an overt ruling-class capture of some state apparatus implies a possibility for a similar capture by different class forces.[10]

Unfortunately, when we are dealing with "hollow" state structures on a sub-national level—Ferguson, for example—that are impacted by blocs of capital with vastly disproportionate economic resources and political power, any local capacity to confront issues of political legitimacy and social costs will be overwhelmed. No version of this outcome is likely to clarify the path ahead for the working class—or for those of us who see ourselves as among its "conscious elements."

The "hollowing" perspective acknowledges that the indeterminism of capitalism's long-term objectives, and the increasing limitations on state structures to pursue them while maintaining vestiges of popular legitimacy, will be reflected in an expansion of state repression. But the quantitative increase of repression is likely to be less important than the changes in its quality. This points to a loosening of the political oversight and centralized controls on the so-called "deep state" and to an increasing involvement of sectors of capital with corrupt rogue fragments of the state apparatus and privatized, non-state forms of repression and oppression. The consequence will be the emergence of territorial and non-territorial forms of warlordism—and there is no reason to equate warlordism with a clearer class polarization. To the contrary, this trajectory can easily wind up on the bad end of the "socialism or barbarism" dilemma, and perhaps on the worse sides of "barbarism."

To put it differently, there are possible outcomes of the merger of "First'" and "Third" world that, in a sense, would be the opposite of the capitalist state enforcing a general class interest on competitive sectors of capital. One outcome could be sectors of the state apparatus acting out of various bureaucratic logics that overlap with some narrow capitalist interests to produce those modern forms of neo-colonial governance (or lack of governance) that play such a large role to our south and in many other parts of our current world—particularly in those locales, and they are increasing in number, where the sectoral interests of fragments of capital and elements of failed state structures don't conform to transnational capital's perceptions of the properly profitable basis for global capitalist stability. The conflicts that emerge are likely to activate a range of armed actors: state, quasi-state, and non-state. I hope people see where I'm going here without the need for further elaboration at this point, since I want to move on to consider some approaches to resistance, again very loosely in the light of Ferguson.

These approaches to resistance involve understanding the objective and subjective sides of the class struggle that we actually have—as opposed to one we wish we had and that some continue to hope for. I've recently read a piece by Jehu Ferguson (2013). He appears to be a remnant of the CWP (ML) who has drifted away from that collapsed brand of statist Maoism in a productive direction.[11] Jehu cited an early Marx position on the working class as follows:

> The separate individuals form a class only insofar as they have to carry on a common battle against another class; otherwise they are on hostile terms with each other as competitors. (Marx and Engels 1845)

A range of other references are possible from Marx or others that address the strategic significance of competition within the working class, perhaps the early IWW* positions on "scabbing," or maybe the position of Gramsci* who said something to the effect that a working class not conscious of its class position is like a bag of potatoes.[12]

Although the competition within the subordinated classes and strata is essential to the hegemony of capital, the erosion of this hegemonic capacity doesn't automatically subordinate the internal class competition to a "common battle against another class." This erosion of hegemony doesn't even necessarily improve the conditions for challenging strife within the class. The modes of competition that perpetuate the essential working-class acquiescence to continued subordination do not evaporate under the pressure of events—even when these events are very dramatic ostensibly "progressive" changes in the political context. They are not limits that are easily surpassed. Instead, they re-emerge within those subsequent "common battles," perhaps in altered form. They must be confronted in the knowledge that common battles have a dismaying tendency to quickly lose their "common" character as the collective will to continue to fight a "common battle" disintegrates.

It's very important to fully grasp the fact that competition is omnipresent in daily working-class routine, while the moments of a genuinely "common battle" are relatively rare and isolated episodes that are eminently reversible. Although such reversals never exactly resurrect a previous status quo, the moments of sharp conflict can provide the cumulative additions needed for the emergence of a revolutionary working class.

The view that the working class within capitalism is "objectively revolutionary" has extensive radical credentials, and with important autonomist amendments it is widely held in our section of the left. It was a pillar of the *operaist** view in general and Facing Reality* in particular. It underlies the "well grubbed old mole" imagery and certainly applies to Sergio Bologna, who was a major popularizer of that image.[13] Although it is easy to appreciate the anti-vanguardist motivations of the position when it comes in autonomist clothing, it is difficult to support empirically. The "objectively revolutionary" forecast tends to discount some facts while elevating others to produce the desired result. A multitude of examples of workers relating to other workers as "competitors" is overlooked, while a handful of examples of workers acting in solidarity, often strained and transitory examples, become an adequate proof of an underlying essence that is supposedly destined to ultimately emerge triumphant.

In my view, while struggles like Ferguson manifest some mass potentials for transcending capitalist "prehistory,"[14] they also throw up new obstacles for realizing such potentials. This is where the competition within the class becomes a factor of overwhelming importance, and why quotation marks around "advances" are perhaps more merited than those around "competition." The differences, the partial interests, the narrowness, the limits presented by this continuing competition necessitate that internal class dynamics be placed in the forefront of any analysis of the developments around Ferguson.

Bromma's *The Worker Elite* (2014) has some relevance to this point. His basic argument is that what the left tends to see as one working class is actually an amalgam of three separate classes with distinct and conflicting interests:

> A meaningful percentage of workers in the developing world—and a majority of workers in the wealthy countries—have a lot more to lose than their chains ... these workers meet the minimum economic requirement for the worker elite. (Bromma 2014, 35)

In my opinion, Bromma's position is superior on many questions to other left analyses of the working class, but on important points it only displaces some questions about an objective grounding for a revolutionary class struggle onto a narrower conception of the global proletariat. Some strategic issues will be more tractable if his "worker elite" is seen as a separate non-revolutionary class or a strategically distinct conservative class fraction, but the unanswered question remains—how will the class, narrowly or broadly conceived, move past the terrain of "better terms" in the struggle within capitalism to the terrain of the abolition of capital? Bromma recognizes this issue in his treatment of the worker elite's "buffer" function in the class struggle:

> The worker elite serves as an object of longing for the proletariat. It embodies living proof that some working-class people can achieve privileged middle-class lives. For many proletarians then, the question becomes not, "how can we make revolution?" but "how can I become a part of the worker elite?" (Bromma 2014, 10)

That is exactly right. One way or another every section and sector of the working class, as well as every individual worker and every working-class family, can look to ameliorate their circumstances within the framework of capitalist possibilities through a process of competition with others like them. What is needed is a rupture, a break with this framework where workers begin to see the universe of possibilities outside of it.

Bromma raises the issue of working-class sectors with "more to lose than their chains" as if that provided some elements of an answer. However, every sector and component of the global working class, including those that he sees as part of the global proletariat and those that he doesn't, always has more to lose than chains. The problem is for them to understand what is available to win outside the framework of capital.

Let me try to illustrate what I'm getting at with a criticism of a couple of passages from a recent piece by Unity and Struggle called "Old Mole Breaks Concrete":

> The US working class is on the move. The Ferguson militants are the vanguard of a rebellion threatening to generalize across the United States.
>
> What is the seemingly endless (up to *ten hours* in some cases) snake march, diverging from one march, converging with another, flowing amorphously from one major infrastructure blockade to another? In our view this is the class groping toward a form of militant action in a period when direct confrontation with the state seems to be off the table. Ferguson has set the tone for the class struggle in the US, but Ferguson, where rioting has flared and at times live ammunition has been fired at the police, is difficult to emulate outside of its context. (JF and Friends 2014)

I completely agree with this sense of the importance of the struggles and actions that are described, and have no quarrel with using some poetic license to impress that importance on others. However, I question this phraseology: "the US working class is on the move," "this is the class groping towards a form of militant action." This language avoids the contradictions and internal dynamics that a radical intervention should clarify—e.g., the issues raised by marginalization and precarious labor—and it substitutes consideration of the real problems of mass, intermediate, and revolutionary organization and the work needed to sustain and build from near-insurrectionary moments with a fetishism of militancy and a spontaneism that assumes a too easy path ahead.

My own position comes with very recognizable problems (and many people in this circle have developed their politics as a response to those problems): vanguardism, elitism, and substitutionism.* It also comes with little practical specificity and frankly I feel a bit foolish to offer it up again in the face of the widespread fragmentation and demoralization among those who have attempted to develop a conscious and collective approach to political activism. I might call my approach Leninist, but my understanding of what is Leninist is certainly not widely shared and is probably not historically defensible. So for now I stick with Badiou*—recognizing some problems there as well—and suggest that people look at *The Rebirth of History* (2012), especially the first few pages of chapter 7, "Event and Political Organization."

## Withering
## January 2017

*The following is an edited version of a longer piece circulated on a private email list of comrades. It was written in response to both Trump's electoral victory and the general rise of social unrest.*

For a couple of decades I've thought that capital was approaching the barriers and limits that Marx forecasts in those famous *Grundrisse* passages in the chapter on machinery.[1] In the capitalist core areas, rent-seeking transnational capital interacts with increasingly "hollow"* structures of bourgeois political rule to marginalize human labor and human life, reshaping relationships between repression, reform, and revolution. The results are evident in the decay of the social-democratic/Fordist* paradigm, the interpenetration of "First" and "Third" worlds (à la Negri*),[2] and the emergence of a mass social base for various neo-fascisms.

Recent developments, notably around the 2016 election, require some rethinking of the implications of this perspective. I've previously argued that the political and economic tensions between financialized transnational capital and the remnants of nationally based capital formations would be manifested in conflicts with forms of populism, and that these conflicts would overwhelmingly tend to favor transnational capital. The first part of this assumption appears plausible ... the second, not so much. Given Trump's victory, Brexit, and the emerging ethno-nationalist right in Europe, this asymmetrical balance of forces appears a good deal less certain—at least in the short run.

A related assumption of mine was that competition between nationally and regionally organized capitalist blocs would be outweighed by the common capitalist interest in preempting and combatting threats from the masses of dispossessed and marginalized populations from both left and radical right. However, recent developments in the Middle and Far East and the Balkans[3] indicate that intra-capitalist competitions and conflicts—including some old and new nation-state rivalries—are growing in importance and that the contradiction between economic nationalism and globalism is not nearly so one-sided. In short, the forces promoting a common global capitalist class political perspective are weaker and more disorganized than I expected, and those hardening capital into antagonistic blocs are stronger.

Beyond such questionable estimates of the objective situation, I may have generally underestimated subjective and historically accidental factors, particularly the impact of ideology and organization that is coalesced in a strong political "will," as Gramsci* would put it. Even when such subjective factors have a short shelf life, they can change the political terrain in important and perhaps irreversible ways.

I'll return to these issues in more detail later in this argument. Since I'm posting this before the election impacts have been clarified, I don't have a lot of confidence in my initial conclusions and expect to do some amending over time.

STO* always considered itself a part of the extra-parliamentary left, and I'd still place myself there. An extra-parliamentary perspective in situations where revolution is not immediately on the agenda is both more than, and different from, electoral abstentionism. It is an attempt to act tactically and strategically "at a distance from the state,"* to incorporate a revolutionary liberatory stance towards the state into immediate questions of practical politics. Badiou* (2012) makes this point in his presentation, "From Logic to Anthropology, or Affirmative Dialectics":

> So we have to be entirely, in some sense, outside of state power, subjectively. But we know that the state is always in the field of political questions and in the space of action. If our political subjectivity is not inside the state ... the state is nonetheless in the field of every political action today.

To take a concrete example, suppose we have to do something about workers who are without papers, who are undocumented workers, say, the African immigrants who are in France. … We will quickly find that the state is in our space. We will have to confront new laws and decisions of the state. And we will have to create something, some new form of organization that will be face-to-face with the state, not inside the state, but face-to-face with it. … We will have to prescribe something that establishes relations with the state but not a relation in the state. And the big difficulty … is to maintain the possibility of being outside, while prescribing something that concerns the inside … because the state is always inviting you inside and asking that you not be outside. (Badiou 2012)

This position provides a basic alternative to the entire range of electoral and anti-electoral arguments that emerged during our recent election, not to mention their outsized role in left history.

After Marx made an ambiguous reference in the Manifesto to the working class "organizing itself as a party," the Second International formations moved quickly towards mass, working class–based parties that were increasingly oriented towards functioning within capitalist parliamentary structures.[4] Most of the non-anarchist sectors of the left became increasingly involved in the maneuvers and mind-sets of parliamentary and trade unionist politics and slid inexorably towards the tame, official social democracy that we know today (Luxemburg's* "Mass Strike" being something of an exception).[5] While the more orthodox sectors maintained a rhetorical commitment to an eventual anti-capitalist revolution for a time, the increasingly reformist and evolutionary sectors moved beyond mere parliamentary participation and joined capitalist governments.

The Leninist "Tribune of the People" stance subordinated participation in parliamentary frameworks to the discipline of an extra-parliamentary "vanguard party."[6] However, all such

"Tribunes" quickly came under heavy pressure to opt for "effectiveness" within parliamentary structures. The more numerous and "influential" the "Tribunes," the greater the likelihood they would weasel at crucial junctures and abandon any commitments to smashing the capitalist state apparatus. With the rapid decay of the revolutionary impetus in "Communism," these principles were increasingly off the table, replaced by various evolutionary incrementalist schemes and reformist conceptions of united and popular fronts.* This decay disoriented any revolutionary social base, and "betrayals" by parliamentary fractions and vanguard party leaderships became routine. This re-posed the strategic question: to what extent should a revolutionary movement seek influence within structures whose essential function is the exercise of class rule, using notions of representation as a substitute for mass movements, class fractions, and individuals that need to become autonomous and "for themselves"?

I became aware of the questions of extra-parliamentary politics on a practical level in 1968, a period that was in some ways similar to the present as well as in some ways significantly different. A few of us in the Communist Party and sections of the left argued that rather than trying to take over, modify, or replace the Democratic Party and make it more "representative," "democratic," or "working-class," our energy should be focused on undermining its legitimacy and fragmenting its organizational structure.

A mixture of naïveté and self-imposed ignorance and the unique historical circumstances led me to think such an extra-parliamentary attempt to smash the Democratic Party could be implemented via the CPUSA. It couldn't, but that's another story. At the time, some fifty years ago, this approach was resisted with arguments that are quite familiar today. The overwhelmingly dominant approach argued that the popular upsurge of the period could and should be harnessed and leveraged to realign parliamentary politics, by either "taking over" the Democratic Party or by creating a mass electoral "people's" or "labor" party. There were a wide range of such perspectives, some openly argued ...

some not so much. All variants advocated taking particular care to protect popular "gains"—by ensuring that various electoral lesser evils suffered no substantial continuing damage.

The second approach was much less widespread. It followed the current Guevarist and Maoist tendencies that treated the existing capitalist state formations as both illegitimate and something of a paper tiger.* This parallels some current variants of insurrectionism by discounting the importance of concrete organized challenges to state legitimacy in favor of a general moralistic revolutionary posture. In the late 60s, this second category was extremely anti-electoral, but was not really extra-parliamentary as laid out in the previous Badiou passage, and within a few years most of its advocates either became politically passive or moved on to one of the infinite variants of the expressly reformist position.

In summary, the modern history of the left in this country has been filled with notions of capturing a "major" party: realigning the Democrats, building a "new" party, a "progressive" party, a "people's" party, a "labor" or "farmer-labor" party, or perhaps a "mass socialist" or "anti-capitalist" party. It's sometimes hard to recall the initial "tragedy" in uncritical reruns of known failures, but the farcical aspects of resurrecting them as real alternatives to the existing political scene are pretty evident.[7]

The reinflation of these shop-worn politics is not surprising. What is surprising is the widespread lack of appreciation that these questions are not unique to this country or this historical moment. Sadly, with marginally different terminology and packaging, similar approaches have emerged over the past century in most areas that are afflicted with parliamentary "democracy."

This historical experience doesn't mean that parliamentary issues "don't matter." At the minimum they should be taken seriously as a window into ruling-class efforts to develop a common class perspective and a coherent political program. Parliamentary and trade union frameworks diffuse and incorporate actual and potential challenges to power and profit in ways that reconstitute capitalist hegemony on a broader and more stable basis. All major issues of reform migrate towards these incorporative structures even if that is not where they originate. They are where the partial victories and the defeats of the reform struggle are generalized and institutionalized. At the same time, however, capitalism's weaknesses and vulnerabilities in this area provide opportunities to undermine its power and hegemony. Neither parliamentary cretinism nor simple abstentionism can take adequate advantage of such opportunities.

The electoral duopoly in this country regularly produces elements that appear to be relatively more responsive to mass grievances and more capable of representing popular demands. These elements function to sanction, shape, and implement reform "victories," and the mechanisms and processes employed legitimate the domination of capital as a collateral cost. In the absence of organized challenges to their underlying logic, they reinforce the notion that electoral and parliamentary politics are an essential path to getting things done. To the extent that the gains are—or appear to be—substantive, more support is generated for treating the state as potentially "neutral" and above class—as a "tool" that might be "captured," not a bulwark of oppression and exploitation that must be smashed.

As noted in the earlier Badiou passage, "the state is always inviting you inside," herding potential antagonists of the system into a subordinate position within the system. This takes on some odd forms when the state is increasingly "hollow" and its capacities to perform its ruling-class functions are increasingly atrophied.

In order to build the ideological and organizational elements of autonomous class power outside the apparatus of the state we have a number of tasks: to present alternatives to bureaucratized authority, target all condescending saviors and their realpolitik narratives, and demystify officialdoms with challenges to their political and technical competence. Inevitably, this will lead to charges that we are undercutting reform potentials, jeopardizing real possibilities for real victories, and alienating potential allies. We need to recognize the elements of truth in such charges in order to effectively respond to them.

Revolutionaries must implement a stance of critique and radical rejection that avoids any "worse is better" attitude towards working-class conditions of life. On the other hand, we can't peddle shop-worn adages that claim that revolutionary struggle will produce the maximum in reform victories as a "byproduct." The limitations of this argument become particularly evident when it is applied to the problems of parliamentarism and the capitalist state. It will be necessary to take some risks and incur some losses in order to maintain a consistent anti-state posture. Frequently, our position will only be a minority, perhaps at times a small and besieged one, but it is only from such refusing and rejecting minorities that an organized radical counter-power with social substance "outside" the state apparatus will be developed.

This has been a lengthy excursion from some more immediate points that may have been distracting. I hope my weak attempt to link these issues to Badiou's "distance from the state" injunction leads some to look further at his position. However, at this point I'd like to approach the same issues in a more practical way by looking at the different social forces and strategies of class rule that Trump, Clinton, and Sanders represented in the outcomes of the 2016 election.

Clinton was clearly the preferred candidate of transnational capital, including some sectors (e.g., extractive industries) that could have been relatively advantaged by Trump's proposed priorities. She had the organized support of an overwhelming majority of the global and national political and economic elites, despite having clear public relations risks as a nominee and as a presidential candidate. The distinctively Clintonesque merger of neoliberal and neoconservative doctrines, disguised for political expediency and appropriately modified for personal rent-seeking, represented continuity with the past half century.

Clinton's social base and political trajectory is hardly in question, so I'd like to spend a little more time on Trump and Sanders. Both were pro-capitalist populists of different hues, and both began their campaigns as half-hearted and equivocal opponents of an "establishment" that had already clearly anointed Clinton—although neither are strongly committed to that stance.

Trump began by merging an economic nationalist "America First" narrative with a clear white supremacist content with some hints of possible "left" populist themes, including a rejection of past and future imperialist "nation building," the horrific ongoing failure in Afghanistan chief among them. Initially more a promotion of a brand than a political program, the Trump primary campaign was packaged in an absurdist theatrical narcissism that combined politics with performance in a manner that seemed destined, if not calculated, to end in a defeat. Although there was little doubt that such a political defeat would be a profitable outcome for the brand. There is some reason to believe that Trump's campaign was initially promoted by some "establishment" forces that were shopping for an ideal foil, a vulnerable "pied piper" that could grease Clinton's election while knee-capping potential Republican opponents who were mistakenly seen as far more challenging than Trump.

As Trump's campaign became less of a joke and it became likely that he would be nominated, as well as that his nomination might fragment the Republican Party, sectors of conservative Republicanism began joining. Under cover of "broadening" Trump's base, they were set on bringing his campaign's excesses and exaggerations under control in the interests of preserving the two-party system and maintaining stability. The watering down of the Trump campaign accelerated after he was nominated and it became apparent that Clinton was a flawed, vulnerable candidate who could conceivably lose—or who might win but be unable to serve.

Now that Trump has won the election, his capture by such establishment forces (if "capture" is the proper term) is fairly complete. Trump is sufficiently hemmed in by neoliberal and neoconservative orthodoxy that only minor rhetorical hints of an anti-establishment "draining the swamp" populism remain—and these are unlikely to survive beyond the inauguration. On the other hand, his actual policy stances that remain in force ensure that the most reactionary aspects of establishment Republicanism will thrive in the pending Trump Administration.

Trump's general shift back towards the capitalist status quo ante will de-emphasize the more overt elements of racism, misogyny, and xenophobia in his campaign persona and his following. If right-wing populism is as vulnerable to buyer's remorse as its left-wing cousin, this will certainly fragment his quasi-fascist support base. Perhaps more relevant for us, it might undermine left strategies that see his election as a big opening for their popular front* politics. In any case, it's important to remember that, even if the programmatic dilution of Trump's populism undermines his ability to effectively speak for potentially subversive constituencies his campaign has energized and mobilized, those constituencies will still be there—affecting what we can and should do, as well as what the ruling class can and will do.

In 2012, Sanders had criticized Obama for abandoning the "change" aspect of the "hope and change" imagery and advocated a presidential primary challenge to Obama's re-election to a second term. However, he wasn't willing to undertake the task himself for fear of losing his Senate seat and its prerogatives. In 2016, Sanders's "new New Deal" "left" populism capitulated to centrist capitalist politics from the outset. Despite the criticisms of Obama policies in the previous election cycle, in 2016, when they would have been effective charges against Clinton, Sanders evaded criticisms of the Obama record on crucial questions, notably including his personal signature issues. No "populism" can gain traction as an insurgent movement if it accepts the major policies of those who have been holding the reins of government power. If Sanders had come a bit closer to winning the Democratic nomination, this basic opportunism would have become more evident. Nevertheless, it is hardly hidden. On questions of militarism, imperialism, and war, Sanders's "populism" accepted the official narratives. He avoided obvious and relevant criticisms of the worst elements of existing policies, even though they clearly would have been popular with his main constituencies.

Quite obviously, the Sanders campaign didn't expect to win the presidential nomination. Instead, it aimed to lay the groundwork for a realignment of the Democratic Party as a step towards transforming it into more of a "people's party" with a clearer political distinction from the Republicans. Rhetoric aside, nothing like a "revolution" was ever intended. At best, the objective was a moderate shake up of the Democratic Party structure, making it more responsive to popular pressure. Sanders and his campaign's key organizers hoped to have some impact on the party platform, to gain some positions in the party hierarchy, and to consolidate an official opposition status. His abject capitulation, and that of much of the leadership of his "movement" after they were summarily discarded at the Democratic Convention, demonstrated the limitations of the venture. The trajectory of the Sanders campaign was shaped by the efforts of its political leadership to dilute and contain his radical populist support within the duopoly's limited range of mindless and bureaucratic electoral busy work. That feature is even more evident in his campaign's dysfunctional efforts in the aftermath of the election season.

The Sanders phenomenon caught its organizers by surprise and outstripped their expectations. At a moment when Clinton's candidacy embodied established power at its most entitled, arrogant, and venal, it was caught up in the same reflexive popular rejection of the "establishment" that benefited Trump. However, a significant difference between the two campaigns is noted in *Counterpunch*'s Jeffrey St. Clair's comment on the primary election process: "Trump prevailed because he was willing, indeed eager to burn down the Republican Party house with him. Sanders failed, in large part, because he wasn't, even when the Democratic Party house, run with the ruthless calculation of any casino, conspired against him" (St. Clair 2016).

Sanders could easily have been a much better "left" candidate—less of a sheep dog. He could have applied his critique of "big money" to a proper range of targets and challenged the permanent war logic of the Military-Industrial Complex and the Global War on Terror. A refusal to concede to Clinton after the convention was certainly within the realm of possibility. If Sanders had launched some kind of independent campaign, as most of his supporters wanted, it could have had a decisive impact on eventual outcomes—perhaps denying the election to both Trump and Clinton. Similar things happen elsewhere in the world, and they are likely to become more frequent. Nevertheless, both history and logic indicate that so long as the range of such outcomes are contained inside the "representative" parliamentary framework, their impact on the power and legitimacy of capital will be neither decisive nor cumulatively enduring.

My main point is that populisms have the potential to be much more radical and come much closer to actual governmental authority than anything we saw in this election. They might even "win" and still wind up with a strengthened capitalist legitimacy. Given the probability of another global financial/economic crisis in the relatively near future, how better to cripple a populist movement than to make it responsible for governing in a recession/depression context without having access to even the normal Keynesian* toolbox? It would be very foolish to believe that the ruling class lacks the capacity to think such thoughts.

This brings us back to the importance of an organized and consistent strategic commitment to remain "outside" the state while attempting to disrupt, not only the system's directly coercive police power, but also its incorporative frameworks for concessions. Without that aspect, populist discontent, even when it takes on organized, radical, and militant "left" aspects, will ultimately produce broader arrays of reformism and reaction, not a systemic alternative to capital.

At this point, I'd like to move back from this particular focus on an election to consider some implications for my general perspective that the transnational capitalist system will increasingly subordinate intra-capitalist conflicts to a perceived existential threat to its survival from the marginalized, dispossessed, and excluded masses of the planet. This will lead back to some of the questions that I raised about problematic elements of my own views at the start of this piece.

I've been working from four assumptions:

1. The transnational capitalist system is an economic reality, but initiatives towards transnational state structures are still in their infancy and are heavily contested, although a range of transnational financial and economic institutions are operational beyond public scrutiny.

2. Transnational capitalism limits and undermines the political and economic capacities of all current capitalist state structures—some much more than others. These conflicts obstruct the development and implementation of a coherent ruling-class political and economic perspective that can effectively contend with the actual and potential oppositions to transnational capital.

3. The "main danger" for transnational capitalism are challenges and disruptions that will emerge from the classes and class fractions of permanently dispossessed and marginalized working and poor people throughout the world. This is both a matter of fact and an implicit ideological premise of this ruling-class strata. However, this prioritization of risks and threats to capital is not fully shared by other fractions of capital, particularly those that have a vested interest in magnifying and manufacturing threats of a different character to buttress their economic and political fortunes.

4. In contrast with the recent past, socially constructed common fears will provide the principal element of social legitimacy for capitalist regimes in the Lockean core.* These will replace most attempts to expand and generalize material advantages (Fordism*) and any ruling-class initiatives towards political and social incorporation through expansion of what is called "democracy."

Ten years ago, I thought that the contradictory elements within capital would produce economic and political competitions between various profit and rent-seeking transnational structures, and the political significance of such contradictions would outweigh political and economic tensions and contestations between capitalist nation-states. However, in the "West," capitalist China or capitalist Russia is increasingly presented as a "near-peer" strategic threat,[8] and tensions of a national bloc character are growing more important, not less. It is also clear that rival national capitalisms are promoting economic nationalist ideologies, movements, and state forms within their own spheres of influence as well as those of their posited national competitors.

There is no denying the increasing importance of such nation-state contradictions, despite the clear risks they raise of exacerbating the "flailing and churning" of global capital (Ranney, 2014). They elevate the possibility of trade and currency wars and undermine the possibilities for a coherent response to capitalist financial and economic cycles. In general, they jeopardize the globalist TINA* narrative. Trump diverged somewhat from this pattern for a political moment, however his general reversion towards the establishment status quo includes a greater focus on "state enemies." His emphasis on China and Iran, as opposed to his ruling-class critics' focus on Russia, is essentially opportunistic and accidental.

This leads to a second point. After 9/11 the "enemy rogue state" narrative morphed into the "Global War on Terror," locating the main strategic threat to capitalist "civilization" in challenges emerging from the massive populations of permanently marginalized working people in zones of chaos and ungovernability—outside of the capitalist "rule set." These positions were prevalent in Western ruling-class circles only a few years ago, but they are scarcely mentioned today. Instead, a ruling-class propaganda theme with a long historical lineage that had been in decline following the implosion of "actually existing socialism"* has been resurrected. Its central feature is the need for permanent national mobilizations against a succession of "enemy" nation-states. (Chomsky, questionably, terms these "fabricated" external enemies, but that is a different discussion.)[9]

At the height of the Iraq War ten years ago, I thought the transnational capitalist class interest in implementing a "War on Terror" against a range of actual and potential radical challenges would increasingly outweigh economic nationalist competitions within capital.[10] For what it's worth, I still think these challenges pose the primary threat to capital when their potential impacts are considered over an appropriate time frame. However, it is hard to deny that this "civilizational challenge" from "barbarism" that raised the "spectre" of the "common ruin of the contending classes," is increasingly ignored by major sectors of the global ruling class.[11] The Russian and Chinese capitalist elites may be something of an exception here, but Russia's increasing promotion of quasi-populist right-wing European nationalist reaction raises the possibility that these differences are eroding.

There is no doubt that ruling-class "anti-fascism" consciously combines fear and xenophobia with an exaggerated threat of terrorism to consolidate a pro-capitalist law and order constituency. Rather than responding to such challenges from "outside" as harbingers of a real and growing common danger, various capitalist state and some non-state actors treat them instrumentally, as tools; possibly to disrupt an emerging Shia arc, or to advantage a particular strategic pipeline routing, or to expedite labor discipline in strategically important areas of resource extraction in the "Third World."

In any case, none of these assumptions looks adequate at the moment. Perhaps it might be argued that it's too early to reach any definite conclusions, and perhaps another global economic tremor or some similar disturbance is needed to show what's right and what's wrong. But, for current purposes, I'm assuming that I was wrong in some important respects and will look at a couple of areas of possible mistakes.

I indicated one of these earlier in this argument. Even when the analysis of interests, institutions, and processes is fairly accurate (and I offer no such guarantees) the reality that is under analysis will be impacted by various accidental or external factors that cannot be accurately foreseen. Despite assertions such as Engels's argument that "amid all the endless host of accidents … the economic movement finally asserts itself as necessary" (Engels 1890) (i.e., that economic factors win out in the "long run"), these factors can undermine or upend structural analyses that aim at objectivity. Before the "long runs" are completed, accidental factors *can* change the nature of the process—and then it can be changed again by conscious and organized interventions. In this manner a range of countervailing impacts can create a basic indeterminacy where outcomes are unexpected and essentially irreversible.

For example, in current conditions a major armed conflict or an environmental disaster could substantially reshuffle the political deck … and how might anyone predict the consequences of some screw-loose attempt to stop Trump because "Putin hacked the election"? Many such developments are within the range of possibility. However, I don't want to push this argument too far. It's hard to see how any such eventualities would undermine capitalist trajectories towards a chaotic end-state where emancipatory revolution must confront barbarism. In any case, what happens in the middle of this process is of far greater concern than where it starts and how it ends.

I hope this second point is more concrete. While I wanted to end on such real-world concerns, I'm determined to finish these final sections in a reasonable time and will undoubtedly leave some points unclear and unfinished—and hence more abstract.

I think I've treated globalization and the associated "hollowing" of nation-states without taking sufficient account of complicating factors, including some that Bromma raised in his recent essay:

Populist opposition to globalization in the West is making breakthroughs not as globalization rises, but as it falters. In fact, the rise of these political movements is probably more a *reflection* of globalization's decline than the *cause* of that decline. What's coming into view, semi-hidden

> underneath the frenzied soap opera of reactionary popu-
> lism, is that the tide of globalization has crested and started
> to recede. It wasn't permanent after all. (Bromma 2017;
> emphasis in original)

I don't agree with Bromma's thesis that globalization "wasn't permanent after all." However, I do agree that the current trajectory
of various capitalist nation-states has exposed important contradictions in the processes of globalization. This is quite distinct
from seeing globalization as a tide that has "crested and started to
recede."

I have based a good deal of my argument on Heinrich's treatment of the capitalist state (2004) that I have described elsewhere.[12]
This approach distinguishes two functions of these state formations: the first involves the adaptive capacity to respond to popular
challenges to profit and authority; the second involves its capacity
to discipline a contradictory array of sectoral capitalist interests
into a general ruling-class perspective.

I've argued that accelerating globalization and the resulting
increase in social and economic inequality accelerate the erosion
of the will and capacity of all capitalist state formations to employ
material concessions and political co-optations to extend ruling-
class hegemony. This "hollowing" of contemporary state formations and of their ability to deliver economic and social goods to
substantial segments of their constituencies is empirically evident.
So is the resulting erosion of popular legitimacy which produces
the various "populist" oppositions in the capitalist center. Bromma
appears to view all of these populist oppositions as right/reaction-
ary in character, while I would expect some will emerge that will
be essentially reformist and social democratic. However, the main
point is these processes are a reflection of the concrete reality of
globalization, not evidence of its reversal.

One question that I haven't considered adequately is whether
the processes that erode the capacities of various state structures
to discipline the contradictory elements within capital will under-

mine the importance of conflicts between nation-states in a parallel fashion. I think that they will not—at least not in a uniform way. This provides the basis for the continued persistence of intra-capitalist conflicts, including some with a national or imperial form.

I think it's useful to supplement Heinrich with Paul Mattick's article "The Withering of the State" (2016). Mattick doesn't mean "withering" in the familiar Leninist context,[13] as the defining element of a post-revolutionary project. He means it as a degenerative process in capitalism, one element of which is marked by "the increasing inability of the state to manage the common affairs of its citizens, within the fairly stringent limits set by the needs of a business economy." Globalization drastically narrows the "affairs" that ruling elites view as "common" and dictates an approach to their management that combines neoliberal ideology with the policies of austerity. The resulting policies combine managing "the *common* affairs" and "within stringent limits" in such a way that "hollow" the material basis for capitalist legitimacy.

Mattick parallels the notion of the "hollowing" of the capitalist state that I have picked up from a variety of sources—Colin Leys and some not so reputable to the left, e.g., John Robb.[14] The withering of the functional capabilities of the nation-state to manage "common affairs" can range from the cynical conservative retrenchments of the incoming Trump Administration to the equally cynical social-democratic capitulations of the Syriza* government.

However, an important distinction emerges when we consider the characteristics of those "fairly stringent limits set by the needs of a business economy" and their impact on the state's capacity to "discipline" capital. Mattick (2016) argues that one outcome of the "autonomization of the state" is the growth of the "public sector," and that "paradoxically, the very growth of the 'public sector' led to the weakening of [the state's] independence." Mattick goes on to cite Hal Draper: "One of the consequences of the relative autonomy of the state is to permit the dominant sectors *within* the capitalist class to secure the main levers of power" (emphasis in original). When this occurs, it reduces the capacity of these states to subordinate and "discipline" the divergent interests of competitive class fractions and enforce a unified ruling-class perspective.

It's in this area where, in my previous thinking, I missed some aspects of globalization that actually elevate the importance of the contradictions and conflicts between nation-state formations. The explosive growth in transnational capital flows far outstrip the efforts to develop a functional framework to "discipline" the sectors of capital (largely financial capital) that are the main beneficiaries of globalization. In the absence of such a framework, blocs of capital pursue their interests by jockeying for access and control over the existing "main levers of power." Beyond police powers, these include various controls over fiscal/monetary issues, controls over regulatory regimes, and way more. That is, in the diminishing set of nation-states where these tools are currently operational and have not been privatized.

Many approaches to transnational capitalism assume this is a temporary stage that will be superseded as transnational governance mechanisms are developed to shore up the global political and economic order against failed states, informal economies, and warlordism. However, this doesn't give sufficient weight to the countervailing impacts from the elements of capital that benefit from maximizing tensions and contradictions between nation-states and building the relative strength of the state that is uniquely "theirs." This is particularly important when these blocs are positioned to capture "main levers" of the national state.

The main example in this country is the Military–Industrial Complex (MIC). The mutual capturing of the MIC and major elements of the state and government are obvious. It is also obvious that the economic, political, and social interests that are incorporated in the MIC need plausible threats and realistic enemies to justify the opportunity costs of their unproductive consumption of scarce resources, not to mention the risks of catastrophe that they present.

When it comes to that justification however, it can be difficult to quantify the threat of "terrorism" at a level that supports militarized social and economic priorities. "Enemy" near-peer nation-states are a more plausible justification than an ambiguous "Global War on Terror" for the mammoth misallocation of resources into navies, air forces, nuclear arsenals, and standing armies. Far larger revenue streams can be tapped for mobilizations against a succession of enemy nation-states than for military initiatives against popular movements of the right or the left. This may not always be true, but it is certainly true now. And if an "enemy" nation-state can be somehow conflated with a threat of "terrorism," it is the best of all possible worlds for capitalist hegemony.

To the extent that the MIC can access the "levers of power" in a given nation-state, it can generate a self-perpetuating militarized nationalist dynamic between its host nation-state and any potential antagonists that can appropriate their own opposing nation-state platform. This dynamic generates feedback loops that perpetuate the antagonism independent of the merits of the initial "threat." Moreover, such nation-state conflict frameworks maximize possibilities to incorporate actual and potential non-state threats to transnational capital, particularly those with a neo-fascist character, as proxy forces in intra-capitalist conflicts. Not so incidentally, arming such "terrorist" elements also provides a lucrative expansion of the MIC customer base.

In all of this it's important to remember that conflicts with partially fabricated enemies can become real wars with actual casualties—usually concentrated on the weaker side—which need not have even chosen to be a side.

It's important to recognize some factors that may work in a different direction. Not only will the escalation of nation-state conflicts have few material benefits for any reformist working-class interests, they also can jeopardize powerful sectoral capitalist interests outside of the MIC. Other distinct sectors of capital are strongly organized across national boundaries; for example, fossil fuel, pharma, industrial agricultural, etc. are not nearly as dependent on the exacerbation of national antagonisms. These sectors also have social and economic incentives to pursue the "main levers" of state power that are functional in those nation-states where they operate. But the results won't necessarily promote nation-state conflicts. For example, consider the current impact of "Big Oil" on relations with Russia, or, more generally, the overall interest of the FANG sector in transnational stability.[15]

This complexity provides substantial elements of indeterminacy to US capitalist politics that can potentially transform apparently viable approaches to stability into new and expanded opportunities for disaster. How will the response to a major downturn in the economic cycle that severely undercuts the rents accruing to global finance capital be impacted if the limits and limitations of economic populism have already been exposed? The ultimate flexibility of capital might be better served by keeping these "economic nationalist" techniques of rule in reserve until the need for them is more pressing. But how will such decisions be reached?

What should be made of all of this? What does it mean for the "What is to Be Done" problems? This is an area that I approach cautiously, expecting some substantial skepticism and even a bit of cynicism. I start with the assumption that the episodes of mass unrest we have experienced in this country and around the world over the past decade are likely to continue and accelerate. Without such a context revolutionaries will be fortunate to survive—and most that do survive will end up dysfunctional.

I'd like to return to Badiou's argument that I raised earlier. What are *we* when we aim to be "outside the state"? In the first place, we must be an organized force. There is no substantial and enduring political significance to being individual irreconcilables outside the state. The situation is not improved with those "revolutionary organizations" that are really accidental and temporary aggregates of such individuals. We need something different and more substantive than that. To take strategic advantage of the emergent weaknesses of capital we need an *organized minority* of irreconcilables with a common subversive project against class power—an "outside the state" resistance that can both organize itself and provide a pole of attraction for a range of political and social rebelliousness that is not yet developed, and which, as it develops, will manifest wide variations in self-organization, self-consciousness, and radicalization.

The search for easy answers—and the painfully repeated attempts to implement deeply flawed candidate answers—has contributed significantly to our current difficulties. Nevertheless, we should have learned some lessons about what doesn't work and, indirectly, perhaps some little about what might. We know, at least I hope that we know, that strategies based on "vanguard" party structures can never produce a clear alternative to the dominion of capital. If such formations aren't crippled from the outset by hierarchy, militarized discipline, and a quasi-religious faith in leadership and doctrine, the nightmare of the party-state is their eventual destiny. At the same time, we should also have learned that no organized opposition to capital can develop without rejecting the solipsistic individualism that sees the accountability and discipline needed to implement a serious collective project as a subtraction from individual autonomy. The negative ramifications of this individualism are widespread, but surely they can be best handled in organizations built around collective experiences of struggle in contrast with those gestated via "principles of unity" and other forms of a priori political agreement.

Rather than either flawed "vanguards" or "autonomous" radicals, we need solid and defined organization where critical participation in the development and implementation of political work and political discussion is expected and facilitated as the norm. We need an organized cadre—linked by political accountability and a discipline that is essentially self-discipline—that is organized to prioritize participatory equality over tactical efficiency. Some will argue that these are utopian organizational objectives—doomed from the outset by the wide differences in circumstances, experiences, and levels of political development across the country. Many more on the left will accept them as formal goals, only to act as if they are impossible. I certainly see the problems in the approach I advocate, but is there a better path to focus the militants who develop out of mass rejections of capital and its state apparatuses into a revolutionary movement for a positive alternative to capital?

Additionally, any organizational approach must grapple with the fact that there is a qualitative difference between mass movements of resistance and negation that refuse capital's command in a variety of ways, and a mass revolutionary challenge that presents and embodies a positive alternative to capital as a social order. We have learned at substantial cost that any radical organizing thrust that can't embody a positive affirmation of a systemic alternative that makes sense to working people will encounter crippling problems shortly down the road—sometimes losing anything that distinguishes it as "revolutionary" in the mass struggle, sometimes taking on the character of a deranged sect, sometimes a combination of both.

Mass struggles are negative responses to features of capitalist oppression and exploitation that are usually contained within the framework of capital and that seldom raise challenges to its basic premises. However, in most genuine struggles some militants move beyond repetitive, episodic cycles of activity and passivity as they discover real social values in acts of collective resistance that are not strictly limited by their potential to achieve reform objectives. In the old STO Gramscian* categories, we might say that *some* participants in struggle experience an epistemological break* that opens up a new horizon of political and personal possibilities. I emphasize "some" because the development of a mass struggle always divides its base—often sharply—and only a part, a relatively small minority, experiences this new sense of possibilities—and even then, usually temporarily. This social layer will provide the basis for any revolutionary alternative to capital, and one major task of revolutionary organization is to develop a political/cultural home for such people without isolating them from their social roots. This requires left organizations that offer expanded opportunities to fight existing power; but equally important, left organizations that are accessible to regular-assed people and that take the injunction to live among them seriously. These organizations must be essentially horizontal, if they are to productively relate to the potentials of mass struggles, and, in my opinion, under current political and security conditions they must at least begin as essentially local.

Instead of "agreement" on political abstractions, the major emphasis in such consolidations should be developing common work—shared organizing projects as contrasted with shared principles of unity—a shared commitment to be accountable to a collective and a willingness to submit one's ideas and activity to its critical review is essential.

Finally, we must also recognize that parallel issues are faced by hundreds of millions across the globe who are on our side—or we on theirs; by millions who have moved into radical oppositional activity—although perhaps only momentarily; and by tens of thousands of consciously anti-capitalist revolutionaries who are dispersed virtually everywhere. That's the good side of the situation. It's not the only side. The difficulties in developing and consolidating revolutionary movements with workable strategies and sustainable organizational forms aren't unique to us either. We are not alone, but there are no clear "revolutionary paths" or "lines of march" to follow.

## Endnotes

Unless otherwise noted, all URLs were accessed Jan. 29, 2023.

## An Introduction to Hamerquist's A Brilliant Red Thread, by Dave Ranney

1. These works and more are available at the STO online archive: www.sojournertruth.net. For more, see Staudenmaier (2012) and also the short Glossary entry on p. 376.

2. David Ranney, *Living and Dying on the Factory Floor: From the Outside In and the Inside Out,* PM Press, 2019.

3. A reference to the *Ever Given* container ship being stuck in the canal and blocking billions of dollars of international shipping for nearly a week in 2021.

4. "About Three Way Fight." http://threewayfight.blogspot.com/p/about.html

## Family History

1. The Smith Act (or "Alien Registration Act") was enacted in 1940. It required all non-citizen adult residents in the US to register with the government and created criminal penalties for advocating the overthrow of the government by force. While the CPUSA supported the early use of the Act against their rivals in the Trotskyist Socialist Workers Party and communists were not prosecuted under it once the US entered the anti-Nazi alliance with the USSR, once the war ended and the Cold War began the Act was primarily used against the CPUSA. In 1948, twelve members of the CPUSA National Board were indicted for violating the Act and after the then longest trial in US history, all eleven who had gone to trial (William Z. Foster was dropped

from the case due to failing health) were convicted and sentenced to 3–5 years each. The case was premised not to a link between specific speech and immediate violence, but rather that the men were communists, communists were for violent revolution, therefore the men advocated the overthrow of the US government by force. In 1951, once the convictions had stood up to appeal, 132 additional lower level CPUSA leaders were indicted across the country. Legal contest would eventually lead to several convictions being overturned in 1957 and jurisprudence that only speech linked to a "clear and present danger" of violence could be prosecuted, which has prevented the use of the Smith Act since 1961. For more information on the Smith Act Trials in Washington state, see https://depts.washington.edu/labhist/cpproject/SmithAct.shtml.

2. Referring to cards issued by unions to cover meals and accommodations, a "piecard" is slang for a union official seen to be careerist, or more on the side of the bosses than the workers.

### A Rough Chronology of My Politics and Work

1. Gus Hall spent most of the 1950s in prison for being a member of the CPUSA leadership—convicted in the first trial which used the Smith Act (see endote above) against the party—and was elected to the top position in 1959, shortly after his release. In the early 1960s he addressed large public meetings as part of an attempt to reclaim legality and public legitimacy for the party.

2. The NCNP brought together various left groups and organizers to attempt to coordinate on a US-wide level, particularly around the upcoming 1968 presidential elections.

3. In August of 1968, Soviet tanks entered Czechoslovakia to suppress mass protests and reverse the efforts to democratize the socialist government that had been initiated in January (known as the Prague Spring).

4. The fractious 1969 SDS National Convention broke down largely into a struggle between the Worker Student Alliance (aka Progressive Labor Party, or PL), the Revolutionary Youth Movement (RYM) and RYM II, a split from the other RYM. While PL and RYM were divided on questions of counter-culture and Black nationalism (PL opposed both while RYM supported them), RYM II emerged as internal opposition to the RYM "Weatherman" statement, and was characterized by being less pessimistic about the political prospects of organizing white workers.

5. The Autonomous Zone, or A-Zone, was an anarchist info-shop in Chicago, open from 1993–2003.

### More on the CP and Me

1. Gus Hall was General Secretary of the Communist Party USA from 1959 to May 2000; he died in October of that year.

2. The sentence in question read, "Revolutionary movements throughout the world are in a state of confusion and crisis at a time of unprecedentedly rapid growth in the numbers of their adherents and participants." The document is not currently publicly available.

3. The CP Convention was in the early summer of 1968 in New York, and the Democratic National Convention was in Chicago in the late summer of that same year. Organizing protests around the DNC became a focal point for much of the left that summer.

4. A wave of militant strikes in France during May of 1968, sparked in part by militant student protests in Paris, were actively suppressed and undermine by the French Communist Party. In August of that same year, Soviet tanks entered Czechoslovakia to suppress mass protests and reverse the efforts to democratize the socialist government that had been initiated in January (known as the Prague Spring).

5. *Towards a Revolutionary Party* (STO 1969) is a pamphlet written largely by Hamerquist. It served as a founding document for the Sojourner Truth Organization. See: www.sojournertruth. net/tarp.html.

### More on STO and After

1. For more on STO, see Glossary. "Industrial concentrations" refers to groupings of militants working and organizing in the same factory.

2. In 1972, US President Richard Nixon visited China, ending a quarter century of no diplomatic ties between the two countries; the goal of the visit was to gain leverage over relations with the Soviet Union, and the normalization of ties culminated in 1979, when the US established full diplomatic relations with China. By "the end of actually existing socialism," Hamerquist is referring to the dismantling of Maoist China's socialist economy and its replacement with a market-driven one, fully integrated into global capitalism. This process began immediately after the ascension of Deng Xiaoping to the top leadership position in December 1978.

3. A reference to Lenin (1917).

4. Tendency building refers to work that incorporated a range of local and regional groupings with generally similar politics. For more on the "tendency building" strategy of STO, see Staudenmaier (2012), pp. 231–66.

5. Referring to radical work that emerged out of the global upswell in struggle in 1968 and that often saw the struggles of that year as key reference points.

6. As explained by Hamerquist in an email to the publisher, "The Midwest Action League (MAL) wanted to focus major resources on our own organizing, which emphasized and prioritized workplace organizing." For more on the split and MAL, see Staudenmaier (2012), pp. 140–46.

7. "Protracted People's War" is a revolutionary strategy often associated with Maoism and guerilla insurgencies and contrasted with the insurrectionary approach traditionally associated with Lenin and the Russian Revolution. A central aspect of Protracted People's War is the development of mass revolutionary consciousness and liberatory ways of life during the prolonged phase of armed struggle.

8. The *Economic and Philosophic Manuscripts* (Marx (1844) presented an approach to class struggle that broke with the flawed "scientific" versions of Marxism that were in vogue at the time, especially those influenced by the orthodox interpretations promoted by the Soviet Union.

## Thoughts about Organization

1. For more on BRICK and this federation, see libcom.org/tags/frac.

2. Brian Dominick, "Anarchists in the Neighborhood," *Arsenal: A Magazine of Anarchist Strategy and Culture* #2, Fall 2000.

3. Referring to *The Communist Manifesto* (1848) and *The State and Revolution* (1917).

4. Active Transformation (AT) was an anarchist collective in Lansing, Michigan that published a newspaper of the same name. It was active throughout the 1990s and were closely associated with Lansing Anti-Racist Action (ARA). For more information, see Clay, Lady, Schwartz, and Staudenmaier (2023).

5. Jumping off the cliff here means an increase in illegal and possibly armed work without adequately considering consequences.

## Thoughts on Naomi Klein

1. Bill Maher is a television host, currently for the program *Real Time with Bill Maher* and formerly for *Politically Incorrect*. He has often been associated with left-liberal politics, but his tendency to deride the significance of "feelings" has led him to take right-leaning positions on many issues, including the #MeToo movement. The Cusack family refers to John Cusack the actor who is a vocal supporter of Klein.

2. Milton Friedman, the University of Chicago economist, and Thomas Friedman, author of *The World is Flat* (2005).

3. MKUltra was an illegal human experimentation program designed and undertaken by the CIA between 1953 and 1973, intended to develop procedures and identify drugs that could be used in interrogations to weaken individuals and force confessions through brainwashing and psychological torture. MKUltra used numerous methods to manipulate its subjects' mental states and brain functions, such as the covert administration of high doses of psychoactive drugs (especially LSD) and other chemicals without the subjects' consent, electroshocks, hypnosis, sensory deprivation, isolation, verbal and sexual abuse, and other forms of torture. Many of these experiments took place at McGill University in Montreal. See https://en.wikipedia.org/wiki/MKUltra.
Structural Adjustment Programs, or SAPs, are an important way in which neoliberal policies have been imposed on Global South nations, generally via the International Monetary Fund and World Bank making various loans conditional on governments adopting certain policies. SAPs have emphasized austerity, selling government assets to transnational corporations, removing tariffs and regulatory policies, and repayment of debts held by the Global North. They have been instrumental in increasing the exploitation of people in the Global South in the period after independence, and as such were a main target of criticism by the left wing of the anti-globalization movement.

4. Lyndon B. Johnson, the Democrat US President from November 1963 to January 1969.

5. These are referencs to the Chicago School of Sociology, centered at the University of Chicago, emphasized biological and ecological metaphors for society, in particular trying to explain the causes of social "disorder"; the US invasion and occupation of the Dominican Republic in 1965; and the FBI's Counter Intelligence Program which targeted domestic social movements for disruption, respectively. Hamerquist has noted that the Chicago School of Sociology was also identified with the US strategic hamlets policy in Vietnam and features of the occupation of the Dominican Republic.

6. Augusto Pinochet was the dictator of Chile from 1973 to 1981, taking power in a US-backed coup that overthrew democratically elected leftist Salvador Allende. "Southern Cone actions" refers to a multinational campaign of state terror in the 1970s, in which tens of thousands of people were killed and several hundred thousand incarcerated, carried out in several South American countries with support from the United States, often under the aegis of Operation Condor.

7. Hugo Chávez was president of Venezuela 1999 to 2013; the regime he founded continues to govern Venezuela and identifies as socialist and anti-imperialist.. Hezbollah is a Shia Islamic political and military formation based in Lebanon and most often identified with a militant stance against Israel. Vladimir Putin has been president or prime minister of Russia since 1999.

### On the Relevance of Old Debates

1. *Khukuri Theory* is no longer in existence, but the original post is accessible via the Internet Archive at bit.ly/3ROvUPu.

## Marx and Revolutionary Politics

1. "Realm of necessity" and "realm of freedom" are from Marx's *Capital*, Vol. 3, Ch. 48, describing the transition out of capitalism. Available here: https://www.marxists.org/archive/marx/works/subject/hist-mat/capital/vol3-ch48.htm.

2. "Diamat" is a contraction of "Dialectical Materialism" and refers to the official interpretation of Marx adopted under Stalin.

3. "The philosophers have only interpreted the world, in various ways; the point is to change it." See all theses here: https://www.marxists.org/archive/marx/works/1845/theses/theses.htm.

## IWW Base Building and Reformism

1. The "Repeal Coalition" was an organization calling for the repeal of the Arizona state law SB1070, which required police to check immigration papers of any "suspected" undocumented immigrants. The coalition involved many radicals who were confronted by questions about participation in electoral-related organizing.

2. The IWW is a radical union founded in 1905, which has historically focused on direct action, direct democratic control of the workplace, and organizing various precarious segments of the working class. Haywood refers to "Big Bill" Haywood, a prominent leader and organizer in the early IWW (see Glossary).

3. Referencing a previous email.

4. From a previous email by N.

## Discussion with Comrade on "Strategy and Struggle"

1. Marx (1845) states that "The materialist doctrine concerning the changing of circumstances and upbringing forgets that circumstances are changed by men and that it is essential to educate the educator himself."

## Angst

1.  Grasmci (1971) writes, "The [current] crisis consists precisely in the fact that the old is dying and the new cannot be born; in this interregnum a great variety of morbid symptoms appear" (276).

2.  From David C. Ranney (2014), especially pages 9–10.

## Recent thoughts on Insurrectionism

1.  Hinton (2021).

2.  Sergey Nechayev was a Russian communist revolutionary and prominent figure of the Russian nihilist movement, known for his single-minded pursuit of revolution by any means necessary, including revolutionary terror. He was the author of the radical *Catechism of a Revolutionary*. https://www.marxists.org/subject/anarchism/nechayev/catechism.htm

3.  Hamerquist is referring here to the problems created by, for example, property destruction and militant confrontation with the police.

4.  Ali La Pointe's trajectory from petty criminal to committed revolutionary is a major plot point in the film *The Battle of Algiers* (1966).

5.  See Luxemburg (1906).

## Three Points on Anti-Globalization Protests

1.  DAN was composed of veteran activists who aimed to coordinate large-scale direct actions, though they were also known for their pacifist inclinations and discouragement of what they perceived as overly disorderly actions.

2.  Hamerquist is referring to an essay released shortly after the Seattle WTO protests by Michael Albert, a former SDS member and the founder of *Z Magazine*, a movement-oriented left

outlet at the time. The essay, titled "On Trashing and Movement Building," claimed that the property destruction by the black bloc (deemed "trashing") was ultimately detrimental to "movement building." Here is a representative quote: "Does this mean, however, that there cannot be a time and place for confrontation and property damage? No, it doesn't mean that at all, at least not in my view. Instead, the time and place for such behavior is when it will meet widespread approval and increase the power of protest rather than providing an excuse for folks to tune out or become hostile to protest. Up to the trashing, anarchists in Seattle added energy, creativity, art, music, and often greatly needed militancy, courage, and steadfastness to many demonstration venues." The original post is no longer available but is still accessible via the Internet Archive here: bit.ly/3JWikYs

3. The official organizers for the IMF protests in Washington, DC (formally referred to as the Mobilization for Global Justice or A16, i.e. April 16th) included the Direct Action Network. They released a document that explicitly called for a non-violent strategy and opposed the militancy of the black bloc. The document is no longer available online. For more discussion of this and other related movement debates, see Wood (2012), especially pages 94–107.

4. Sunday was April 16th (A16), the most publicized day of protests.

### Madison & Egypt

1. For more on *Khukuri*, see Glossary. The piece by Hamerquist presented here is available via the Internet Archive at: bit.ly/3YFg7Vv. The piece as presented here has been edited and somewhat abridged.

2. While Badiou's article was later included as an appendix in the book *The Rebirth of History: Times of Riots and Uprisings* (2012), it had been previously posted as a stand-alone piece on *Khukuri Theory* on February 28, 2011.

3. In philosopher G.W.F. Hegel's dialectics, "negative" means that something is a term in a transformative contradiction, not "bad" in the sense of political or moral judgment. See also Glossary entry on Hegel on p. 363–64.

4. Palingenesis means rebirth or re-creation. The term is here associated with the work of Robert Griffin, a scholar of fascism whose work has been influential on Hamerquist as well as the "Three Way Fight" approach (see: http://threewayfight.blogspot.com/). Griffin claims that the defining feature of fascism is a "palingenetic nationalism," i.e., a national rebirth or a quest for to re-create a mythic national past. See especially Griffin (1991).

5. For the full text of Blake's poem see bit.ly/3jQRvug.

## Email on the Historical Situation

1. "The tradition of all dead generations weighs like a nightmare on the brains of the living," Marx wrote in *The 18th Brumaire* (1852).

2. See "Perspectives on Occupy Atlanta from Revolutionary Voices," Unity and Struggle October 16, 2011. http://www.unityandstruggle.org/2011/10/perspectives-on-occupy-atlanta-from-revolutionary-voices/.

3. A reference to Lenin (1902).

4. See, for example, Badiou (2012).

## Initial Thoughts on Longview

1. In 1968, a grouping of radical Black workers at the Dodge Main factory in Detroit formed an organization called the Dodge Revolutionary Union Movement (RUM) in order to advance a militant rank-and-file strategy. Workers at other factories and workplaces were inspired to form their own "RUM"s (for example the Ford Revolutionary Union Movement aka FRUM). In 1969, these groups joined to form the League of Revolutionary

Black Workers. For more see Dan Georgakas and Marvin Surkin, *Detroit: I Do Mind Dying: A Study in Urban Revolution*, Chicago: Haymarket Books, 2012.

2. Lowell May was a founding member of the Bread and Roses Workers Cultural Center in Denver, CO. He was also a former member of STO.

3. Nick Paretsky, also a recipient of this email, is a former STO member and longtime interlocutor of Hamerquist.

## Email on Longview

1. In Oakland and Portland (as well as other cities), elements of the Occupy movement organized protests that shut down the ports. This was viewed as a way to bring the movement to a new disruptive anti-capitalist level and to connect more directly with workers.

2. For more on the notion of "recognize and record," see Glossary.

3. EGT stands for Export Grain Terminal LLC is the operator of a major grain export terminal at the port of Longview and the main opponent during the struggle there.

4. In *Capital Vol. 1* (1867) Marx says that, "It follows therefore that in proportion as capital accumulates, the lot of the labourer, be his payment high or low, must grow worse." For more of this chapter see https://www.marxists.org/archive/marx/works/1867-c1/ch25.htm.

## Militancy After Occupy

1. Steve Biko was a leader of the South African liberation struggle against apartheid, largely known for his emphasis on culture and consciousness in struggle. The quote Hamerquist refers to here is, "The most potent weapon in the hands of the oppressor is the mind of the oppressed" (Biko 1978, 68).

## Third Position

1. The Church of the Creator was a neo-Nazi organization. Following the sentencing of its then leader Matt Hale to forty years in prison (for encouraging an informant to kill a judge) it split into two successor organizations: the Creativity Movement and the Creativity Alliance. The American Front (AF) is a neo-fascist skinhead organization that publicly stated that they were nationalist but not white supremacist. The two organizations featured prominently in Hamerquist's essay "Fascism & Anti-Fascism," included in the volume *Confronting Fascism* (2002).

2. The Montoneros (Movimiento Peronista Montonero) was a paramilitary organization in Argentina from the 1970s to the 1980s. The Montoneros represented the left wing of the Peronist political coalition and were purged from the movement during the start of Juan Perón's second term as President of Argentina—hence the allusion to the expulsion of the Strasserites. However, unlike Strasserites, the Montoneros were unquestionably of the left.

3. "Larouchies" and "Moonies" refer to cult-like organizations that operated adjacent to political circles, especially in the 1980s. "Larouchies" refer to followers of Lyndon Larouche, who was a conspiracy-minded political figure who originally emerged from the left until turning to far-right politics. The "Moonies" refer to followers of Sun Myung Moon who founded the Unification Church. Both organizations are still active, though with substantial shifts and developments having followed the deaths of Larouche and Moon in the 2010s.

## Response to Bring the Ruckus on Fascism

1. Bring the Ruckus (BTR) was a multi-tendency revolutionary left organization active from 2002 to 2012, which prioritized the struggle against white supremacy as an anti-capitalist strategy. Their website and documents are available on the Internet Archive at https://bit.ly/3HP5nwP.

329

2. The BTR discussion was in part responding to Hamerquist's "Fascism & Anti-Fascism" in *Confronting Fascism* (2002). Some of the original discussion can be found here: https://theanarchistlibrary.org/library/ruckus-collective-debates-on-fascism.

3. These quotes refer to the BTR discussion.

4. The NSDAP is the full name of the Nazi party, translating to the National Socialist German Workers Party. The liquidation Hamerquist refers to here was epitomized by the Night of the Long Knives. See Glossary for more on this Night of the Long Knives and Strasserism.

5. For more on the concept of herrenvolk democracy, see Joel Olson, *The Abolition of White Democracy* (University of Minnesota Press, 2004).

6. A reference to the quote by Mao Zedong, "a single spark can start a prairie fire," and to its legacy in the American revolutionary left, where it was famously used in the 1974 political document by the Weather Underground Organization, *Prairie Fire: The Politics of Revolutionary Anti-Imperialism*, as well as by the related aboveground organization the Prairie Fire Organizing Committee.

7. In the editor's opinion, this laundry list of major political events in the 1960s is best handled by the reader with Google.

8. Hamerquist is referring to certain socialist-led municipal governments in the early twentieth century, often referred to as the "sewer socialists." These administrations are often lauded for their pragmatism and focus on infrastructure development (hence "sewer" socialists) but they were also known for their racist attitudes and prioritization of European-descended working-class communities' interests.

9. Pat Buchanan is a leading paleoconservative and a career Republican operative; Tom Tancredo is a Republican politician from Colorado who served in the US House of Representatives

from 1999 to 2009. Both are well known for their ultra-nationalist and anti-immigrant views.

## Email to K on Fascism

1. See Glossary under "Third Position" for more.

2. A reference to Hardt and Negri 2003.

3. A reference to key events in the rise to power of both Mussolini and Hitler.

4. "Strategy of tension" refers to a far-right strategy of fomenting political violence and instability, the goal being to provoke popular support for authoritarian rule. The term is often associated with the violence of the late 1960s and early 1970s in Italy, which included a number of massacres of civilians carried out by far-right forces.

5. See for example https://libcom.org/article/british-jobs-british-workers.

6. This is a reference to the work of fascism scholar Roger Griffin; "palingenetic" from "palingenesis," meaning "rebirth." See for example Griffin (1991).

7. The piece by Hamerquist referenced here is titled "Thinking and Acting in Real Time and A Real World" (2009) and was framed as a response to a blog post by Kali Akuno (2008).

8. Kingsley Clarke is a long-time comrade of Hamerquist and former STO member.

9. Referring to Lenin's *What is To Be Done?* (1902) and the *Organisational Platform of the General Union of Anarchists (Draft)* (1926) by the Delo Truda Group. The latter is the founding document of the anarchist tendency of "platformism," so called because it is premised on agreement with Delo Truda's proposal.

10. Hardt and Negri 2003 and 2004.

11. The global financial crisis of 2008–9.

12. Quote from Hegel's Preface to his *Elements of the Philosophy of Right* (1820). The phrase arises from the Latin form of Aesop's Fables; in the fable, a boastful athlete brags that he once achieved a stupendous long jump in competition on the island of Rhodes. A bystander challenges him to repeat his accomplishment on the spot: "Here is Rhodes, jump here!" I.e., put up or shut up. The phrase was also famously garbled in Marx's *The Eighteenth Brumaire of Louis Bonaparte* (1852): "proletarian revolutions ... constantly criticize themselves, constantly interrupt themselves in their own course, return to the apparently accomplished, in order to begin anew; they deride with cruel thoroughness the half-measures, weaknesses, and paltriness of their first attempts, seem to throw down their opponents only so the latter may draw new strength from the earth and rise before them again more gigantic than ever, recoil constantly from the indefinite colossalness of their own goals—until a situation is created which makes all turning back impossible, and the conditions themselves call out: *Hic Rhodus, hic salta!* Here is the rose, here dance!"

## Mistakes in Our Previous Approaches to Fascism

1. At the onset of WWII, the Soviet-centered Communist International (Comintern) and Information Bureau (Cominform) advocated for the "popular front" strategy. For more on the popular front and Comintern, see Glossary.

2. For an example of STO and Ken Lawrence's evolving analysis of US fascism at the time, see Lawrence (1982).

3. The organizations referenced here are as follows: PLP is the Progressive Labor party, a China-oriented split from the Communist Party famous as a main player in the internal politics of Students for a Democratic Society; SWP is the Socialist Workers Party, one of the original Trotskyist organization in

the United States; Workers World, refers to the Workers World Party, which was founded in a split from the Socialist Workers Party that was pro-China and defended the Soviet suppression of the 1956 Hungarian revolution; CLP is the Communist Labor Party, which was founded in part by sections of the League of Revolutionary Black Workers and went on to become the League of Revolutionaries for a New America; the RCP is the Revolutionary Communist Party (USA), a Maoist-aligned organization very much revolving around promoting its leader Bob Avakian. The May 19th Communist Organization (May19) and Prairie Fire Organizing Committee (PFOC) were actively involved in the John Brown Anti-Klan Committee (see Glossary). In addition, both organizations were heavily involved in supporting militant anti-imperialist struggles especially domestically. The Workers Viewpoint Organization (WVO) became the Communist Workers Party; see the Glossary entry for the Greensboro massacre.

4.   All organizations mentioned were anti-fascist and anti-racist projects reacting to the rise of the British National Party and the National Front. *Searchlight* is a UK publication reporting on the far right from an anti-fascist perspective; it began in 1964 and became a regular magazine in 1975. Anti-Fascist Action (AFA) was founded in 1985 by a range of anti-racist and anti-fascist organizations, including *Searchlight*. AFA was notable as a more militant and less compromising alternative to existing anti-fascist organizing spearheaded by the Socialist Workers Party (SWP) through the Anti-Nazi League (ANL). The SWP's efforts had become prominent a decade earlier through the success of Rock Against Racism.

5.   The Racketeering Influenced and Corrupt Organizations (RICO) Act is a federal statute that officially is meant to target organized crime, but that is often used against radical political movements, both left and right.

6.   Examples of government repression aimed at the Puerto Rican independence movement during this period include, among many others: the repressive use, between 1975 and 1985, of a series of grand jury investigations in New York, Chicago, and elsewhere that led to prison time for more than a dozen activists who refused to testify against their comrades; the capture and imprisonment in the early 1980s of more than thirty alleged armed combatants, many of whom served sentences of more than fifteen years; the assassination of two young independence activists in 1978 after they were entrapped by government agents; the 1979 death in custody under suspicious circumstances of Ángel Rodríguez Cristobal, an activist who had been arrested during mass protests against the US Navy's control of the small island of Vieques; and the eventual exposure in 1987 of a system of secret police files known as "las carpetas" that documented governmental spying on almost 75,000 individuals and organizations across Puerto Rico.

7.   The Southern Poverty Law Center is a non-profit organization that monitors and reports on far-right organizations. They have often been criticized for their pro-state, liberal approach, which has at times involved their smearing of left and anarchist radical groups.

8.   Clara Zetkin was a German communist and feminist; in 1933 she went into exile in in the USSR following the Nazi rise to power. Her analysis of fascism can be found in her 1923 document "The Struggle Against Fascism" available at Marxists.org.

9.   For more on Third Position see the Glossary entry and also the so-titled essay in this volume on p. 133. "Fourth Position" refers to the Fourth Political Theory proposed by Russian neo-fascist theoretician Aleksandr Dugin, in a 2009 book of the same name, as a supposed development beyond liberalism, communism, and fascism. The theory is vaguely defined but builds on themes that Dugin has long advocated, such as National Bolshevism, traditionalist theology, anti-globalization, and Eurasianism.

### Lenin, Leninism, and Some Leftovers

1.  This quote appeared on the now-defunct Kasama website (August 8, 2009). For more on Kasama, see Glossary.

2.  Referring to the Jacobin radicals of the French revolution, but also a general term for the forces that advance an uncompromising, principled program.

3.  See Badiou 2010.

4.  The USSR's New Economic Policy (NEP) allowed some market reforms and private accumulation in the name of reviving the war-torn economy at the expense of the egalitarian aims of the revolution. It was ended by Stalin in 1928.

5.  The founding head of the FBI J. Edgar Hoover published a conspiratorial book in 1958 titled, *Masters of Deceit: The Story of Communism in America and How to Fight It.* In it he argued that American communist claims to support the poor and oppressed were bad faith lies covering for their real objective, which was to cynically support the state agenda of the USSR.

6.  In Maoist China, "capitalist roader" was an epithet used by members of the Chinese Communist Party against fellow party members who allegedly supported a return to capitalism.

7.  See Badiou 2010, 79.

8.  From Marx (1845), "Theses on Feuerbach," thesis VII.

9.  See, for example, Lenin (1905), (1906), (1917a).

10.  The 10th (1921) and 11th (1922) Party Congresses of the Soviet Communist Party are notable for, among other things, approving Lenin's "New Economic Policy." The general turn away from more radical state policies was defended by Lenin in his book referenced above, *"Left-Wing" Communism: An Infantile Disorder* (1920).

11.  See Lenin (1902), chapter 2.

12. Karl Kautsky was an important theorist in the German Social Democratic Party and in the Second Intenational.

13. See Rosa Luxemburg's "Leninism or Marxism" (1904). https://www.marxists.org/archive/luxemburg/1904/questions-rsd/index.htm.

14. Third International orthodoxy refers to the official interpretations of Lenin promoted after his death in the Soviet-controlled Third International of socialist organizations, the Comintern.

15. In *What is To Be Done?* (1902) Lenin states that, "We have said that there could not have been Social-Democratic consciousness among the workers. It would have to be brought to them from without. The history of all countries shows that the working class, exclusively by its own effort, is able to develop only trade union consciousness, i.e., the conviction that it is necessary to combine in unions, fight the employers, and strive to compel the government to pass necessary labour legislation, etc. The theory of socialism, however, grew out of the philosophic, historical, and economic theories elaborated by educated representatives of the propertied classes, by intellectuals." https://www.marxists.org/archive/lenin/works/1901/witbd/ii.htm.

16. In *"Left-Wing" Communism* (1922) Lenin says, "The mere presentation of the question—'dictatorship of the party or dictatorship of the class; dictatorship (party) of the leaders, or dictatorship (party) of the masses?'—testifies to most incredibly and hopelessly muddled thinking. These people want to invent something quite out of the ordinary, and, in their effort to be clever, make themselves ridiculous. It is common knowledge that the masses are divided into classes, that the masses can be contrasted with classes only by contrasting the vast majority in general, regardless of division according to status in the social system of production, with categories holding a definite status in the social system of production; that as a rule and in most cases—at least in present-day civilised countries—classes are led by political

parties; that political parties, as a general rule, are run by more or less stable groups composed of the most authoritative, influential and experienced members, who are elected to the most responsible positions, and are called leaders. All this is elementary. All this is clear and simple." (https://www.marxists.org/archive/lenin/works/1920/lwc/ch05.htm) Clear and simple indeed ...

17.   This refers to Gramsci's (1968) essays on workers' councils in Italy, which, though written in the years immediately following the Bolshevik revolution, were only made available in English in the late 1960s. These had a major impact on STO's early political practice.

18.   Eurocommunism was a political tendency that came to dominate the Communist Parties of Western Europe in the 1970s and 80s. It was characterized by a normalized participation in the parliamentary process and a diminishing of openly revolutionary rhetoric and practice.

19.   In an unabridged version of Mao (1957), he writes, "Stalin was 70 percent a Marxist, 30 percent not a Marxist" (MacFarquhar, et. al., ed. 1989). For more on the Soviet critique of Stalin after 1956, see Khrushchev's Secret Speech in the Glossary.

20.   Palmiro Togliatti held a number of positions in Italian governments following the fall of fascism, including Deputy Prime Minister and Minister of Justice.

21.   Alexander Kolchak and Anton Denikin were prominent leaders of the anti-communist (aka "White") forces in the Russian Civil War that followed the Bolshevik seizure of power. The "Allied Intervention" refers to the combined military forces of a range of capitalist powers—including the United States, Britain, France, Italy, and Japan—which invaded the new, post-revolutionary Russia in 1918, supporting the counter-revolutionary Whites; following the defeat of the Whites in 1922, the "allies" withdrew their forces. The final phrase is a reference

to the dynamic between Paris and the rest of France, wherein, from the 1789 revolution through the proletarian Paris Commune of 1871, Paris represented the leading edge of revolutionary fervor, while much of the rest of the country (especially the rural areas) remained committed to the traditional power structures.

22.  "One-man management" is in contrast to the collective management of workplaces in the early stages of the Soviet revolution.

23.  This is a term for Marxisms which place primary emphasis on technical and technological developments, rather than social relations, believing that historical materialism consists in placing the cart of technical "forces of production"/"productive forces" before the horse of "(social) relations of production." It is a form of technological determinism.

24.  See Wetzel 2005 and 2006.

25.  The Kasama website had a changing masthead. At one point, it read as Hamerquist references. For more on the Kasama Project, see Glossary.

26.  Many versions of Marxism use the contrasting categories of a "class in itself" and a "class for itself." A class-in-itself is a class formed by the objective relations of production (those who own the means of production, those who must sell their labor). Such a class becomes a class-for-itself when it becomes conscious of itself as a class and can turn to shaping the world in its class interests.

27.  See Lynd (2012).

28.  "Individuals — each of whom desires what he is impelled to by his physical constitution and external, in the last resort economic, circumstances" (Engels 1890).

29.  See Gramsci (1971).

30.  The Hundred Flowers Campaign was a period of a few months in 1957 during which citizens' criticisms of the Communist Party and the People's Republic of China were

encouraged. Its name comes from Mao's poetic summation in "Contradictions Among the People" (1957): "Let a hundred flowers bloom, let a hundred schools of thought contend." Within a year the campaign was ended and immediately replaced by a wave of persecutions known as the Anti-Rightist Campaign (1957–59).

31.   See Khrushchev (1956). See also entry for Khrushchev's Secret Speech in Glossary.

32.   Hamerquist here is listing a number of events in the aftermath of WWII which contributed to debate, acrimony, and splits among Communists around the world. In 1948 a split became public between the USSR and Yugoslavia, which was framed as being over central political principles; in 1955, in the wake of Stalin's death, there was a partial rapprochement. In 1956 the Soviet military suppressed a revolution in Hungary that featured significant worker self-management. This is the same year as the "Suez Crisis," where the Soviet-friendly populist leader of Egypt, Gamal Abdel Nasser, nationalized the Suez Canal, leading to the invasion of the country by Israel, the UK, and France. In 1954–55, an armed conflict (now referred to as the First Taiwan Strait Crisis) between the Peoples Republic of China (PRC) and Kuomintang-controlled Taiwan began when the PRC began shelling two Kuomintang-held islands a few miles off the coast of the mainland: Quemoy and Matsu. The conflicts regarding China's borders with India and USSR reference issues that ultimately led to armed conflicts in the 1960s. The "Three Peacefuls" refers to the Soviet policies of peaceful coexistence, peaceful competition, and peaceful transition to socialism, which were seen by many Communists as a retreat from the effort to overthrow global capitalism, favoring instead geopolitical stability.

33.   Alonzo Alcazar is a European leftist active in the anti-globalization movement who Hamerquist was in conversation with.

34.  In January and June of 2009, oil refinery workers at many sites in the UK conducted wildcat strikes to protest subcontracting to non-British firms and other issues. The events were closely watched as an early response by workers to the financial crisis and also demonstrated the strength of nationalism among workers. See for example https://libcom.org/article/2009-strike-lindsey-refinery-struggle-entangled-nationalism.

35.  In *The German Ideology* (1845), Marx and Engels wrote that "the ideas of the ruling class are in every epoch the ruling ideas, i.e. the class which is the ruling material force of society, is at the same time its ruling intellectual force." https://www.marxists.org/archive/marx/works/1845/german-ideology/ch01b.htm.

36.  See Gramsci (1971), especially pages 323–43.

37.  For more on the phrase "An Injury to One is an Injury to All" see "IWW, Base Building, Reformism" in this volume.

38.  The phrase "it is right to rebel" comes from a speech given by Mao in 1939. It became one of the most important slogans of the Cultural Revolution and, by extension, of movements around the world that were inspired by the Chinese example.

39.  In *The Mass Strike* (1906), Rosa Luxemburg says, "An artificially arranged demonstration of the urban proletariat, taking place once, a mere mass strike action arising out of discipline, and directed by the conductor's baton of a party executive, could therefore leave the broad masses of the people cold and indifferent. But a powerful and reckless fighting action of the industrial proletariat, born of a revolutionary situation, must surely react upon the deeper-lying layers, and ultimately draw all those into a stormy general economic struggle who, in normal times, stand aside from the daily trade-union fight." https://www.marxists.org/archive/luxemburg/1906/mass-strike/ch05.htm.

40.  *Revolutionary Suicide* (1973) is the title of Huey P. Newton's autobiography.

41.  For more on "Fourth Generation Warfare," see Robb (2004).

42.  In an email to the publisher, Hamerquist explains that "The question I wanted to raise involved the difficulty of materializing a dual power out of a terrain of struggle where the 'progressive' side (essentially militant trade unionism) was still substantially influenced by the existing structures and ideologies of capitalist domination. So while 'counterpower' is not the best term, I'd like some working that clarified that capitalist ideological and cultural domination (hegemony) would not 'wither', but would have to be actively overthrown."

43.  For example, see Guillen (1973).

44.  Wetzel (2009) originally appeared on Znet and included this exchange. This form of the article, however, is no longer accessible.

45.  "Boring from within" was the strategy of taking over existing unions adopted by the early Communist Party USA, especially under the leadership of William Z. Foster in the 1920s. The strategy was eventually abandoned in favor of one that sought to establish opposing "dual" unions closely tied to Communist leadership.

46.  During World War I, UK shop stewards (workers who act as the lowest level of union representation on the shop floor) became active organizers of wildcat action, often against the wishes of higher levels of union leadership. The movement both stemmed from and resulted in a rise in the number of work-places with elected shop stewards and in an increasing posture of stewards representing their fellow workers against the bosses (and the union if necessary) rather than representing the union to the workers. The Shop Stewards Movement was criticized at the time by anarcho-communist Guy Aldred for being an essen-tially economistic movement where those producing the mate-rials of slaughter of the international working class fought to be paid more for doing so, rather than opposing the war. For more

on CWC and the movement in Scotland, see Organise Ireland!, "1915-1920: Red Clydeside and the shop stewards' movement," (Libcom, 2006) https://libcom.org/article/1915-1920-red-clydeside-and-shop-stewards-movement. For more wide-ranging coverage, see Branko Pribićević, "Shop Stewards' Movement and Workers' Control 1910-1922" (1959), https://www.marxists.org/archive/pribicevic/.

47. See Badiou 2010, 182.

## Repression

1. Jaggi Singh and the Germinal 5 were all activists in Quebec who were arrested in the lead-up and aftermath of the Summit of the Americas, held in Quebec City in April 2001.

## On Some Historical Examples of Repression

1. A reference to Marx's *Capital*.

2. See Marx's *Capital* Vol. 1 (1867), especially chapters 2 and 6.

3. A "Red Squad" is a section of the police force dedicated to monitoring and disrupting leftist activity.

4. The National Lawyers Guild is an organization of progressive lawyers well known for supporting leftist protest movements. *Counterspy* and the *Covert Action Information Bulletin* were publications that tracked and reported on covert activity by assorted intelligence and repressive agencies.

5. The Mississippi State Sovereignty Commission was an official Mississippi state agency tasked with surveilling and disrupting the Black liberation movement.

6. Frank Kitson and Robin Everleigh were high-ranking officers in the UK armed forces who participated in the suppression of numerous anti-colonial insurgencies; they are associated with the use of "pseudo-gangs," discussed in the entry of that name in the Glossary.

7. Doug Durham was an active FBI informant within the American Indian Movement (AIM). William O'Neil was an informant in the Chicago Black Panther Party and partly responsible for chapter chairman Fred Hampton's murder at the hands of the Chicago Police in coordination with the FBI. Jack and Morris Childs were informants deep within the CPUSA as part of an FBI operation code-named "Solo" (more information further in this essay on pages 233–34). Jon Dial was a police infiltrator in Southern California who was involved in support work for armed Mexican revolutionary organizations. When he disappeared from movement work a rumor circulated that he had been kidnapped by the CIA and the Mexican state, sparking some left organizations to launch a "Where is Jon Dial?" campaign. Some months later however, by sheer coincidence, Dial was discovered working the front desk of the Riverside Police Department and the truth was obvious.

8. The US Congress's House Un-American Activities Committee (HUAC) was tasked with investigating and exposing "disloyal" or "subversive" elements, principally Communists. Larry McDonald was a virulently anti-Communist politician in the late 1970s and early 1980s, a kind of spiritual successor to Joseph McCarthy. Months before dying aboard a commercial airliner shot down by Soviet fighter jets in 1983, he became chairman of the far-right John Birch Society while still a sitting US Congressman.

9. Wael Ghonim was a Google employee who gained international recognition after being imprisoned during the 2011 Egyptian Revolution.

10. For more on the 1956 20th Congress and Khrushchev's "Secret Speech," see Glossary. The "Statement of 81 Communist and Workers Parties Meeting in Moscow" was a 1960 document released in the Western media shortly after the meeting itself and marked an important turn in the split between the Soviet and Chinese Communist Parties.

11. J. Edgar Hoover, the long-time director of the FBI.

12. For more current and extensive discussion of the Solo operation, as well as various other important state repression operations, see *A Threat of the First Magnitude* (Leonard and Gallagher 2018).

## On Transnational Capitalism

1. "Black Swan" refers to events that are highly transformative and completely unexpected, but are retrospectively seen to be predictable (often incorrectly), like the discovery of black swans by Europeans, who had assumed swans were white by definition.

2. See, for instance, Lewis and Leys (2010) and Robb (2009).

3. Yves Smith is the founder of the *Naked Capitalism* blog (www.nakedcapitalism.com) and Michael Hudson is a Marxist economist whose work includes *Super Imperialism: The Economic Strategy of American Empire* (1972).

## Email to K on the Iraq War

1. The neoconservatives are a right-wing tendency which favors US military action and intervention abroad, especially in the Middle East where they favor strong support for Israel. Their influence peaked during the George W. Bush presidency.

2. This phrase is a reference to the rhetoric used by the G. W. Bush administration to justify the invasion of Iraq.

3. John Kerry was the Democratic candidate who lost against George W. Bush in the 2004 US presidential election.

4. This phrase is from Barnett (2005) and refers to zones of turmoil and war in the international system which are "unintegrated" into the capitalist core. For more discussion of these concepts, see the following essay in this volume, "Barack, Badiou, and Bilal al Hasan."

5. Ferguson and Barnett are academics who took strong public positions in support of the US invasion of Iraq.

6. Halliburton is an energy corporation of which G. W. Bush Vice President Dick Cheney was a long-time executive.

7. General Smedley Butler was an officer in the US Marines and participated in the "Banana Wars," where the US initiated a number of occupations in Latin America and the Caribbean to protect their interests and the interests of businesses such as the United Fruit Company.

8. In 1973, the Organization of the Petroleum Exporting Countries (OPEC) limited oil production in response to the West's support for Israel in the Yom Kippur war. This caused the price of oil to quadruple, with predictable political shock waves.

### Barack, Badiou, and Bilal al Hasan

1. Hamerquist is referring to an exchange between himself and anti-war activist Stan Goff in 2004 and 2005. The exchange can be found here: http://threewayfight.blogspot.com/2010/03/new-fascism-dead-imperialism.html. An earlier draft of this paper can be found here: http://threewayfight.blogspot.com/2010/01/barack-badiou-and-bilal-al-hasan.html.

2. See, for instance, Don's articles "Thinking and Acting in Real Time and A Real World," http://threewayfight.blogspot.com/2009/01/thinking-and-acting-in-real-time-and.html; and "Response to Paretsky," http://threewayfight.blogspot.com/2009/04/response-to-paretsky-21909.html.

3. On December 1, 2009, then President Obama gave a widely publicized speech expressing his administration's strategy regarding the war in Afghanistan. It can be read here: https://obamawhitehouse.archives.gov/blog/2009/12/01/new-way-forward-presidents-address.

4. "Kasama" refers to the *Kasama Project* website founded by Mike Ely, discussed in the Glossary. "Znet" refers to the Z-Network and *Z Magazine* website founded by Michael Albert. The Kasama text can be viewed using the Internet Wayback Machine: bit.ly/3DXMKpj. The Miles text is here: https://znet-work.org/znetarticle/imperial-inertia-by-jim-miles/

5. The Naxalite insurgency is an armed Maoist movement in rural Eastern India.

6. Neo-fascist tendencies in the ruling Hindu elites refers to the Bharatiya Janata Party (BJP) and the affiliated Rashtriya Swayamsevak Sangh (RSS); India's Prime Minister Narendra Modi is a member of both. National Bolshevism is a far-right Russian nationalist movement that emerged following the fall of the Soviet Union that blends Soviet iconography and fascistic nationalism.

7. Gabriel Kolko was a US-born Canadian historian who wrote extensively on the connections between economics, economic elites, and US state policy, both foreign and domestic.

8. See, for example, Gindin and Panitch (2012) and Harvey (2005).

9. Obama (2009 and 2010).

10. See Robb (2004).

11. Zbigniew Kazimierz Brzeziński was President Jimmy Carter's National Security Advisor. The USSR's military engaged in a protracted war in Afghanistan against US-backed Islamist rebels from 1979 to 1989.

12. See Barnett (2005). Barnett claims that the primary dynamic in the twenty-first century will involve the relationship between the "functioning" core and those parts of the globe that cannot successfully integrate into the established order, the "gap."

13. A reference to Mao's "paper tiger" metaphor; see Glossary.

14.  General Stanley A. McChrystal was the commander of the Joint Special Operations Command (JSOC) from 2003 to 2008. In June 2009 he was appointed to lead all forces in Afghanistan. JSOC directs special operations and specific teams that span multiple branches of the US military (for example, the US Navy's Seal Team Six).

15.  FLUOR is a construction and engineering company heavily involved in post-invasion Iraq and Afghanistan. DYNCORP (now Amentum), L-3 (now L3Harris), and XE Services (formerly Blackwater, now Constellis) were private military contractors active in Iraq and Afghanistan.

16.  The Pinkerton detective agency, founded in 1850, became synonymous with corporate militia-like forces often used to suppress strikes.

17.  In the late nineteenth century, in coal mining regions in Pennsylvania, a secret workers' organization known as the Molly Maguires was heavily persecuted on behalf of business interests. While the organization likely existed and was part of a movement of popular militancy, it was used by the government and employers to justify widespread repression including the arresting and execution of prominent worker leaders for things it has later been established they were innocent of. The Moyer, Pettibone, and Haywood trial was a highly publicized court case in 1906–7 in Idaho involving Charles Moyer, George A. Pettibone, and "Big Bill" Haywood after the former Idaho Governor was assassinated. The three men were leaders of the Western Federation of Miners (WFM), a radical and militant union. They were ultimately acquitted and the tactics of the state as well as the publicity around the trial helped raise Haywood and the WFM's profile in conjunction with the union's incorporation into the newly formed Industrial Workers of the World (IWW), discussed in the Glossary.

18. The notion of "trans-capitalist" fascism is meant in the sense of fascism being "beyond" capitalism and draws on the writing of Alfred Sohn-Rethel (1987).

19. "Bandung modernization" refers to the Afro-Asian Conference held in Bandung, Indonesia in 1955. The conference was attended by many leaders from former colonies and is credited as a starting point for the Non-Aligned Movement.

20. Hassan was a member of the Democratic Front for the Liberation of Palestine and a former editor of the journal *Shu'un Filasteeniya* (Palestine Affairs), the seminal journal of the Palestinian national movement in the late 1960s up until the 1980s. The quote in question comes from an unofficial translation by Toufic Haddad of a text by Hasan which had been published in *Al Sharq al Awsat*, July 19, 2009.

## Financialization and Hegemony

1. The original essay by Hamerquist remains available via the Internet Wayback Machine at bit.ly/3jUZeY1. For more on *Khukuri Theory*, see Glossary.

2. Quoted in Bosteels (2011), 136.

## Ferguson

1. This refers to a grouping of revolutionaries doing workplace organizing in St. Louis in the 1970s, known as the Worker Unity Organization. They eventually became part of a federation of such groups in the Midwest; while many in this federation joined STO, the St. Louis grouping did not. See Staudenmaier (2012), 118–19.

2. FIRE stands for "Finance, Insurance, and Real Estate."

3. The "Great Society" was the name given to federal anti-poverty programs enacted by the administration of Lyndon B. Johnson.

4.   For more information on the situation Hamerquist is refer-
ring to see the following news reports: "JPMorgan To Lose
$842 Million In Toxic Ala. Sewer Deal," by Jason M. Breslow,
*Frontline*, June 5, 2013 (http://bit.ly/3YE6LJI) and "Alabama's
Jefferson County Declares Biggest Muni Bankruptcy," by William
Selway, Margaret Newkirk, and Steven Church, *Bloomberg*,
November 10, 2011 (http://bit.ly/40N9t1q).

5.   Referring to austerity expectations that all state expenses be
balanced with immediate revenue.

6.   TBTF stands for Too Big To Fail, a designation popularized
following the 2008 financial crisis and the recognition by regulators that certain financial institutions were so important to the
system that their failure would have a disastrous impact throughout the economy; as such, the state had an interest in preventing
their failure at all costs.

7.   The quote that "we are all Keynesians now" is often
attributed to Richard Nixon, though it had some precedent.

8.   The German Sociologist Max Weber, in his 1918 lecture
titled *Politics as a Vocation*, defined the state as "monopoly of the
legitimate use of physical force."

9.   A term often used in neoclassical economics that claims markets will tend toward the most efficient allocation of resources.

10.   The Third Period is an ideological approach adopted
by the Communist International (Comintern, see Glossary for
more) at its 6th World Congress, held in Moscow in the summer
of 1928. During this period the Comintern called for militant
and uncompromising organizing as well as an open hostility to
reformism, known as its "class against class" policy. Famously, the
social democratic parties were referred to as "social fascists" and
the distinct threat of fascism was minimized. This was abruptly
reversed in 1935 at the Comintern's 7th World Congress, where
General Secretary Georgi Dimitrov called for the creation of a
united anti-fascist front that included support for anti-fascist government coalitions (the Popular Front strategy—see Glossary).

349

11.   The Communist Workers Party (Marxist-Leninist), which eventually became the Workers' Viewpoint Organization, organized the ill-fated Greensboro anti-fascist action (see Glossary).

12.   "This continuous effort to separate out the 'international' and 'unitary' elements in national and local reality is true concrete political action, the sole activity productive of historical progress. It requires an organic unity between theory and practice, between the intellectual strata and popular masses, between rulers and ruled. The formulae of unity and federation lose a great part of their significance from this point of view [the organic unity between theory and practice], whereas they retain their sting in the bureaucratic conception, where in the end there is not unity but a stagnant swamp, on the surface calm and 'mute,' and no federation but a 'sack of potatoes,' i.e. a mechanical juxtaposition of single 'units' without any connection between them" (Gramsci 1971, 190). The phrase "sack of potatoes" is itself a reference to Marx's *18th Brumaire of Louis Bonaparte* (1852).

13.   "Well grubbed old mole" is a line Marx uses in his *18th Brumaire* (1852). A reference to Shakespeare's *Hamlet*, the image is often used to evoke the belief that the revolution is always progressing forward, even if at times beneath the surface. Sergio Bologna is a theorist associated with Italy's Autonomia (see Glossary); for an example of his use of Marx's mole image see https://libcom.org/article/tribe-moles-sergio-bologna.

14.   In the *Preface to A Contribution to the Critique of Political Economy* (1859), Marx states that, "the productive forces developing within bourgeois society create also the material conditions for a solution of this antagonism. The prehistory of human society accordingly closes with this social formation." This preface is often seen as an especially mechanistic and deterministic example of Marx's thought.

## Withering

1. "Forces of production and social relations—two different sides of the development of the social individual—appear to capital as mere means, and are merely means for it to produce on its limited foundation. In fact, however, they are the material conditions to blow this foundation sky-high" (Marx 1939, 693). The section from page 690 to 695 is often referred to as the "fragment on the machine."

2. See pages 249–50 for more on Antonio Negri's comment that Hamerquist refers to.

3. Hamerquist is referring here most especially to situations such as the Syrian Civil War and Ukraine, where the interventions of Russia have been geopolitically significant. As well as sabre-rattling by China in the South China Sea.

4. In *The Communist Manifesto*, Marx and Engels do not ever directly explain the nature and role of the communist political party. They do say that "this organisation of the proletarians into a class, and, consequently into a political party, is continually being upset again by the competition between the workers themselves. But it ever rises up again, stronger, firmer, mightier. It compels legislative recognition of particular interests of the workers, by taking advantage of the divisions among the bourgeoisie itself" (Marx and Engels 1848). The Second International was an organization of self-described Marxist parties and the premier body claiming to work for socialist revolution prior to the First World War.

5. Luxemburg (1906).

6. In *What is to Be Done?* (1902) Lenin refers to the role of the communist party as the "tribune of the people," meaning an organization that gives voice and action to the collective will of the oppressed. His distinct perspective on the role of the party was an important issue in the split from the Second International following the successful Bolshevik revolution.

7.   The pairing of "tragedy" and "farce" here is a reference to the opening sentence of Marx's *18th Brumaire* (1852): "Hegel remarks somewhere that all great world-historic facts and personages appear, so to speak, twice. He forgot to add: the first time as tragedy, the second time as farce."

8.   The term "near-peer" has been increasingly used in US national security circles to describe a change in threats to American hegemony. It highlights the contrast between the sporadic and asymmetrical threats from global terrorist networks and those from competition with large and growing national blocs, China and Russia in particular.

9.   Cf. Chomsky and Herman (1988).

10.   See "Email to K on the Iraq War" on page 238 in this volume.

11.   The opening of Marx and Engels's *The Communist Manifesto* (1848) reads, "A spectre is haunting Europe — the spectre of communism," and a few sentences later it is stated that, "The history of all hitherto existing society is the history of class struggles. Freeman and slave, patrician and plebeian, lord and serf, guild-master and journeyman, in a word, oppressor and oppressed, stood in constant opposition to one another, carried on an uninterrupted, now hidden, now open fight, a fight that each time ended, either in a revolutionary reconstitution of society at large, or in the common ruin of the contending classes."

12.   See "Ferguson" on page 283 in this volume.

13.   See chapter 5 of Lenin's *The State and Revolution* (1917), "The Economic Basis of the Withering Away of the State."

14.   See, for example, Robb (2009) and Lewis and Leys (2010).

15.   FANG is an investing acronym for big tech companies, and stands for Facebook, Amazon, Netflix, and Google.

# Glossary

*Actually existing socialism*
A sympathetic term for countries with officially "Communist" governments, especially before the collapse of the Soviet bloc.

*The administration of people vs. the administration of things*
In his book *Anti-Dühring* (1877), Friedrich Engels writes of the future development of communism: "The interference of the state power in social relations becomes superfluous in one sphere after another, and then ceases of itself. The government of persons is replaced by the administration of things and the direction of the processes of production. The state is not 'abolished,' it withers away." This is a core aspect of many Marxist approaches to the state and is usually interpreted as describing the priority of transforming the material conditions of society so that social institutions, such as the state, are no longer viable. The "administration of people," therefore, is usually understood to mean coercive control and exploitation, whereas the "administration of things" refers to coordination to meet social needs and achieve abundance without coercion and exploitation.

*Althusser, Louis (1918–1990)*
Althusser was a leading intellectual of the French Communist Party and one of the foremost Marxist theorists of ideology, which he understood as the mechanism by which a society constitutes the individual as a subject (a process he called "interpellation") and thus reproduces relations of production, particularly through the means of what he called "Ideological State Apparatuses." His "structuralist" interpretation of Marxism emphasized the ability to "scientifically" analyze society and downplayed the role of agency and contingency in history. In some ways and at some times, Althusser was strongly critical of the Soviet and French

Communist Party's direction. This made him appealing to certain Maoists and elements of the New Left of the 1960s. However, Hamerquist and STO categorically rejected his position of hostility to the radicalism of the French General Strike of 1968. For further criticism of Althusser's attitude towards the French Communist Party's Eurocommunist turn, see pages 184–86.

### Anti-Racist Action (ARA)

ARA was a network of anti-fascist groups in North America in the 1990s and 2000s that prioritized militant confrontation with the far right; many of the network's members also had anti-capitalist politics. It was formed out of a number of anti-fascist crews largely from the punk and skinhead subculture, especially from the Midwest. Hamerquist worked closely with members of the network, especially in Chicago, and a number of the pieces in this volume emerged from this relationship. For more, see Shannon Clay, Lady, Kristin Schwartz, and Michael Staudenmaier, *We Go Where They Go: The Story of Anti-Racist Action*, Oakland, CA: PM Press/Working Class History, 2023.

### "At a distance from the state"

French philosopher Alain Badiou (2010) describes politics "at a distance from the state" as "an obligatory refusal of any direct inclusion in the State, of any request for funding from the State, of any participation in elections, etc." (192), and advocates this as the appropriate orientation for revolutionaries today. For more on Hamerquist's use of this notion, see "Withering" in this volume, page 293. See also "Badiou, Alain."

### Autonomia

The name given to the new forms of "autonomous" revolutionary left politics in Italy in the late 1960s and early 1970s, which emphasized militancy, mass action, and cultural resistance, in contrast to the traditional left approaches that prioritized trade unionism and parliamentary politics. Autonomia emerged from connections between radical student movements and rank-and-file worker militancy, notably in the context of the Italian Hot Autumn (see entry below). Autonomist or Autonomous Marxism can also be used in a more general sense to refer to forms of left communism that emphasize the agency of working-class people and criticize state-centric approaches, especially support for "actually existing socialism" (see entry above). While emerging from Marxism, it was influenced by (and influential on) anarchism. The "autonomous" adjective most significantly refers to autonomy from trade union and (parliamentary or vanguard) party structures. STO's direct action–oriented approach to workplace organizing was very much in the spirit "autonomia," and they had active dialog with some groupings in Italy. For more, see Steve Wright, Harry Cleaver, Riccardo Bellofiore, and Massimiliano Tomba, *Storming Heaven: Class Composition and Struggle in Italian Autonomist Marxism*, second edition, London: Pluto Press, 2017.

*Badiou, Alain (1937–)*
A French philosopher; in the 1970s, he was one of the most important intellectuals in the *Union des communistes de France marxiste-léniniste*, a Maoist organization; subsequently, he was a founding member of *L'Organisation politique* (1985–2007), which intervened in a wide range of issues (including immigration, labor, and housing). In North America, Badiou's later work was initially promoted by former members of the Revolutionary Communist Party USA and various independent Marxists who came together around the Kasama and Khukuri Theory websites. See also "At a distance from the state," "Communist invariant," and "Event" in this Glossary.

*Bombard the Headquarters*
Mao Zedong's short text, "Bombard the Headquarters—My first big-character poster [dàzìbào]," released in August 1966 in the earliest days of the Cultural Revolution, is one of the most signif-

icant documents in the history of the period. Competing understandings of the Cultural Revolution (or, more specifically, of
Mao's role in it) will see the document differently: broadly, either
as a barely veiled attack on his rivals at the top of the Chinese
Communist Party or as an injunction for the masses in China to
continue the revolutionary process even though socialism had
been established, most significantly by opposing those "leading
comrades from the central down to the local levels" who had
"adopt[ed] the reactionary stand of the bourgeoisie." "Bombard
the headquarters" became—for the Cultural Revolution and
afterwards, in China and beyond—a potent symbol for rallying
resistance to "Communist" parties and governments which had
ossified into counter-revolutionary structures. The original text
can be found at https://www.marxists.org/reference/archive/mao/
selected-works/volume-9/mswv9_63.htm.

### Bring the Ruckus (BTR)

BTR was a multi-tendency revolutionary left organization active
from 2002 to 2012 that, among other positions, prioritized the
struggle against white supremacy as an anti-capitalist strategy.
Many former STO members (see below), including Hamerquist,
were in close conversation with BTR members. See for example "Response to Bring the Ruckus: Four Points" on page 136 in
this volume. BTR's website and documents are available on the
Internet Archive at http://bit.ly/3HP5nwP

### The Chicago School (of Economics)

The "Chicago School" of economics refers to a school of thought
around economics and public policy named for the University
of Chicago. Milton Friedman was a key figure in the school, and
its defining approach was advocating market-driven solutions
to social problems and opposing direct public investments. It is
often referred to as "neoclassical," because it claimed to support
a return to pre–Depression era perspectives. Its theories laid the
basis for what became known as neoliberalism.

## Christian Identity

Christian Identity is a racist version of Christianity that believes Anglo-Saxons or northern Europeans more generally are the real descendants of the ancient Israelites, that today's Jews are evil imposters, and that people of color are subhumans. Several key white nationalist groups of the 1980s espoused Christian Identity, including the Aryan Nations and many Posse Comitatus members.

## COINTELPRO

The FBI's "Counter-Intelligence Program" (COINTELPRO) was a large-scale program of surveillance and disruption targeting movements within the United States. Targeted individuals could be slandered or blacklisted or, in more severe cases, could be set up for assassination. In many cases radicals would be turned against each other, using informants or falsified documents to suggest that some genuine activists were working for the police ("snitch-jacketing"), were engaged in improper activities, or were conspiring against other radicals. A group of activists exposed the existence of the program in 1971 by breaking into the FBI field office in Media, PA and retrieving documents which they then released to journalists. It and other programs were investigated by the Pike Committee in the US House of Representatives and the Church Committee in the Senate. For more, see Ward Churchill and Jim Vander Wall, *Agents of Repression: The FBI's Secret Wars against the Black Panther Party and the American Indian Movement*, South End Press, 1988.

## Comintern (The Third International)

Founded in 1919, the Communist International (Comintern) was composed of Communist Parties throughout the world aligned with and under the leadership of the newly victorious Soviet government in Moscow. It was also known as the Third International, in reference to the two previous generations of international socialist coordination (Marx was a significant figure in the First International, the International Workingmen's Association). In 1947, the Comintern was dissolved and replaced with an even more centrally controlled body: the Information Bureau of the Communist and Workers' Parties, generally known as the Cominform. This was in turn disbanded in 1956 following the Soviet government's turn away from Stalinism. See "Khrushchev's Secret Speech" below.

*Communist invariant*

Alain Badiou's concept of the "communist invariant" refers to the principles of communism in the most general sense—equality, collectivity, the contribution of each to the well-being of all—and the presence of such principles in wildly different historical situations: from slave revolts in the Roman Empire to peasant rebellions in Qing China to the George Floyd uprising. As Hamerquist writes on pages 122–23: "The communist invariant includes the concepts of equality and justice; the conception that resistance to oppression and rebelliousness is 'right'; the intuition/conviction that the experiences of cooperation in production and social life generally point to a universal potential; and the perception/intuition that people have the capacity to think and to comprehend the truth of their situation and its possibilities. In my opinion, these relate to the elements of a dual consciousness that develop among participants in collective struggles, and the more fundamental and widespread the struggle, the more pronounced these elements become. They are ephemeral and extremely resistant to being captured in any continuing organizational form—union, party, popular assembly—but they are both the points of departure and those of arrival." See also Badiou (2010), and "Badiou, Alain" in this Glossary.

### Condescending saviors

This phrase comes from the song *The Internationale*, which was originally written by French radicals and became a de facto anthem for the communist movement across the world. In the popular English translation by Charles H. Kerr, a verse reads:

> We want no condescending saviors.
> To rule us from a judgment hall;
> We workers ask not for their favors;
> Let us consult for all.

### Construct acts to the end

The course on dialectics that the Sojourner Truth Organization (STO, see entry below) developed for its members—which Hamerquist frequently taught—included the following discussion question: "What does it mean to 'construct acts to the end'?" This was in reference to the following passage from Lerone Bennett Jr.'s discussion of John Brown: "In the end, Brown made of himself an act of transcendence. The act he chose—the tools, the means, the instruments—does not concern us here. His act, as it happened, was violent and apocalyptic; but it could have been as gentle as rain in spring, a word perhaps, yes, or a name or a life committed to a piece of paper. Acts to the end grow out of the lineaments of men's lives and it is up to each man to create and invent not only his act but also the occasion of his act" (1964, 102). For more on STO's dialectics course, see Michael Staudenmaier, *Truth and Revolution: A History of the Sojourner Truth Organization, 1969–1986*, Oakland, CA: AK Press, 2012, esp. pp. 220–23. For the full syllabus and discussion questions from the course, see https://www.marxists.org/history/usa/pubs/sojournertruth/htt.html

### The Cultural Revolution

The Cultural Revolution in China was a complex period of political unrest which began in 1966. Its meaning, fundamental function, and nature remain the subject of wide disagreement. While most commonly viewed as a power play by Mao to restore himself to the head of the Party and oust his challengers (or worse, as "mass hysteria"), the Cultural Revolution is seen by Maoists as a very important, if ultimately unsuccessful, stage in the revolutionary process, intended to prevent the bureaucratization of the socialist party-state and/or its return to capitalism. Newly formed organizations of tens or hundreds of thousands of people fought each other or the Party, while everyone involved identified themselves as the true supporters of Mao's vision. Leadership struggles at the top of the Party opened up space for political activity outside of and even against Party structures; this space was then filled with people with a vast array of interests and political beliefs who, in conformity with the limits of the space, articulated those interests and views in the language of Mao Zedong Thought. By the summer of 1968, a full repression of Red Guards organizations by the army (and led by Mao) had begun, and the Cultural Revolution entered a new phase, much more characterized by a party-state orchestration of events. This lasted until 1976, when Mao died and the "Gang of Four"—who were the most prominent figures identified with the Cultural Revolution at the upper echelons of the party—were arrested.

*Epistemological break*

Hamerquist uses the term "epistemological break" to denote a dramatic and often sudden shift in consciousness. Such shifts, in Hamerquist's perspective, are not gradual evolutions nor the product of quiet reflection, but rather the result of participating in mass action and engagement with historical events as they unfold. Elsewhere he has described epistemological breaks to be "where social actors emerge from passivity and assume political roles that would have been unthinkable 'yesterday'" (2020). Academically, the concept is often associated with Louis Althusser (1969), though Hamerquist attributes his meaning to the work of Antonio Gramsci (1971) and C.L.R. James (1980). See, for example, Gramsci's comment that, "if yesterday the subaltern element [the working class—ed.] was a thing, today it is no longer a thing but an historical person, a protagonist ... an agent, necessarily active and taking the initiative" (1971, 337).

## Event
In the political philosophy of Alain Badiou, an "event" is "a rupture in the normal order of bodies and languages as it exists for any particular situation," and in particular it is "not a realization of a possibility that resides within the situation or that is dependent on the transcendental laws of the world. An event is the creation of new possibilities" (2010, 181–82). Hamerquist uses this concept to highlight the ways that constraints and limitations on what's possible may change quickly and dramatically, and to argue that revolutionaries must always be prepared to change their approach to respond to surprising and expansive possibilities. See also "Badiou, Alain" in this Glossary.

## Facing Reality
Facing Reality was an organization founded by C.L.R. James, Grace Lee Boggs, Martin Glaberman, and others formerly associated with the Johnson-Forest Tendency (see entries on C.L.R. James and Johnson-Forest below). The organization's politics heavily prioritized the ability and tendency for working-class people to discover their own forms of liberatory activity outside of the active intervention and "leadership" of a vanguard party. One formulation of this approach claimed that the role of a Marxist organization was to "recognize and record" the activities of the working class, in particular those practices which indicate the organic emergence of a "new society." The group's politics and philosophy were described in a book of the same name (for the above quote, see C.L.R. James and Grace C. Lee, *Facing Reality: The New Society: Where to Look for It & How to Bring It Closer*, Sixties Series, Chicago: Kerr, 2006, especially p. 134.)

*Fordism*

A strategy and regime of capitalist accumulation that emphasizes higher wages, especially in industrial manufacturing work, in order to create demand for the goods produced. Its name comes from the fact that Henry Ford chose to offer higher wages to workers on his assembly lines (in part to prevent unionization) and publicly claimed this was so the workers could purchase the cars they produced. While it began to be introduced in the 1920s, it came into its own and is often associated with the post–World War II class regime, especially in the United States, and the emphasis on selective access to a share of social wealth for some sectors of society in order to prevent unrest. The phenomenon was also extensively discussed and analyzed by Antonio Gramsci in his *Prison Notebooks* (1971).

*Genoa G8 Protests 2001*

On July 20, 2001, during protests against the G8 summit in Genoa, Italy, 23-year-old Carlo Giuliani was murdered by the police. His death is widely seen as an inflection point, ending a period of large and militant counter-summit demonstrations which began with those in Seattle in 1999 against the World Trade Organization.

*Gramsci, Antonio (1891–1937)*

An Italian Communist intellectual, imprisoned by Mussolini for several years. Gramsci's work, most of which consists of a series of notes written in prison (his "prison notebooks"), only became widely available in English in the late 1960s. In them, he examines a multitude of questions, notably including the importance of consciousness and ideology, ruling-class hegemony (the means by which society is controlled, particularly in ways that rely on consent not coercion), and the "war of position" (the development of alternative consciousness and counter-hegemony preceding a revolutionary outbreak, or "war of maneuver"). His work, which can be interpreted in wildly different ways, was very influential on the Sojourner Truth Organization.

362

*Greensboro Massacre*
On November 3, 1979, a group of Klansmen and Nazis opened
fire on an anti-Klan rally in Greensboro, NC organized by the
Communist Workers Party (CWP), killing five people and injur-
ing ten. The far-right caravan that day was led by Ed Dawson,
a former FBI informant who had founded the North Carolina
Knights in 1969 with FBI backing, and who was at the time an
informant for the Greensboro Police Department. Two days
before, the police had given Dawson a copy of the anti-Klan
march route and permit (which stated that marchers were not
allowed to carry weapons). Bernard Butkovich, an agent of the
federal Bureau of Alcohol, Tobacco and Firearms, was also
working undercover at the time in the area's far right. In the
days leading up to the November 3 demo, both Dawson and
Butkovich urged far rightists to confront the CWP, and both
attended planning sessions to that effect. According to court
testimony, Butkovich not only urged Nazis to take guns to the
confrontation but also encouraged them to illegally convert semi-
automatic weapons to fully automatic and offered to obtain explo-
sives for them. Although the massacre was captured on video and
witnessed by many people, two criminal trials before all-white
juries resulted in acquittals. Finally, in 1985, the killers and the
Greensboro Police Department were found liable in a civil trial
and ordered to pay $350,000 in damages to the widow of one
of those killed. See Matthew N. Lyons, *Insurgent Supremacists:
The U.S. Far Right's Challenge to State and Empire*, Montreal/
Oakland: Kersplebedeb and PM Press, 2018, pp. 170–71.

*Hegel, G.W.F. (1770–1831)*
Hegel was one of the most important German philosophers of
his day and continues to be one of the landmark reference points
in European philosophy—not least because of his significant
influence on Karl Marx. His work is famously opaque and subject
to many interpretations, but it is usually seen to prioritize the
philosophical importance of historical development and human

activity. Additionally, it advances a radical "idealism" that sees the development of logic and reason as fundamental to reality. Hegel emphasizes that limitations and contradictions are essential to all phenomena and bring about continual development and change, especially through dramatic reversals where something becomes its apparent opposite. This process is often referred to as "dialectical," in reference to the way in which it highlights the fact that what something "is" is necessarily dependent on what it "is not." This opposition or contradiction is often referred to as "negation." For those interested in exploring his ideas more, see C.L.R. James's *Notes on Dialectics* (1980) and Susan Buck-Morss's *Hegel, Haiti, and Universal History* (2009).

*Hollowing*

A term with some currency across the political spectrum, which refers to the current tendency for nation-states to become less and less able to deliver political goods or for their bureaucratic structures to act in a coordinated and functional fashion. As Hamerquist explains, "The basic economic premise of this transnational capitalist system ... constantly undermines and hollows the brittle and corrupt state and regulatory institutions that are its major hopes for maintaining and renewing a stable legitimacy." (245) This also relates to the "withering of the state" described by Paul Mattick and discussed by Hamerquist as "a degenerative process in capitalism, one element of which is marked by 'the increasing inability of the state to manage the common affairs of its citizens, within the fairly stringent limits set by the needs of a business economy.' Globalization drastically narrows the 'affairs' that ruling elites view as 'common' and dictates an approach to their management that combines neoliberal ideology with the policies of austerity. The resulting policies ... 'hollow' the material basis for capitalist legitimacy." (317) This framework draws on notions taken from Colin Leys (Lewis and Leys 2010) and John Robb (2009).

*Industrial Workers of the World (IWW)*

The IWW is an anti-capitalist union founded in 1905 and still active to this day. In its first decades it came to constitute a powerful force of militancy and strategic innovation. It was characterized by an orientation toward workers the existing labor movement had neglected, especially migrant workers, and was one of the most successful revolutionary organizations in US history. Prominent organizers of this first generation include "Big Bill" Haywood and Elizabeth Gurley Flynn. Following a period of sharp decline in the wake of World War I, the union has been slowly regaining some strength since the 1970s, though remaining nowhere near its previous peak. The IWW has been a positive reference point for both anarchists and Marxists, as it was for several STO members. In the twenty-first century, it has seen a number of high-profile organizing drives in the fast-food industry, including the Starbucks Workers Union, the Jimmy Johns Workers Union, and the Burgerville Workers Union. IWW members are also active in less visible direct actions in defense of workers' rights on an ad hoc basis, such as are seen in "solidarity networks."

*Italian Hot Autumn*

The Italian Hot Autumn refers to a period of mass militant strikes in Northern Italy in 1969 and 1970, most significantly in the giant factory complexes of the auto industry. This famously included collaboration between militant workers and radical students, armed activity against managers and informants, and an apparent break between the radical workers and both the Communist Party and the trade union movement. Small radical groups were quickly transformed into organizations with tens of thousands of members, in a turning point in the development of Italy's Autonomia.

## James, C.L.R. (1901–1989)

An important Trinadadian Marxist who worked closely for many years with Raya Dunayevskaya (James and Dunayevskaya lent their pseudonymous names to the Johnson-Forest tendency) before breaking with her over the role of the revolutionary organization. He is known both for his theoretical and historical work opposing Stalinism and white supremacy as well as for an approach that paid close attention to popular culture and to the everyday lives of working-class people, especially Black workers. James was highly influential on the Sojourner Truth Organization, some of the members of which knew him during his time in the United States. Hamerquist was specifically influenced by James's work on Hegel in *Notes on Dialectics* (1980) and was more critical of James's approach to organization and political intervention.

## John Brown Anti-Klan Committee

The John Brown Anti-Klan Committee (JBAKC) was a national anti–white supremacist organization active from the late 1970s through the 1980s which shared much of the same anti-imperialist politics and personnel as the Prairie Fire Organizing Committee. The organization conducted community organizing, coalition building, and public demonstrations to combat the rising public presence of white supremacist organizations, including the KKK and various neo-Nazi organizations. JBAKC had an active presence in Chicago throughout the 1980s and at times worked in coalition with STO. For more, see Hilary Moore and James Tracy, *No Fascist USA! The John Brown Anti-Klan Committee and Lessons for Today's Movements*, Open Media Series, San Francisco: City Lights Books, 2020.

## Johnson-Forest Tendency

A tendency within the Trotskyist Workers Party in the United States in the 1940s. It took its name from the pseudonyms of C.L.R. James and Raya Dunayevskaya (J.R. Johnson and Freddie Forest, respectively). Grace Lee Boggs is often described as being the tendency's third founder. Following a split in the 1950s, Boggs would go on to help found the group Facing Reality (see entry above).

## Kahl, Gordon

Gordon Kahl was a Posse Comitatus member who died in a shootout with US marshals in 1983 and was hailed as a martyr of the emerging far-right movement.

## Kasama Project

A project active from approximately 2007 to 2013 that sought to reconstitute a militant communist pole in North America, heavily influenced by Maoism. Kasama began as a website (kasamaproject.org) to discuss a document by Mike Ely (2007) called "Nine Letters to Our Comrades," a critique of the Revolutionary Communist Party (USA), which Ely and several others in the Kasama scene had recently split from. Later, a loose association was formed to explore organized experimentation with Kasama's ideas.

## Keynesianism

John Maynard Keynes (1883–1946) was an English economist working largely in the first half of the twentieth century. His ideas focused on ensuring the existence of adequate economic demand to avoid capitalist crises, in particular the appropriate role the state has in doing so. Keynesians generally advocate for increased social spending and argue against other economists (such as the "Chicago School," see entry above) who view state interventions as dangerous distortions to markets. Historically, Keynesian policies were adopted by all of the core capitalist countries in the years following the Great Depression, and neoliberalism is often understood as rolling back these policies.

*Khrushchev's Secret Speech*
In 1956, three years after Stalin's death, Soviet leader Nikita
Khrushchev made a speech to a closed session of 20th Congress
of the Communist Party of the Soviet Union, titled "On the
Cult of Personality and Its Consequences." In it, he criticized
Stalin for displaying intolerance, brutality, and abusing his
power; amongst the many examples he provided, he noted: "It
was determined that of the 139 members and candidates of the
party's Central Committee who were elected at the 17th congress,
98 persons, that is, 70 percent, were arrested and shot." Despite
not being public, the speech was leaked to the Western media
quickly after its delivery, and the revelations of the Soviet leadership's reconsideration of Stalin's legacy caused tremendous
turmoil and realignment throughout the international communist movement. See "Speech to 20th Congress of the C.P.S.U.
(Feb. 24–25, 1956)" at https://www.marxists.org/archive/
khrushchev/1956/02/24.htm.

*Khukuri Theory*
A militant communist blog whose subtitle was "toward radical reconception of revolutionary theory," closely related to
the *Kasama Project* (see entry above). It took its name from a
machete-like knife popular in the Himalayas, in a nod to the
Maoist movement active in Nepal in the 2000s.

*Lockean Heartland*
Dutch political scientist Kees van der Pijl uses the term "Lockean
Heartland" to refer to the parts of the global system considered
"home" for the anglophone core societies, such as Britain and the
United States. The term refers to English political theorist John
Locke.

*Love and Rage*
The Love and Rage Revolutionary Anarchist Federation began
in 1989 as a North America–wide (though primarily US-

based) project centered on a newspaper of the same name. It transitioned from being a "network" to a formal organization, emphasizing its nature as a "federation" to highlight a balance of centralism and autonomy. During the decade it was in existence, it played an important role in both practical activism and theoretical debates within the North American anarchist movement and signaled a high point in social anarchist organizing, while also integrating important insights from the feminist and Black liberation movements. Its dissolution in 1998 was in part because a small section of the organization had become increasingly critical of anarchism, moving closer to a Maoist (or post-Maoist) perspective.

### Luxemburg, Rosa (1871–1919)

Rosa Luxemburg was a Polish communist who spent most of her adult life in Germany. Joining the illegal Polish Proletariat Party at the age of 15, she rose to prominence in the left wing of the Social Democratic Party of Germany (SPD) prior to WWI. Though critical, she would not fully break with the SPD until their decision to support the German Empire's war effort in WWI. Freed from her imprisonment for anti-war agitation by the German Revolution of 1918–19, she was killed by the far-right Freikorps militias (with the approval of the new SPD government) just two months later. In addition to her theorization of imperialism and criticism of reformist social democracy, Luxemburg's intellectual work is notable for her articulation of the stark choice between "socialism or barbarism" as capitalism collapses, for her internationalist opposition to an emphasis on national independence, for her criticism of Lenin and the Bolsheviks (see "Marxism or Leninism?" [1904] and "The Russian Revolution" [1918]), and for her emphasis on the importance of a "dialectic of organization and spontaneity," which charted a course between what she saw as the mirrored dead ends of a spontaneist anarchism and an anti-democratic and repressive Bolshevism.

*March through the institutions*
This is a reference to a strategy proposed in the late 1960s by Rudi Dutschke, a leader in West Germany's left-wing Socialist German Students Federation. The complete name of the concept is the "long march through the institutions," in a nod to the year-long set of arduous retreats by the Chinese Communist Party's forces in 1934 and 1935. Dutschke advocated setting up counterinstitutions, while identifying dissatisfied elements within the establishment that might be won over or subverted; however, perhaps predictably, it would come to be associated with individuals and groups which sought to exercise pressure by holding positions of power within various capitalist institutions.

*Mass vanguard*
A term used by some members of the Italian Autonomia movement (see entry above) to refer to social formations that emerge and act to push historical processes forward, without themselves constituting a distinct and formal organization.

*May 68*
In France, during May of 1968, a struggle of students in Paris eventually led to a nation-wide wave of strikes and factory occupations. This is often considered a particularly potent example of radical activity outside of and against trade union and political party structures (the French Communist Party, for example, coordinated with the government to suppress the movement). The legacy of the events dramatically shifted the political traditions of France and beyond.

*National Alliance*
The National Alliance is a neo-Nazi organization founded by William Luther Pierce in 1974. It played a major role in the revival of neo-Nazi ideology and organization in the 1970s and 1980s in the United States. Pierce was also the author of the fascist propaganda novel *The Turner Diaries*, which was highly

influential in the American far right in the 1980s and 1990s, notably for Timothy McVeigh who bombed the Oklahoma City Federal Building in 1995. The National Alliance degenerated into infighting and political insignificance in the years after Pierce's death in 2002.

### National Anarchism

National Anarchism is an offshoot of the neo-Nazi movement that advocates a decentralized society of racially segregated communities. National Anarchism first emerged in Britain in the 1990s and briefly established a small presence in the US in the 2010s. Relatedly, but also distinct from National Anarchism, pan-secessionism is a political strategy proposed by Keith Preston, founder of the right-wing anarchist website Attack the System, which calls for dismantling the United States through a broad alliance of groups across the political spectrum that want to secede and establish self-governing regions or enclaves.

### Negri, Antonio (1933–)

An important Italian Marxist intellectual; in the 1960s he was one of the leading members of the Potere Operaio group, part of Italy's Autonomia. During the repression of the Italian radical left, he was charged with terrorism-related offenses. Following a period of exile in France, he returned to Italy in 1997 to serve six years of what had initially been a thirty-year sentence. He is the author of numerous books, including several written with American political philosopher Michael Hardt. Negri and Hardt have grappled with changes in global capitalism, arguing that distinctions between nation-states have become less important than the overarching global system ("empire") and that the working class has been superseded by multiple sectoral struggles and identities (the "multitude").

*Night of the Long Knives*
A violent purge within the Nazi Party, from June 30 to July 2, 1934, during which a number of Hitler's rivals were killed, mainly by the SS. The aim was to reassure the German ruling class that unruly and proletarian elements could be reined in. Both Ernst Röhm and Gregor Strasser (see entry on Strasserism below), who were seen as leading figures in the Nazis' "anti-capitalist" wing, were killed during the purge.

*Occupy Wall Street*
A protest movement that began as an occupation of Zuccotti Park, located in New York City's Wall Street financial district, in September 2011, in the wake of 2008–9 Financial Crisis and associated bailouts. This gave rise to a wider Occupy movement, in which various public spaces were occupied by encampments around the world. The framing was "we are the 99%," and while the movement tended to the left, this provided space for a range of eclectic politics, as well as for right-wing and far-right elements.

*The Order*
The Order, also known as *Bruderschweigen* ("Silent Brotherhood") or Aryan Resistance Movement, was an underground neo-Nazi cell formed in 1983 that "declared war" on the US government and carried out a series of robberies, killings, bombings, etc. before its members were arrested or killed in shootouts with police.

*Paper tiger*
Mao used this metaphor to describe the weakness of capitalist powers often enough that there is a chapter in his "Little Red Book" titled "Imperialism and All Reactionaries are Paper Tigers." The gist of the metaphor can be gathered by this passage: "In appearance [US imperialism] is very powerful but in reality it is nothing to be afraid of, it is a paper tiger. Outwardly a tiger, it is made of paper, unable to withstand the wind and the rain. …

The day will come when the paper tigers will be wiped out. But they won't become extinct of their own accord, they need to be battered by the wind and the rain." ("US Imperialism Is a Paper Tiger," July 14, 1956).

*Penitenti*
Italian for "penitents," *penitenti* refers to those imprisoned by the Italian state during the 1970s who accepted amnesty in exchange for renouncing their politics and testifying against their former comrades. More broadly, it applies to captured revolutionaries (especially those associated with armed politics) who recant.

*Plekhanov, Georgi (1856–1918)*
Plekhanov was an early promoter and translator of Marxism in Russia. His approach to philosophy and history is considered notoriously deterministic and mechanistic, often arguing that certain things were not possible (and therefore not worth struggling for) due to "historical conditions" or the "historical stage" that had been reached by the society in question.

*Popular Front*
Starting in 1935, Russia-aligned Communist Parties pursued a strategy known as the "popular front" in response to the Nazi ascension to power in Germany. The strategy called for Communist Parties to form alliances with non-communist parties (specifically, Social Democrats) in opposing fascism. The term is also often used for refer to strategies that advocate deprioritizing revolutionary politics in favor of alliances with non-communist or even ruling-class elements to achieve immediate goals. The "Popular Front" strategy was a reversal of the Comintern's previous "Class against Class" strategy. See Georgi Dimitrov, "The Fascist Offensive and the Tasks of the Communist International in the Struggle of the Working Class against Fascism," August 2, 1935, available at https://www.marxists.org/reference/archive/dimitrov/works/1935/08_02.htm.

*Posse Comitatus*

Posse Comitatus was an antisemitic, white supremacist network that rejected the legitimacy of all government above the county level. It helped shape the revolutionary white nationalist movement of the 1980s in the United States and served as a source of inspiration for certain elements in the Patriot/militia movement of the 1990s and later. It takes its name from the principle in English common law (which carried over to the US and other former British colonies), wherein a group of citizens may be temporarily mobilized by an officer of the law and given policing powers. This where the word "posse" comes from.

*Prairie Fire*

A reference to a quote from Mao Zedong: "a single spark can start a prairie fire." It was famously cited in the 1974 political document by the Weather Underground Organization, *Prairie Fire: The Politics of Revolutionary Anti-Imperialism*, as well as in the name of the related aboveground organization the Prairie Fire Organizing Committee, which centered on support for militant anti-imperialism.

*Primitivism*

Anarcho-primitivism is a strain of ecologically oriented anarchism which views civilization (usually defined as agriculture and societies based upon it) as fundamentally oppressive and unsustainable, admiring and aspiring to forms of life thought to be typical of "primitive" hunter-gatherer societies. John Zerzan is the tendency's most important theorist, and anarcho-primitivists from Eugene, OR (where Zerzan lives) constituted a significant portion of the black bloc in Seattle in 1999.

*Pseudo Gangs*

The term "pseudo gang" is taken from military counterinsurgency theory. It refers to militant organizations formed by security forces that present themselves as legitimate parts of an insurgent or criminal milieu. They are often used to conduct operations at a plausibly-deniable distance from the state, in order to disrupt oppositional forces either by infiltration, discrediting, or violence. For more on pseudo gangs and counterinsurgency, especially their application to domestic communities and political movements, see *Life During Wartime: Resisting Counterinsurgency* (Oakland: AK Press, 2013), edited by Kristian Williams, Lara Messersmith-Glavin, and William Munger. See also: "Pseudo-Gangs" in J. Sakai, *The Shape of Things to Come: Selected Writings and Interviews*, Kersplebedeb 2023, pp. 233–57.

*Recognize and record*
Drawing on the work of C.L.R. James, the group Facing Reality proposed that the role of the Marxist organization was to "recognize and record" the activities of the working class, in particular those practices which indicate the organic emergence of a "new society." Hamerquist outlines some problems with this approach on pp. 159–61.

*Secular crisis*
In this context, "secular" indicates a long-term tendency; for instance, a secular trend is one that plays out over decades or centuries, even though there may be periodic, even quite extensive, countermovements. Cyclical crises, for example, recessions and inflation, can be manifestations of the more long-term secular crisis of capitalism.

*Serve the people*
A slogan which originates in Maoist China and is one of the principal mottoes of the Chinese Communist Party. It has also been widely adopted wherever Maoism's influence is felt, including by the Black Panther Party. It is often associated with direct support and mutual aid initiatives, such as the Panthers' free breakfast for children program.

*Sojourner Truth Organization (STO)*
STO was a revolutionary organization that Hamerquist helped found in 1969 and that existed through the mid-1980s. It was the main vehicle for his political work for over a decade and a primary nexus to many of his political relationships. The organization was notable for its varied and changing strategies, yet these consistently prioritized mass militancy, refusal to engage with parliamentary politics, and a high level of intellectual engagement. Early strategies focused on building direct action committees in industrial workplaces, while later strategies focused on solidarity work with Third World liberation struggles and developing a tendency in the US left that centered opposition to imperialism, while avoiding uncritical support for "socialist" political movements and governments. Notable members at various times included Noel Ignatiev, David Ranney, and Ken Lawrence. For more on STO, see Staudenmaier (2012) and the online archive of STO material, http://www.sojournertruth.net/

*Stalin Renunciation*
See: Khrushchev's Secret Speech.

*Strasserism*
Otto and Gregor Strasser were early leaders in the German Nazi party and political rivals of Hitler. They advocated an explicitly anti-capitalist, worker-oriented, and revolutionary (but still highly racist and nationalistic) version of national socialism. Gregor Strasser was expelled from the party in 1930, and his tendency was violently suppressed under Hitler's direction in the 1934 "Night of Long Knives," in which he was killed. Otto survived by fleeing Germany (he spent World War II in Canada) and remained active in the German far right until his death in 1974. See entry on Night of the Long Knives.

*Students for a Democratic Society (SDS)*
SDS was the premier New Left student organization, founded in 1960 and largely defunct by the 1970s. Its membership was primarily young and white, promising a radical approach distinct from previous left-wing movements such as the Communist Party. At its height it had dozens of chapters across the country, with tens of thousands of members. Members of SDS went on to be a part of or found numerous organizations, including the Weather Underground and most of what is known as the New Communist Movement.

*Substitutionism*
A term used to criticize approaches to revolutionary politics that "substitute" the activity of an organization or party for that of working-class people.

*Syriza*
Syriza was a left-wing political party that formed the government in Greece in 2015, in the midst of a financial crisis around that country's place in the European Union. Its victory followed many years of militant and radical struggle and marked an attempt by sections of the left to execute a populist governance strategy. Ultimately, it failed to achieve any substantial improvements in negotiations with European financial leaders and came to administer many of the austerity policies it had campaigned against.

*Taylorism*
Frederick Winslow Taylor (1856–1915) promoted the notion of "scientific management" around the turn of the twentieth century as an approach that sought to standardize and optimize as many aspects of workers' labor as possible. In particular, this marked a qualitative shift in working conditions for many manufacturing workers, dramatically reducing their control of their labor. Taylorism in general refers to the effort to remove any aspect of workers' control and spontaneity.

*There Is No Alternative (TINA)*
A term coined by Margaret Thatcher, the Conservative prime minister of the United Kingdom from 1979–90, largely reflecting the perceived failure of self-proclaimed socialist governments, which left Western dominated capitalism as the only viable social system. Closely associated with the rise of neoliberal ideology, the phrase argues that austerity measures and "free market" policies are inevitable. As Hamerquist explains on page 213, "The primary manifestation of the dominance of the ruling ideas on popular attitudes is the mass buy-in to the 'There Is No Alternative' mantra: the acceptance of the inevitability and essential rightness of the major features of the status quo and the ultimate folly and futility of collective resistance to it. For the majority of people, this attitude predominates even while they are engaged in struggles and resistance that stretch the framework of capitalist legitimacy." See also "Chicago School."

*Thinking head vs. acting body*
This refers to an approach to politics and especially organization often associated with Stalin, which considers that the central bodies of revolutionary organization have the role of deciding on the strategy and direction that the rest of the organization—and even the rest of the working class—executes, much as the body is seen to relate to the head. For example, in *The Foundations of Leninism* (1924), Stalin says, "The Party must stand at the head of the working class; it must see farther than the working class; it must lead the proletariat, and not drag at the tail of the spontaneous movement. ... Only a party which adopts the standpoint of advanced detachment of the proletariat and is able to raise the masses to the level of understanding the class interest of the proletariat—only such a party can divert the working class from the path of trade unionism and convert it into an independent political force."

*Third Position*
A strain of fascism that claims to be against both capitalism and communism and to be neither of the left nor the right. Many adherents trace their lineage to the Strasser brothers and those purged in the Night of Long Knives (see entries above) in the Hitler period. Hamerquist discusses the phenomenon, which he sees as having great potential for growth, in the text of the same name, on page 133.

*War of position vs. war of maneuver*
Antonio Gramsci's (see entry above) concept of "war of maneuver" refers to the phase of social struggle characterized by open conflict for power. It is contrasted to the concept of the "war of position," where revolutionary forces accumulate within capitalist society and ruling-class hegemony is undermined, establishing the conditions for ideological transformation. See Gramsci (1971), especially pp. 229–39.

*Withering of the state*
While Marxists normally associate this term with a hoped-for eventuality along the road to communism (see entry "The administration of people vs. the administration of things"), in Hamerquist's usage in the texts in this volume, he plays off of this association in order to discuss the process through which nation-states are becoming fragmented and atrophied under the pressures of transnational capitalism. See Hollowing.

*Young, Andy (1932–)*
Andy Young has been a US politician, diplomat, and activist. During his tenure as ambassador to the UN during the Carter administration, he was a prominent and vocal critic of white-minority rule in southern Africa, and as such was instrumental in establishing the neocolonial neutralization of the liberation movement, especially in Zimbabwe. See also, "What Happened to the Zimbabwe Revolution" in J Sakai, *The Shape of Things to*

*Come: Selected Writings and Interviews*, Montreal: Kersplebedeb, 2023, pp. 265–97.

*ZANU*
The Zimbabwe African National Union was a national liberation movement against white minority rule in what became Zimbabwe. In 1978, there was a split in ZANU that was heavily debated in leftist circles and intertwined with USSR vs. Chinese foreign policy. One wing, ZANU-PF, eventually took power with the support of the Chinese and of the Carter administration, installing Robert Mugabe as the head of the new state. See also "What Happened to the Zimbabwe Revolution," in J. Sakai, *The Shape of Things to Come: Selected Writings and Interviews*, Montreal: Kersplebedeb, 2023, pp. 265–97.

*Zerzan, John*
See "Primitivism."

## Bibliography

Akuno, Kali. 2008. "Navigating the Storm: A Strategic Orientation for Confronting the Advance of Reaction and National Oppression in the 'Obama' Era." *Navigating the Storm* (blog). October 28. http://navigatingthestorm.blogspot.com/2008/11/navigating-storm-strategic-orientation.html.

Albert, Michael. 1999. "On Trashing and Movement Building." *Znet* (blog). December 1. https://web.archive.org/web/20100224010500/www.zcommunications.org/on-trashing-and-movement-building-by-michael-albert.

Althusser, Louis. 1977. "On the Twenty-Second Congress of the French Communist Party." https://www.marxists.org/reference/archive/althusser/1977/22nd-congress.htm.
———. 2005. *For Marx*. Radical Thinkers. London/New York: Verso.

Arrighi, Giovanni. 2010. *The Long Twentieth Century: Money, Power, and the Origins of Our Times*. London/New York: Verso.

Badiou, Alain. 1975. *Théorie de la contradiction*. Paris: Maspero.
———. 1999. "Philosophy and Politics." *Radical Philosophy*, no. 096, August. https://www.radicalphilosophy.com/article/philosophy-and-politics.
———. 2008. "Is the Word Communism Forever Doomed?" https://www.lacan.com/thevideos/1108.html.
———, dir. 2012. *From Logic to Anthropology, or Affirmative Dialectics*. The European Graduate School. https://www.youtube.com/watch?v=wczfhXVYbxg.
———. 2015. *The Communist Hypothesis*. Translated by David Macey and Steve Corcoran. Paperback edition. London/New York: Verso.

Badiou, Alain, and François Balmès. 1976. *De l'idéologie*. Collection Yenan. Paris: F. Maspero.

Badiou, Alain, and Jason Barker. 2011. *Metapolitics*. English-Language ed. Radical Thinkers. London/New York: Verso.

Badiou, Alain, and Gregory Elliott. 2012. *The Rebirth of History*. London/New York: Verso.

Bakunin, Mikhail. 1870. "Letter to Albert Richard." https://www.marxists.org/reference/archive/bakunin/works/1870/albert-richard.htm.

Barnett, Thomas P.M. 2005. *The Pentagon's New Map: War and Peace in the Twenty-First Century*. Berkley trade paperback edition. New York: Berkley Books.

Barron, John. 2014. *Operation Solo: The FBI's Man in the Kremlin*. Paperback edition. Washington, DC: Regnery History.

Bello, Walden. 2008. "The Coming Capitalist Consensus." *Foreign Policy in Focus* (blog). December 24. https://fpif.org/the_coming_capitalist_consensus/.

Bennett, Lerone, Jr. 1964. *The Negro Mood, and Other Essays*. Chicago: Johnson Pub. Co.

Bernes, Jasper. 2019. "Revolutionary Motives." *Endnotes 5*. https://endnotes.org.uk/articles/revolutionary-motives.pdf.

Biko, Steve, and Aelred Stubbs. 2002. *I Write What I Like: Selected Writings*. Chicago: University of Chicago Press.

Bosteels, Bruno. 2011. *Badiou and Politics*. Post-Contemporary Interventions. Durham, NC: Duke University Press.

Brighton Solidarity Federation. 2009. "Strategy and Struggle: Anarcho-Syndicalism in the 21st Century." https://libcom.org/article/strategy-and-struggle-anarcho-syndicalism-21st-century.

Bromma. 2014. *The Worker Elite: Notes on the "Labor Aristocracy."* Montreal: Kersplebedeb Publishing.

———. 2016. "Notes on Trump." *Kersplebedeb* (blog). December 2016. https://kersplebedeb.com/posts/notes-on-trump/.

Buck-Morss, Susan. 2009. *Hegel, Haiti and Universal History*. Illuminations. Pittsburgh, Pa: University of Pittsburgh Press.

Clay, Shannon, Lady, Kristin Schwartz, and Michael Staudenmaier. 2023. *We Go Where They Go: The Story of Anti-Racist Action*. PM Press/Working Class History.

Connelly, Joel. 2004. "In the Northwest: Bush-Cheney Flip-Flops Cost America in Blood." *Seattle Post-Intelligencer*, September 28. https://www.seattlepi.com/news/article/In-the-Northwest-Bush-Cheney-flip-flops-cost-1155271.php.

Delo Truda Group. 1926. "Organizational Platform of the General Union of Anarchists (Draft)." https://www.anarkismo.net/article/1000.

Dhondt, Geert, and Joel Olson. 2008. "On 'Fascism and Anti-Fascism': A Review of Don Hamerquist's Essay." https://theanarchistlibrary.org/library/ruckus-collective-debates-on-fascism.

Dominick, Brian. 2000. "Anarchists in the Neighborhood." *Arsenal 2*, Fall.

Ely, Mike. 2007. "Nine Letters to Our Comrades." https://www.marxists.org/history/erol/ncm-7/nine-letters.pdf.

———. 2009. "Class against Class? Real World Alignments for Revolution." *Kasama Project* (blog). August 19. https://web.archive.org/web/20121021205346/http://kasamaproject.org/2009/08/19/class-against-class-allignment-and-wellsprings-for-revolution/#more-12772.

———. 2009. "Opposing Obama's War: Let's Be Real." *Kasama Project* (blog). December 2, 2009. https://web.archive. org/web/20121030154819/http://kasamaproject. org/2009/12/02/opposing-obamas-war-lets-get-serious/

Engelhardt, Tom. 2009. "The Nine Surges of Obama's War." *CBS News*, December 10. https://www.cbsnews.com/news/ the-nine-surges-of-obamas-war/.

Engels, Friedrich. 1890. "Letter to J. Bloch In Königsberg." https://www.marxists.org/archive/marx/works/1890/ letters/90_09_21.htm.

Engels, Friedrich. 1877. *Anti-Dühring*. https://www.marxists. org/archive/marx/works/1877/anti-duhring/.

Ferguson, Jehu. 2013. "Proletarian Consciousness Can Only Be Global: A Reply to Chris Cutrone." *The Real Movement* (blog). July 10. https://therealmovement.wordpress. com/2013/07/10/proletarian-consciousness-can- only-be-global-a-reply-to-chris-cutrone/.

Ford, Glenn. 2015. "Changing the Guard in Black America." *The Black Agenda Report* (blog). January 28. https://web.archive.org/web/20150321192912/https:// www.blackagendareport.com/node/14642.

Friedman, Thomas L. 2005. *The World Is Flat: A Brief History of the Twenty-First Century*. 1st ed. New York: Farrar, Straus and Giroux.
———. 2010. "What's Our Sputnik?" *The New York Times*, January 17, sec. Opinion. https://www.nytimes.com/ 2010/01/17/opinion/17friedman.html.

Gambone, Larry. 2009. "THE STATE AND REVOLUTION— An Anarchist Viewpoint." June 16. http://porkupineblog. blogspot.com/2009/06/state-and-revolution-anarchist. html.

Garrow, David J. 1981. *The FBI and Martin Luther King, Jr: From "Solo" to Memphis.* 1st ed. New York: W.W. Norton.

Garvey, John. 2014. "No More Missouri Compromises." *Insurgent Notes* (blog). November 18. http://insurgent-notes.com/2014/11/no-more-missouri-compromises/.

Georgakas, Dan, and Marvin Surkin. 2012. *Detroit: I Do Mind Dying: A Study in Urban Revolution.* 3rd ed. Chicago: Haymarket Books.

Gindin, Sam, and Leo Panitch. 2012. *The Making of Global Capitalism: The Political Economy of American Empire.* London/Brooklyn, NY: Verso.

Gramsci, Antonio. 1968. "Soviets in Italy." *The New Left Review* I (51). https://newleftreview.org/issues/i51/articles/antonio-gramsci-soviets-in-italy.
———. 2012. *Selections from the Prison Notebooks of Antonio Gramsci.* Repr. London: Lawrence & Wishart.

Griffin, Roger. 1993. *The Nature of Fascism.* London/New York: Routledge.

Guillén, Abraham. 1973. *Philosophy of the Urban Guerrilla: The Revolutionary Writings of Abraham Guillén.* Translated by Donald C. Hodges. New York: Morrow.

Haddad, Toufic. 2009. "Where Is Fatah Headed?" *Socialist Worker* (blog). August 6. https://socialistworker.org/2009/08/06/where-is-fatah-headed.

Hamerquist, Don. 2009a. "Thinking and Acting in Real Time and a Real World." *Three Way Fight* (blog). January 27. http://threewayfight.blogspot.com/2009/01/thinking-and-acting-in-real-time-and.html.
———. 2009b. "Lenin, Leninism, and Some Leftovers." *Kersplebedeb* (blog). September 23. https://kersplebedeb.com/posts/lenin-leninism-and-some-leftovers/.

———. 2010. "Barack, Badiou, and Bilal al Hasan." *Three Way Fight* (blog). January 24. http://threewayfight.blogspot. com/2010/01/barack-badiou-and-bilal-al-hasan.html.

———. 2020. "Don Hamerquist: Distinguishing The Possible From The Probable: Contending Strategic Approaches within and against Transnational Capitalism." *Kersplebedeb* (blog). June 14, 2020. https://kersplebedeb.com/posts/ distinguishing-the-possible-from-the- probable-contending-strategic-approaches-with- in-and-against-transnational-capitalism/

Hamerquist, Don, and J. Sakai. 2017. *Confronting Fascism: Discussion Documents for a Militant Movement*. 2nd ed. Montreal: Kersplebedeb Publishing.

Hardt, Michael, and Antonio Negri. 2003. *Empire*. 1. Harvard University Press paperback ed., [Nachdr.]. Cambridge, MA: Harvard University Press.

———. 2004. *Multitude: War and Democracy in the Age of Empire*. New York: Penguin Books.

Harvey, David. 2005. *The New Imperialism*. Oxford/New York: Oxford University Press.

Heinrich, Michael. 2012. *An Introduction to the Three Volumes of Karl Marx's Capital*. New York: Monthly Review Press.

Herman, Edward S., and Noam Chomsky. 2002. *Manufacturing Consent: The Political Economy of the Mass Media*. New York: Pantheon Books.

Hinton, Elizabeth Kai. 2022. *America on Fire: The Untold History of Police Violence and Black Rebellion Since the 1960s*. New York: Liveright Publishing Corporation.

Hudson, Michael, and Kin Chi Lau. 2021. *Super Imperialism: The Economic Strategy of American Empire*. Third edition. Dresden: ISLET.

James, C. L. R. 1980. *Notes on Dialectics: Hegel, Marx, Lenin.* Westport, Conn.: L. Hill.

James, C.L.R., and Grace C. Lee. 2006. *Facing Reality: The New Society: Where to Look for It & How to Bring It Closer.* Sixties Series. Chicago: Kerr.

Jappe, Anselm. 2011. "Who Is to Blame." Libcom.Org. 2011. https://libcom.org/article/who-blame-anselm-jappe.

JF and Friends. 2014. "The Old Mole Breaks Concrete." *Unity and Struggle* (blog). December 11. http://www.unityandstruggle.org/2014/12/the-old-mole-breaks-concrete/.

Keynes, John Maynard. 1936. *The General Theory of Employment, Interest, and Money.* New York: Harcourt, Brace & World.

Khrushchev, Nikita. 1956. "Speech to 20th Congress of the C.P.S.U." https://www.marxists.org/archive/khrush-chev/1956/02/24.htm.

Klein, Naomi. 2008. *The Shock Doctrine: The Rise of Disaster Capitalism.* 1st Picador ed. New York: Picador.

Lapavitsas, Costas. 2015. "The Syriza Strategy Has Come to an End Lapavitsas." *Verso Books* (blog). April 30. https://www.versobooks.com/blogs/1967-costas-lapavitsas-the-syriza-strategy-has-come-to-an-end.

Lawrence, Ken. 1982. "The Ku Klux Klan and Fascism." http://www.sojournertruth.net/kkkandfascism.html.
———. 1985. "The New State Repression." https://itsgoingdown.org/wp-content/uploads/2019/05/510.lawrence.new_.state_.repression.1985.pdf.

Lenin, V.I. 1902. *What Is to Be Done?* https://www.marxists.org/archive/lenin/works/1901/witbd/.

———. 1905. *The Reorganisation of the Party.* https://www.
marxists.org/archive/lenin/works/1905/reorg/index.htm.

———. 1906. "Freedom to Criticise and Unity of Action." https://
www.marxists.org/archive/lenin/works/1906/may/20c.
htm.

———. 1917. *The State and Revolution.* https://www.marxists.
org/archive/lenin/works/1917/staterev/.

———. 1920. *"Left-Wing" Communism: An Infantile Disorder.*
https://www.marxists.org/archive/lenin/works/1920/lwc/
index.htm.

———.1956 [1923]. "'Last Testament' Letters to the Congress."
https://www.marxists.org/archive/lenin/works/1922/dec/
testamnt/index.htm.

Leonard, Aaron J., and Conor A. Gallagher. 2017. *A Threat of the
First Magnitude: FBI Counterintelligence & Infiltration
from the Communist Party to the Revolutionary Union—
1962-1974.* London: Repeater Books, an imprint of
Watkins Media Ltd.

Lewis, Edward, and Colin Leys. 2010. "The Dictatorship
of the Market: Interview with Colin Leys."
MRonline. June 9. https://mronline.org/2010/06/09/
the-dictatorship-of-the-market-interview-with-colin-leys/.

Luxemburg, Rosa. 1906. "The Mass Strike, the Political Party
and the Trade Unions" https://www.
marxists.org/archive/luxemburg/1906/mass-strike/.

Lynd, Staughton. 2013. *Accompanying: Pathways to Social
Change.* Oakland: PM Press.

Mao, Zedong. 1957. "On the Correct Handling of Contradictions
Among the People." February 27. https://www.marxists.
org/reference/archive/mao/selected-works/volume-5/
mswv5_58.htm.

Marx, Karl. 1844. *Economic & Philosophic Manuscripts of 1844.* https://www.marxists.org/archive/marx/works/1844/manuscripts/preface.htm.

———. 1845. "Theses on Feuerbach." 1845. https://www.marxists.org/archive/marx/works/1845/theses/theses.htm.

———. 1852. *The Eighteenth Brumaire of Louis Bonaparte.* https://www.marxists.org/archive/marx/works/1852/18th-brumaire/.

———. 1859. "Preface to a Contribution to the Critique of Political Economy." https://www.marxists.org/archive/marx/works/1859/critique-pol-economy/preface.htm.

———. 1894. *Capital Vol. 3.* https://www.marxists.org/archive/marx/works/1894-c3/.

———. 1939. *Grundrisse.* https://www.marxists.org/archive/marx/works/1857/grundrisse/.

Marx, Karl, and Friedrich Engels. 1845. *The German Ideology.* https://www.marxists.org/archive/marx/works/1845/german-ideology/.

———. 1848. *Manifesto of the Communist Party.* https://www.marxists.org/archive/marx/works/1848/communist-manifesto/.

Mattick, Paul Jr. 2016. "The Withering of the State." *Communists in Situ* (blog). June 7. https://cominsitu.wordpress.com/2016/06/07/the-withering-of-the-state/.

Miles, Jim. 2009. "Imperial Inertia." *Znet.* December 2, 2009. https://znetwork.org/znetarticle/imperial-inertia-by-jim-miles/.

Moore, Hilary, and James Tracy. 2020. *No Fascist USA! The John Brown Anti-Klan Committee and Lessons for Today's Movements.* Open Media Series. San Francisco, CA: City Lights Books.

Nappalos, Scott Nicholas. 2011. "Direct Action? Who Cares!" https://libcom.org/book/export/html/35997.

Nechayev, Sergey. 1869. "The Revolutionary Catechism." https://
www.marxists.org/subject/anarchism/nechayev/catechism.
htm.

Pontecorvo, Gillo, dir. 1966. *The Battle of Algiers*.

Ranney, David C. 2014. *New World Disorder: The Decline of U.S.
Power*. CreateSpace Independent Publishing Platform.

Robb, John. 2004. "4GW—FOURTH GENERATION
WARFARE." *Global Guerrillas* (blog). May 8. https://
globalguerrillas.typepad.com/globalguerrillas/2004/05
/4gw_fourth_gene.html.
———. 2007. *Brave New War: The Next Stage of Terrorism and
the End of Globalization*. Hoboken, NJ: John Wiley &
Sons.
———. 2009. "HOLLOW STATES vs. FAILED STATES."
*Global Guerrillas* (blog). March 24.
https://globalguerrillas.typepad.com/globalguerrillas/
2009/03/hollow-states-vs-failed-states.html.

Seymour, Richard. 2014. "Torture Works." *Lenin's Tomb* (blog).
December 10. http://www.leninology.co.uk/2014/12/
torture-works.html.

Sohn-Rethel, Alfred. 1978. *Economy and Class Structure of
German Fascism*. London: CSE Books. https://mronline.
org/wp-content/uploads/2019/05/The20Economy20and
20Class20Structure20of20German20-20Alfred20Sohn-
Rethel.pdf.

Sojourner Truth Organization. 1971. "Towards a Revolutionary
Party." http://www.sojournertruth.net/tarp.html.

St. Clair, Jeffrey. 2016. "That Magic Feeling: The Strange
Mystique of Bernie Sanders." *Counterpunch*
(blog). December 16. https://web.archive.org/
web/20161222033335/http://www.counterpunch.
org/2016/12/16/that-magic-feeling-the-strange-mystique-
of-bernie-sanders/.

Stalin, Joseph. 1953. *The Foundations of Leninism.* https://www.marxists.org/reference/archive/stalin/works/1924/foundations-leninism/.

Staudenmaier, Michael. 2012. *Truth and Revolution: A History of the Sojourner Truth Organization, 1969-1986.* Oakland: AK Press.

Steele, John. 2011a. "Why is Badiou of Political Value?" *Khukuri Theory* (blog). May 1. https://web.archive.org/web/20120103123525/http://www.khukuritheory.net/why-is-badiou-of-political-value/.
———. 2011. "Marxism or Anarchism." *Khukuri Theory* (blog). August 1. https://web.archive.org/web/20110919133444/http://www.khukuritheory.net/marxism-or-anarchism-or/.

Tilly, Charles. 1984. *Big Structures, Large Processes, Huge Comparisons.* Russell Sage Foundation. https://www.jstor.org/stable/10.7758/9781610447720.

Trautmann, W.E. 1912. "Why Strikes Are Lost! How to Win!" https://libcom.org/article/why-strikes-are-lost-how-win-we-trautmann.

Unity and Struggle. 2009. "Economic Crisis in the Third World." *Unity and Struggle* (blog). November 7. http://www.unityandstruggle.org/2009/11/economic-crisis-in-the-third-world/.

Weather Underground Organization. 1974. *Prairie Fire: The Politics of Revolutionary Anti-Imperialism.* https://archive.org/details/PrairieFire_20170422.

Wetzel, Tom. 2005. "Workers Power and the Russian Revolution a Review of Maurice Brinton's For Workers Power." https://theanarchistlibrary.org/library/tom-wetzel-workers-power-and-the-russian-revolution.

———. 2006. "Workers' Liberation and Institutions of Self-Management." https://theanarchistlibrary.org/library/tom-wetzel-workers-liberation-and-institutions-of-self-management.

———. 2009. "Anarchism, Class Struggle and Political Organization." https://theanarchistlibrary.org/library/tom-wetzel-anarchism-class-struggle-and-political-organization.

Williams, Kristian, William Munger, and Lara Messersmith-Glavin, eds. 2013. *Life During Wartime: Resisting Counterinsurgency*. Oakland, CA: AK Press.

Wohlleben, Adrian. 2021. "Memes without End." *Ill Will* (blog). May 16. https://illwill.com/memes-without-end.

Wood, Lesley J. 2012. *Direct Action, Deliberation, and Diffusion: Collective Action after the WTO Protests in Seattle*. Cambridge Studies in Contentious Politics. Cambridge: Cambridge University Press.

Wright, Steve, Harry Cleaver, Riccardo Bellofiore, and Massimiliano Tomba. 2017. *Storming Heaven: Class Composition and Struggle in Italian Autonomist Marxism*. Second edition. London: Pluto Press.

Zerzan, John. 1993. "Rank-and-File Radicalism within the Ku Klux Klan of the 1920s." https://theanarchistlibrary.org/library/john-zerzan-rank-and-file-radicalism-within-the-ku-klux-klan-of-the-1920s.

Zetkin, Clara. 1923. "The Struggle against Fascism." https://www.marxists.org/archive/zetkin/1923/06/struggle-against-fascism.html

# HARD CRACKERS
## CHRONICLES OF EVERYDAY LIFE

*Hard Crackers Magazine* is a journal that chronicles everyday life, both to demonstrate that a better world is possible and to examine the barriers to it, including the barriers erected by those who must build it. The editors believe that we need to be alert to the possibilities of "the beach underneath the pavement" and that life on the ground is not necessarily determined by the grand structures. Our material reflects that belief. *Hard Crackers* is political but not defined by party or program, literary but not pretentious, and scholarly but not academic. Our content covers a lot of ground.

Hard Crackers produces a print magazine semi-regularly and publishes more regular contributions on our website. We are always open to new submissions and will consider all on their merit. We appreciate good writing. Check us out at www.hardcrackers.com. All electronic communications and new submissions can be sent to editor@hardcrackers.com. Our street address is P.O.Box 22155, Brooklyn, NY 11201.
Past issues are available.

# Three Way Fight:
## an insurgent blog on the struggle against the state and fascism

**http://threewayfight.blogspot.com/**

Three Way Fight is a blog that promotes revolutionary antifascist analysis, strategy, and organizing. Unlike liberal antifascists, we believe that "defending democracy" is an illusion, as long as that "democracy" is based on a socio-economic system that exploits and oppresses human beings. At the same time, unlike many on the revolutionary left, we believe that fascists and other far rightists aren't simply tools of the ruling class, but represent an autonomous political force that clashes with capitalist interests in real ways.

Radicals need to confront both the established capitalist order and an insurgent or even revolutionary right, while recognizing that these opponents are also in conflict with each other. Our blog confronts complexities in the dynamics between these three poles that are often glossed over. We point out, for example, that repression isn't necessarily fascist—antifascism itself can be a tool of ruling-class repression (as was the case during World War II, when anti-fascism was used to justify strike-breaking and the mass imprisonment of Japanese Americans, among other measures). And we warn against far right efforts to build alliances with leftists as well as fascistic tendencies within the left (as when leftists promote conspiracy theories rooted in anti-Jewish scapegoating).

Three Way Fight was initiated in 2004 as a collaborative project by several radical antifascist organizers. From the beginning, Three Way Fight has brought together anarchist and independent Marxist perspectives, and has sought to promote inclusive discussion and debate among revolutionary leftists. Our work is intended as a contribution to larger conversations among all those who are committed to liberatory change.

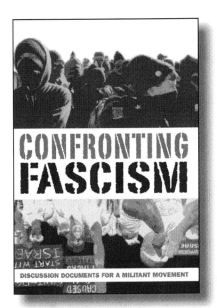

**KER**
**SPL**
**EBE**
**DEB**

Since 1998 Kersplebedeb has been an important source of radical literature and agit prop materials.

The project has a non-exclusive focus on anti-patriarchal and anti-imperialist politics, framed within an anticapitalist perspective. A special priority is given to writings regarding armed struggle in the metropole, the continuing struggles of political prisoners and prisoners of war, and the political economy of imperialism.

The Kersplebedeb website presents historical and contemporary writings by revolutionary thinkers from the anarchist and communist traditions.

Kersplebedeb can be contacted at:

Kersplebedeb
CP 63560
CCCP Van Horne
Montreal, Quebec
Canada
H3W 3H8

email:  info@kersplebedeb.com
web:    www.kersplebedeb.com
        www.leftwingbooks.net

# Kersplebedeb